The *Malleus Maleficarum* and the construction of witchcraft

STUDIES IN EARLY MODERN EUROPEAN HISTORY

This exciting series aims to publish challenging and innovative research in all areas of early modern continental history. The editors are committed to encouraging work that engages with current historiographical debates, adopts an interdisciplinary approach, or makes an original contribution to our understanding of the period.

SERIES EDITORS
Professor Joseph Bergin, William G. Naphy and Penny Roberts

The *Malleus Maleficarum* and the construction of witchcraft

Theology and popular belief

HANS PETER BROEDEL

Manchester University Press

Manchester and New York

distributed exclusively in the USA by Palgrave

Published by Manchester University Press
Oxford Road, Manchester M13 9NR, UK
and Room 400, 175 Fifth Avenue, New York, NY 10010, USA
www.manchesteruniversitypress.co.uk

Distributed exclusively in the USA by
Palgrave, 175 Fifth Avenue, New York NY 10010, USA

Distributed exclusively in Canada by
UBC Press, University of British Columbia, 2029 West Mall,
Vancouver, BC, Canada V6T 1Z2

British Library Cataloguing-in-Publication Data
A catalogue record for this book is available from the British Library

Library of Congress Cataloging-in-Publication Data
A catalog record for this book is available from the Library of Congress

ISBN-10: 0 7190 6441 4

ISBN-13: 978 0 7190 6441 8

First published 2003 by Manchester University Press

First digital, on-demand edition produced by Lightning Source 2006

Contents

Acknowledgments

I am much indebted to the generous assistance of a number of people on this project. I would like to thank especially Robert Stacey for his tireless assistance and encouragement in all aspects of this work. I also owe much to Mary O'Neal's incisive comments and encyclopedic knowledge of early-modern witchcraft history. I would like also to thank Henning Sehmsdorf, Fritz Levy, and Gerhild Scholz Williams who read this manuscript at various stages and offered valuable criticism. I owe special thanks to my wife, Sheryl Dahm Broedel, not only for her patience, but also for her invaluable criticisms of my writing and ideas.

Note on translation

The popularity of the *Malleus* in the English-speaking world stems in large part from the ready availability of the Montague Summers translation, but, as has often been noted before, this translation suffers from serious defects. In particular, Summers relied upon very late Latin editions, which differed substantially from the original. In this book I have used as my primary Latin text the 1991 photographic reprint of the first edition of the *Malleus* (1487), supplemented by the 1519 Jean Marion edition. I have retained the original Latin throughout in the notes; in addition to noting apparent errors in the Latin, where necessary I have given the alternative Latin from the 1519 edition within brackets. The English translations are my own and are my responsibility, but I have benefited from the advice and assistance of Professors Barbara Gold and Carl Rubino of Hamilton College's Classics Department, and from the dedicated revisions of the readers for Manchester University Press.

1
Introduction:
contested categories

On the morning of October 29th, 1485, dignitaries began to assemble in the great meeting room of Innsbruck's town hall. They included Cristan Turner, licentiate in the decretals and the special representative of Georg Golser, bishop of Brixen, Master Paul Wann, doctor of theology and canon law, Sigismund Saumer, also a licentiate in the decretals, three brothers of the Dominican Order, a pair of notaries, and the inquisitor, Henry Institoris.[1] They were there to witness the interrogation of Helena Scheuberin, who, along with thirteen others, was suspected of practicing witchcraft. Scheuberin would have been familiar to at least some of these men: an Innsbruck native, she had been married for eight years to Sebastian Scheuber, a prosperous burger. She was also an aggressive, independent woman who was not afraid to speak her mind, a trait which on this occasion had landed her in serious trouble. From the formal charges against her, we learn that not long after the inquisitor had first arrived in Innsbruck with the stated intention of bringing witches to justice, she had passed him in the street, spat, and said publicly, "Fie on you, you bad monk, may the falling evil take you."[2] Worse still, Scheuberin had also stayed away from Institoris' sermons and had encouraged others to do likewise, even going so far, as the next charge against her reveals, as to disrupt one sermon by loudly proclaiming that she believed Institoris to be an evil man in league with the devil – a man whose obsession with witchcraft amounted to heresy.[3]

It is possible that Scheuberin was aware that she had a reputation for harmful sorcery, and that her fear of suspicion led her unwisely to take the offensive when the inquisitor appeared. If such were the case, her tactics were spectacularly ill-conceived. Institoris was a man who treasured his orthodoxy above all things, and we may well imagine that he was deeply offended by Scheuberin's slander; more seriously, though, her attack upon the work of the Papal Inquisition was manifest evidence that she was herself either a heretic or a witch. A searching investigation of Scheuberin's life and character ensued, producing additional charges: she had kept company with suspected heretics; she had caused a woman's illness in order to have her husband as her lover; and, most seriously, in January of the previous year she had killed, either through witchcraft or through poison, a knight with whom she wished to have an adulterous affair.[4] Scheuberin thus stood accused of using magic to cause injury and death, of causing *maleficium* in the jargon of the court. Since this was a charge familiar to all those in attendance at her interrogation, the various members of the tribunal must have expected to hear testimony directly relevant to this crime. If so, they were in for a surprise.

In the preamble to the charges against Scheuberin, the inquisitor alluded to sorcery only indirectly; instead he dwelt upon the relationship between witchcraft and sexual immorality, the one being, in his opinion, a necessary complement to the other. Institoris observed that,

> [just as it is hard to suspect an upstanding and decent person of heresy,] so on the contrary a person of bad reputation and shameful habits of faith is easily defamed as a heretic, indeed it is a general rule that all witches have been slaves from a young age to carnal lust and to various adulteries, just as experience teaches.[5]

Helena Scheuberin was an ideal example of this principle: a woman of questionable morals, rumored to be sexually promiscuous, and with a reputation for maleficent magical power. Hence, for Institoris, she *was* a witch, and, by definition, once this identification was made, she also became guilty of demonolatry and of personal and sexual commerce with the devil. For Institoris, such an identification was crucial to his thinking about witches, and the function of an inquisitorial proceeding was in large part to provide a context in which this identification could be made and proved. To this end, he began his interrogation with a series of questions about Scheuberin's virginity and sexual history that made his fellow commissioners exceedingly uncomfortable.[6] Soon Bishop Golser's representative asked the inquisitor directly to cease this line of questioning since it seemed to him improper and irrelevant to the case at hand. Institoris then began to question the witness about several specific points of her testimony, but again his manner was so offensive to the episcopal commissioners that they protested and called a halt to the morning's proceedings.

When the court reconvened, it was with a telling addition: the bishop's representatives had sanctioned the presence of Johann Merwais, whom the documents reveal to be a licentiate in the decretals and a doctor of medicine. From Institoris' perspective, though, his calling was infinitely more sinister: he was an advocate for the defense – a lawyer. Merwais immediately raised questions about the trial's validity, accusing the inquisitor of asking leading

questions and of making a variety of serious procedural errors. Upon investigation, the defense council's motion to dismiss was approved, and over
Institoris' vehement objections the commission vacated the process and
released the suspects.

Through this little drama we see clearly revealed the extent to which the
category "witch" was contested in late-fifteenth-century Germany. All the
learned men at Scheuberin's trial believed in witchcraft. If, up to this point,
Bishop Golser and his representatives had supported the inquisitor with no
real enthusiasm, they certainly had not interfered with his investigation. Nor
did they object to prosecuting those who caused injuries through magic. They
and the inquisitor simply disagreed about how a witch should be recognized,
and, on a more fundamental level, about what a witch actually was. Moreover,
this was not simply an isolated confrontation between inquisitorial and local
authorities but rather a reflection of a much more widespread debate within
the learned, ecclesiastical community over these same issues. Thus, inspired
by this local humiliation, Henry Institoris retired to Cologne to write a
detailed and comprehensive defense of his beliefs. And so, in a way, the insults
of an otherwise obscure woman were responsible for one of the best-known,
most quoted, and, indeed, most infamous of all medieval texts, the "Hammer
of Witches," the *Malleus Maleficarum*.

The study which follows examines the problem of the construction of witchcraft in fifteenth-century Europe, with particular reference to this text. Prior
to the fifteenth century, people spoke in terms of heretics, of *maleficium*, of
monstrous female spirits – the *lamiae* and *strigae*, but not of a single composite category, "witch." By the mid-sixteenth century, however, educated men
generally agreed upon the definitions of "witch" and "witchcraft," definitions
which drew upon, but were clearly distinguished from, older categories. Since
the *Malleus* played a significant role in this evolution of terms, it seems reasonable to focus upon this text, and to determine how its authors arrived at
their particular conception of witchcraft, how the idea of witchcraft functioned within wider cognitive fields, and where the witch of the *Malleus* fit into
the learned discourse of fifteenth-century witchcraft.[7]

First, however, we must understand the basic arguments of the text, its
origins, structure, and methods. This study, taken up in chapter 2, locates the
text and its authors in space and time, as the products of both Dominican and
German experience. The arguments of the *Malleus* are a response to failure
and an answer to critics both numerous and hostile. They aim in the first place
to demonstrate the existence and prevalence of witchcraft and the terrible
threat it poses. Secondly, the text provides sufferers from witchcraft with a
broad range of remedies, both legal and spiritual, of proven effectiveness.

Finally, the text is a guide for civil and ecclesiastical authorities to the successful detection and prosecution of witches. In the course of these prolonged
discussions, Institoris and Sprenger provide a remarkably complete picture of
their witch, along with descriptions of her origins, habits, and powers.

Before this image could be plausible, even intelligible, to a theologically
sophisticated audience, however, Institoris and Sprenger had to define appropriate relationships between witchcraft and established conceptual fields. This
problem was pressing because, as will be argued throughout, the authors' conception of witchcraft was ultimately grounded in traditional beliefs and practices, neither of which had an inherent theological component. In order to
construct a category of "witch" on the basis of such beliefs, theoreticians were
obligated to make it compatible with a learned, theologically informed worldview. An examination of the relationships between witchcraft, God and the
devil, the projects of chapters 3 and 4, follows in the inquisitors' footsteps,
and reveals how they reconciled data from testimony and experience with their
assumptions about the nature of the universe.

That witchcraft was necessary in the first place seems much the product
of a peculiarly late-medieval way of looking at the devil and diabolic power.
Many witch-theorists, Institoris and Sprenger prominent among them,
embraced an oddly bifurcated devil, a being of transcendent but mechanical
power for evil, and a creature whose physical presence was more often of an
almost trivial appearance. This disjunction between impressive diabolic power
and minimal diabolic presence demanded a mediator who could channel and
direct disordering and harmful forces on earth. The witch neatly filled this
void. A comparison of the beliefs of various fifteenth-century witch-theorists
reveals that those who held different, more unitary, conceptions of the devil
conceived of witches that were correspondingly less powerfully threatening.
Their witches remained firmly subordinate to devils, fully dependent upon
their masters for leadership and agenda.

A second problem faced by all witch-theorists was to explain why a just
God would grant permission for witches to wreak such havoc upon the world.
Here again, the belief in a powerful, aggressive, threatening witch corresponded to a mechanical and liberal view of divine permission. Where God
provided meaningful oversight to demons, witchcraft was not particularly
threatening. If, however, God was so offended by human sin that virtually all
diabolic requests to visit punishment upon it were approved, witches were free
to utilize the power of the devil almost automatically. This was a view of diabolic and divine power that was intensely anthropocentric; although the source
of power was ultimately supernatural, it was deployed only by the will and
effort of men and for their own purposes.

In a universe where God and the devil had to such an extent abandoned their traditional roles, learned theologians had plenty of space in which to carve out the new category of witchcraft. In the *Malleus*, the witch becomes the effective agent of diabolic power, a living, breathing, devil on earth in respect to those around her. On the other hand, the witch's power was to some extent balanced by the power of the Church, which could deploy divine power in the form of sacraments and sacramentals for the protection of the faithful. While God and the devil retreated into mechanical passivity the efforts of their human followers became increasingly important. For this reason, the arguments of the *Malleus* focus as much upon spiritual remedies as upon the power of witches, and upon the thin but critical line that separates the diabolic power from the divine.

Although the broad contours of late-medieval learned conceptions of witchcraft were determined by basic metaphysical assumptions, the specific form these conceptions took was primarily the result of the evidence and experience available to various authors. In chapter 5 I take up the epistemological problems posed by belief in witchcraft. In the case of Institoris and Sprenger, their category "witch" responded to their experience as inquisitors, experience which included extensive familiarity with the oral testimony of victims of witchcraft and of accused witches themselves. Institoris and Sprenger did not preside over the trials of learned individuals or even of locally prominent ones; their witches were the common people's witches, those unpleasant and unpopular individuals held responsible for damaging crops, souring milk, and causing illness out of petty malice. In their trials, rumor, hearsay, and legend played an important part. Moreover, because of their Dominican training, the authors were predisposed to accept almost any consistent body of testimony at face value. They repeatedly report as fact anything authenticated by the testimony of "reliable witnesses." As a result, Institoris and Sprenger's notion of witchcraft retained a congruence with traditional beliefs lacking in the constructions of authors with different experience or epistemological orientations.

For all theorists, late-medieval witchcraft was a composite – a combination of motifs derived from a number of quite different traditions: those associated with monstrous female spirits, animal transformation, demonolatrous heresy, maleficent magic, and superstition are among the most prominent. Chapters 5 and 6 set these categories in relation to one another, and show how witch-theorists combined them according to the evidence available to them and their assumptions about the world. The resulting composite figures were in no way haphazard; rather, each theorist used one of these established categories as a kind of conceptual template to provide the underlying principles around which his version of witchcraft was ordered and constructed. In the *Malleus*, as in some other German texts, the witch was defined through her *maleficium* and practice of magic. Throughout southern Europe authors tended to center witchcraft around those traditions earlier associated with the *bonae res* and other female spirits. Many French models of witchcraft depicted the witch more as a demonized heretic – a being defined by her willing entry into the demonic pact and her worship of the devil. In every case, however, the template originally chosen by the witch-theorist both defined and restricted the field of his inquiry and the scope of his investigation, while determining at the same time the inherent plausibility of his definition of "witch" and "witchcraft" and the extent to which these categories could be used to drive witchcraft persecutions.

I will argue that the strength of the category "witchcraft" in the *Malleus* was that the narrative paradigms by which evaluations of witchcraft and the identification of witches were made on the local level in daily life informed its construction. In villages, witchcraft was created within a discursive field of "words and deeds," in narrative accounts of unexpected or otherwise unexplainable harm.[8] In these narratives, the various threads that comprised *maleficium* were woven together to decide the identity of witches beyond reasonable doubt. In the *Malleus*, Institoris and Sprenger raised these explanatory mechanisms to the level of learned discourse, by integrating them (however uncomfortably) into a more theologically sophisticated conception of the world. In essence, the authors provided their audience with a window onto the discursive field in which their informants constructed witchcraft themselves, and in so doing gave their own construction of witchcraft a utility and persuasive force not found in its competitors.

Necessary to the success of this model was the close identification of the theorists' witches with the persons of reputed local *maleficae*, and to make this identification stick, Institoris and Sprenger had to admit that an astonishingly wide array of practices and behaviors were tantamount to witchcraft: magic of almost any kind, rumors of animal transformation, stories of fairies or changelings, magical flight, the evil eye, all could be interpreted as direct evidence of witchcraft. Moreover, for this same reason it is plausible to assume that the description of the persons of witches themselves in the *Malleus* corresponded closely to Institoris and Sprenger's actual experience; hence the final chapter of this study argues that their much noted emphasis upon women as the overwhelming practitioners of witchcraft is quite probably descriptive rather than prescriptive in nature. Nonetheless, Institoris and Sprenger's interpretation of this apparent fact was very much their own, and depended closely upon their intense fear of the disordering power of female sexuality. Just as the person of the witch is closely identified with that of the devil in the *Malleus*, so too does unbridled female sexuality come to be all but indistinguishable from demonic power.

The conception of witchcraft which emerges from this examination of the *Malleus* is idiosyncratic, one of a large number of competing notions of what witchcraft was all about in the late fifteenth century. Yet within fifty years of the text's publication, the learned definition of witchcraft had stabilized, and a category of witchcraft that closely resembled that in the *Malleus* was widely accepted. In large part, I would suggest that this growing consensus was due to the accord between the witch of the *Malleus* and perceived reality. In all probability, to most learned observers, "witches" and "witchcraft" in the world about them would look more like those described in the *Malleus* than those in similar texts. Nor was the conception of witchcraft in the *Malleus* as vulnerable to criticism as were witches modeled after notions of heresy or night-flying women. Perhaps as important, though, was Institoris and Sprenger's explicit claim to the status of authority combined with the ready availability of their text. The authors of witch-treatises were men with an acute sensitivity to the value of textual authority, yet prior to 1500, authoritative texts on witchcraft were not widely available. There are virtually no references to contemporary texts on witchcraft in fifteenth-century witch-treatises, except to Nider's *Formicarius*, which was not, in any case, really a witch-treatise at all. This complete absence of textual references allowed authors to give full reign to their own experience, with consequent regional variations.

The publication of the *Malleus* changed this picture dramatically. By 1500, eight editions of the *Malleus* had been published, and there were five more by 1520. By the time of Institoris' death around 1505, his work could be found in many libraries and judicial reference collections throughout Europe, although especially in Germany.[9] The simple presence of a comprehensive, authoritative guidebook created a certain uniformity of discourse in subsequent witchcraft debate. Almost immediately, authors of witch-treatises began to refer to Institoris and Sprenger as accepted authorities on the subject. In an extensive treatise written in the early sixteenth century, the Dominican inquisitor Sylvester Prieras treats the *Malleus* throughout as *the* authoritative witchcraft text, and refers to Institoris as a *vir magnus*.[10] At about the same time, Gianfrancesco Pico della Mirandola praises the *Malleus* at length in his dialogue on witchcraft, and lists its authors along with Augustine and Gregory the Great as authorities on the subject.[11] Furthermore, as Wolfgang Behringer has pointed out, "Although throughout Europe between 1520 and 1580 no new edition of the *Hexenhammer* was published, it remained the authoritative work and was present in regional libraries."[12]

When the witchcraft debate heated up again in the second half of the sixteenth century, authors no longer bothered to argue about what witchcraft was; instead, they argued over whether it existed. Almost everyone accepted the basic terms of the category "witch," a category substantially similar to that presented in the *Malleus* and in subsequent texts. When, for example, Johann Weyer attacked the reality of witchcraft in his *De Praestigiis Daemonum*, he argued explicitly against the witch of the *Malleus*.[13] When Jean Bodin prepared his counter-blast, *Démonomanie des sorciers*, he did nothing to alter the terms of the debate; he simply refuted Weyer's argument.[14] At this time, too, the *Malleus* enjoyed a second surge of popularity, as sixteen new editions were produced between 1576 and 1670. George Mora estimates that between thirty and fifty thousand copies were distributed during this time by publishers in Frankfurt and the Rhineland, Lyon, Nuremburg, Venice, and Paris.[15]

It is this shift from idiosyncratic text to generally accepted reference work that is most perplexing. Even granting that the *Malleus* offered one of the most persuasive constructions of late-medieval witchcraft, this does not explain its continued popularity a century later. Moreover, by the late sixteenth century there were a number of more recent works, notably those of Bodin and Delrio, in which the treatment of witchcraft was as comprehensive as the *Malleus*. To an extent, however, the very antiquity of the *Malleus* made it an attractive text. The *Malleus* was in this sense a kind of classic of the genre, a text whose rough edges were dulled by age. Because of it, sixteenth and seventeenth-century authors were no longer compelled to write of the new sect of witches; their witches had a short, but well-documented history. The *Malleus* was an agreed-upon starting point for the discourse of witchcraft, a position graphically illustrated by the collections of demonological texts that began to be produced in the 1580s. These texts were usually multi-volume collections of sources drawn from a variety of periods, but all began with the *Malleus*. Thus for generations of scholars, investigations into the problem of witchcraft began quite literally with Institoris and Sprenger's famous text, and appropriately too, since the very notion of "witchcraft" owed so much to their fertile imaginations.

Notes

1 Although the trial records themselves have been lost, detailed notes of the proceedings were made for Bishop Golser, and survive in Brixen's episcopal archives; they have been partially edited by Hartmann Ammann, "Der Innsbrucker Hexenprocess von 1485," *Zeitschrift des Ferdinandeums für Tirol und Vorarlberg* 34 (1890): 1–87. See also Eric Wilson, "Institoris at Innsbruck: Heinrich Institoris, the *Summis Desiderantes* and the Brixen Witch-Trial of 1485," in R.W. Scribner and Trevor Johnson, eds., *Popular Religion in Germany and Central Europe, 1400–1800* (New York: St. Martin's Press, 1996): 87–100.

2 "Pfie dich, du sneder minch, daz dich das fallend übel etc." Ammann, "Innsbrucker Hexenprocess," 40.

3 When Institoris asked her to explain her remark, Helena replied that she had said it "because you preach nothing except heresy" ("Ideo dixi, quia nunquam predicatis nisi heresim"). And when Institoris asked, "how so?" she continued "because you do not

preach except against witches" ("Quia non predicatis nisi contra maleficas"). *Ibid.*, 36.

4 Ammann, "Innsbrucker Hexenprocess," 36; Heide Dienst, "Lebensbewältigung durch Magie: alltägliche Zauberei in Innsbruck gegen Ende des 15. Jahrhunderts," in Alfred Kohler and Heinrich Lutz, eds., *Alltag im 16. Jahrhundert* (Vienna: Verlag für Geschichte und Politik, 1987): 91–3. Scheuberin had a reputation for folk medicine and had lent the knight, one Leopold von Spiess-Friedberg, her expertise. When he did not recover, he turned instead to a learned Italian physician, who also failed to effect a cure, but did apparently induce the dying knight to accuse Scheuberin of witchcraft.

5 "per oppositum personam male fame et inhonestam in fidei moribus de heresi faciliter infamari, ymo et regula generalis est, quod omnes malefice a iuventute carnalitatibus et adulteriis servierunt variis, prout experiencia docuit." Ammann, "Innsbrucker Hexenprocess," 39–40.

6 For the interrogation of Helena Scheuberin and the response of the episcopal commissioners, see *ibid.*, 65–72.

7 In a general sense, this approach to the problem of late-medieval witchcraft is inspired by Stuart Clark's ground-breaking work and, in particular, *Thinking with Demons: The Idea of Witchcraft in Early Modern Europe* (Oxford: Oxford University Press, 1997); more specifically, the ideas of semiotic and symbolic anthropologists informs my emphasis upon the conceptual power of category construction. See especially the work of Clifford Geertz, Edwin Ardener, James Fernandez, Rodney Needham, Malcolm Crick, George Lakoff, and Dan Sperber.

8 Since witchcraft, as Institoris and Sprenger observe, invariably comes to light through the witch's "words and deeds." "Hoc enim est maleficarum proprium concitare adversum se, vel verbis inutilibus aut factis, puta quam petit sibi praestari aliquid, aut infert ei damnum aliquod in orto [sic] et similia hoc ut occasionem recipiant et se manifestant in verbo vel in opere." Henricus Institoris and Jacobus Sprenger, *Malleus Maleficarum* (1487; facsimile reprint, Göppingen: Kümmerle Verlag, 1991), pt. 3, qu. 6, p. 201.

9 André Schnyder, "Der *Malleus Maleficarum*: Fragen und Beobachtungen zu seiner Druckgeschichte sowie zur Rezeption bei Bodin, Binsfeld und Delrio." *Archiv für Kulturgeschichte* 74 (1992): 325–64; Sigrid Brauner, *Fearless Wives and Frightened Shrews: The Construction of the Witch in Early Modern Germany*, ed. Robert H. Brown (Amherst: University of Massachusetts Press, 1985), 32. Although not translated into German until the eighteenth century, the message and ideas in the *Malleus* were disseminated to those unversed in Latin. "For example," writes Brauner, "at the request of the city of Nuremburg, Kramer provided a manuscript with trial instructions in both Latin and German" for the benefit of municipal judges with no knowledge of Latin (33).

10 Sylvester Prieras (c. 1456–1523), *De Strigimagarum, Daemonumque Mirandis, Libri Tres* (Rome: 1521), a.1.

11 Gianfrancesco Pico della Mirandola, *Strix* (Argentoratum [Strassburg]: Carole Weinrichius, 1612), 131–2.

12 "Obwohl in ganz Europa zwischen 1520 und 1580 keine Neuauflagen des Hexenhammers gedruckt wurden: er blieb das maßgebende Werk und war in den regionalen Bibliotheken vorhanden." Wolfgang Behringer, *Hexenverfolgung in Bayern* (Munich: R. Oldenbourg, 1988), 82. Behringer also observes that knowledge of the *Malleus* informed the composition of interrogatories in late-sixteenth-century German trials (132).

13 Although Weyer quotes a variety of witch-treatises, he relies most extensively upon the *Malleus* to provide him with erroneous notions of witchcraft. See George Mora, introduction to Johann Weyer, *Witches, Devils, and Doctors in the Renaissance*, trans. John Shea (Binghamton: Medieval and Renaissance Texts and Studies, 1991), li–lvi.

14 Gerhild Scholz Williams, *Defining Dominion: The Discourses of Magic and Witchcraft in Early Modern France and Germany* (Ann Arbor: University of Michigan Press, 1995), 68.

15 Mora, lxxxiv.

2

Origins and arguments

The *Malleus* is an idiosyncratic text, reflective of its authors' particular experiences and preoccupations. It is, in the first place, an expression of a distinctively clerical worldview, the product of two lifetimes of academic, spiritual, and pastoral experience within the Church. But more than this, it is also the result of a peculiarly Dominican encounter between learned and folk traditions, an encounter determined in part by the demands of inquisitorial office, and in part by the requirements of effective preaching and pastoral care. Yet although the *Malleus* is certainly a Dominican text, it is not necessarily representative of Dominican or even inquisitorial thought as a whole. Dominicans in France, Spain, and, to a lesser extent, in Italy had quite different notions of what witches were all about, and of the means required to curb their spread. Despite the book's subsequent popularity throughout the continent, the *Malleus* is very much a book written by and about people living in southern Germany and the Alps, and reflects this more or less coherent cultural tradition. Finally, the authors themselves were unusual figures in their own right, whose personal histories – especially that of Institoris – manifest themselves in their writing.

When Henry Institoris began to compose the *Malleus*, some time in 1485–86, he was well into his fifties, in other words, by medieval standards, he was already an old man.[1] Indeed, early in 1486, after a particularly unpleasant encounter with the inquisitor's zeal, Georg Golser wrote to a friend that Institoris seemed "completely childish on account of his age."[2] Yet Golser's appraisal was almost certainly wrong: despite his age, Institoris was not senile. Rather, he was a man capable of inspiring profound animosity in those he met, and his "childishness" seems to have been a permanent feature of his personality, perhaps exacerbated by, but not the result of, his advancing years. The casual insult does, however, make the point that despite a career that left him exceptionally well qualified to tackle his subject, Institoris was not someone who was so well respected by his peers that his views on witchcraft would be accepted without question. Quite the contrary, he was widely (and perhaps even charitably) regarded as being somewhat eccentric.

Undeniably, Institoris was a well-educated man. At a young age he had entered the Dominican convent in his home town of Schlettstadt, a house well known for its excellent library and provincial school.[3] There, Institoris received training in the humanities before matriculating to the four-year course in the arts required of all Dominicans.[4] The curriculum of the Dominican *studium artium* centered upon rational philosophy, and above all upon the works of Aristotle. Students began with grammar and logic, and then proceeded to natural philosophy, metaphysics, and moral philosophy. But at the same time they were also prepared for their work in the ministry by attending courses of practical lectures on basic theology, scriptural interpretation and effective preaching. Graduates of these schools could then claim the title of Master of Arts, and a rank comparable to that of graduates of the universities.

The most promising of students, however, among whom Institoris was plainly numbered, were encouraged to continue their education at a school for advanced theology; and Institoris probably studied theology at the *studium generale* at Cologne, which, after St. Jacques in Paris, was the most prestigious Dominican school in fifteenth-century Europe. There he would have studied and lectured on sacred scripture, the *Sentences* of Peter Lombard, and the theology of Thomas Aquinas. All in all a degree of Master of Theology required at least fourteen years of higher education, but, since friars were required to teach as lectors at provincial schools for between five and seven years before they could be awarded their degrees, all of this time need not have been spent at the university. Hence, Institoris probably spent at most three or four years at Cologne, before leaving with the titles of Master of Arts and Lector in Theology, and, though his subsequent career would seem to have left him scant time for further study, he nonetheless continued to lecture, eventually receiving his doctorate in theology at Rome in 1479.[5]

Institoris' most important pursuit, however, was always a vigorous, zealous and uncompromising war against the enemies of the faith, whomever he might perceive them to be. Heretics and witches had this much in common with the emperor and reforming clergy: all were the objects of Institoris' righteous wrath. This aggressive zeal for the faith, combined with his considerable personal ambition, secured rapid advancement for Institoris within the Order. Although little is known of his early career, we do know that in 1467, at about the age of 37, he received an important position in the papal commission assigned to combat the Hussites in Bohemia and central Germany. Institoris' job was to preach against heresy and to collect money to assist the campaign; in October of 1467, we find the head of the commission, Rudolf, bishop of

Wratislava and papal legate, writing to encourage and assist Institoris by del-
egating to him the power to remit sins and the authority to grant plenary indul-
gences.[6] In another letter, written four years later, Institoris agreed to lift the
interdict he had placed upon the town of Lipczk in retaliation for the continued presence of "supporters of Bohemian heretics," which would indicate that
he had also been provided with a corresponding stick with which to beat the
intransigent.[7]

Institoris' success and apparent popularity in Rome obtained an appointment for him as inquisitor in 1474, with all of the privileges of a preacher-
general of the Order. His appointment was unusual, however, in that instead
of being appointed to a particular province, Institoris was authorized "to carry
out the office of the Inquisition, either where there is no inquisitor, or, where
there is, by [that inquisitor's] permission and pleasure."[8] By the terms of this
assignment, Institoris was now free to choose his own residence and move
about as he pleased, an unusual honor for one so new to the Holy Office. In
the Inquisition Institoris found his calling, and soon received additional promotion for his successful prosecution of heretics and witches. In 1478, Pope
Sixtus IV appointed him inquisitor to upper Germany, a position to which
he was reappointed in 1482 with Jacob Sprenger as colleague. In the mean-
time, as Schlettstadt's most famous son, he had been elected prior of the
Dominican convent there in 1481, although just two and one half years later
he was released from the obligations of that office, possibly to allow him to
devote his energies more fully to the Inquisition.

By 1485 Institoris was easily the most experienced inquisitor in
Germany, and was held in high esteem in Rome: in the letter confirming his
position as inquisitor for upper Germany, Pope Sixtus was unstinting in his
praise, commending him as a man notable for his "zeal for religion, knowledge
of letters, integrity of life, constancy of faith, and other praiseworthy virtues
and merits."[9] Nonetheless, there was also a sharply contrasting side to Institoris' life and character, hard to reconcile with such a glowing endorsement,
unless we see Brother Henry as one of those people adept at ingratiating themselves with their superiors while systematically alienating their subordinates
and peers.

Certainly Institoris was widely disliked, and the belligerence, self-
righteousness, and refusal to compromise that served him so well on the
inquisitor's bench caused him difficulty in other contexts. For example, at
exactly the same moment as he was receiving his first appointment to the
Inquisition in 1474, Institoris was facing a lengthy prison sentence, the result
of his typical inability to restrain himself when fired with zeal for a just cause.
In a sermon defending the temporal powers of the pope against imperial
infringement, Institoris had allowed himself to make several personal and slan-

derous remarks about the emperor himself. The emperor was not amused and nor was the Dominican general chapter, which ordered Institoris to be jailed for detracting from the majesty of the emperor.[10] Indeed, only the intervention of the master-general of the Order saved Institoris from prison: the same letter that gave him his promotion suspended his sentence, a suspension that was eventually made permanent in 1479.

But if it was easy to pardon an excess of enthusiasm on behalf of the papacy, it was less simple to excuse Institoris' frequent quarrels and misadventures within his own Order. In April of 1475, the master-general was again compelled to intervene in Institoris' affairs, this time to authorize the prior of the convent at Basel to settle a dispute between Institoris and two other Schlettstadt friars, each of whom had charged the other with the theft of a sum of money.[11] The matter was settled, apparently in Institoris' favor, but it is indicative of his ability to carry a grudge that four years later the unfortunate prior at Basel was still receiving instructions from the master-general, this time authorizing him to resolve Institoris' charges of slander against his opponents.[12]

A more serious matter arose in 1482, when Institoris had been given the job of collecting money donated for the war against the Turks, and was strongly suspected of embezzling funds. On March 26th he was summoned to present himself in Rome within nine days or face "the gravest penalties," including, but not limited to, the loss of all goods, privileges, offices and rank, to be followed by expulsion from the Order, excommunication and imprisonment.[13] Nor was Rome entirely convinced of the effectiveness of its draconian threats, for just six days later a papal commission also wrote to the bishop of Augsburg, asking him to determine "as secretly and cautiously as could be done" whether Institoris was still in the city and ordering him to be detained if he was. The commission further specified that all money, silver, and jewels which Institoris had deposited with "a certain widow" were to be recovered by any expedient means and entrusted to someone of greater reliability.[14] Although the conclusion of the affair is undocumented, Institoris was evidently not convicted of anything serious since he retained his position within the Inquisition, and was back in papal good graces by the following summer. He was not, however, given further financial responsibilities.

It is hard to know what to make of these scandals, but they dogged Institoris' career.[15] Though Institoris never mentions his troubles in his writings, it seems likely that they contributed to the keen hostility with which he greeted any hint of criticism, and to his self-image as a man unjustly persecuted by numerous enemies. To Institoris' superiors, however, it seems that, when weighed in the balance, Institoris' devotion to the papacy and the Church – as well as his capacity for hard work – counted for more than his occasionally serious lapses in judgment. In consequence, despite his constant bickering with his colleagues and his intermittent brushes with more serious displinary proceedings, Institoris retained his position as inquisitor for most of his long life and he was still pursuing witches and heretics in Bohemia when he died, probably in 1505.

For most of his life, then, Institoris was involved with the fight against heresy. At the beginning of his career we find him participating in the trial and execution of the Waldensian "bishop," Frederick Reiser – an event which, Institoris tells us, confirmed his belief in the ever-increasing power of heresy in Christendom.[16] Soon afterwards, Institoris was preaching against the Hussites, and his experience with Utraquism goes far toward explaining his concern with sacramental heresies of all kinds. Such were his chief concerns at least through 1480, when, while in Augsburg, he perceived "a dangerous error concerning the daily communion of the laity," and initiated inquisitorial proceedings accordingly.[17] Indeed, a great deal of Institoris' writing – even that on witchcraft – is closely tied to his conceptions of the sacrament and the ways in which a physical object can mediate between the natural and supernatural worlds. The *Malleus* was Institoris' only work on witchcraft, but he wrote about the sacrament on several occasions, attacking eucharistic errors, great and small.[18]

By 1480, however, Institoris had become concerned by the dangers of witchcraft, and he accordingly began to prosecute suspected witches with vigor. Unfortunately, the precise extent of the inquisitor's campaign is not clear. Though Institoris claimed extensive personal experience in witch prosecutions both in the *Malleus* and his personal correspondence (for instance in a report written in 1490 to the Nürnberg city council, he boasted of having been responsible for the discovery and execution of more than two hundred witches[19]), there is an almost complete lack of corroborating evidence. Indeed, on the basis of contemporary documents, the only witch-trials in which Institoris' participation can be proven are those which took place in Ravensburg in 1484 and in Innsbruck in the following year. Though additional records might easily have been lost, it seems certain that Institoris' own account of the extent of his personal experience in witchcraft prosecutions is greatly exaggerated.

Whatever his previous experience, however, in the autumn of 1484 Institoris arrived in Ravensburg and began at once to preach against witchcraft.[20] In response to his request that Ravensburgers come forward to denounce "hechsen ald unholden," a number of suspects were arrested, and eventually eight women were convicted and burned. Yet although Institoris seems here to have had the support of the mayor and other civic officials, elsewhere he met with opposition from local officials, both secular and ecclesiastical, who resented the sudden expansion of inquisitorial activity against foes even more nebulous than usual.

In response, Institoris went to Rome that winter, carrying a letter, signed both by him and his colleague, Jacob Sprenger, asking for explicit authority to prosecute witchcraft. By early December he had received an entirely satisfactory reply in the form of the famous "witch-bull," the *Summis Desiderantes* of Innocent VIII, which recognized the existence of witches and the authority of inquisitors to do what was necessary to get rid of them; Institoris and Sprenger, the pope commanded, were neither to be molested nor hindered in any manner whatsoever by any authority, under pain of excommunication and worse.[21] Further, the bishop of Strassburg was asked to enforce the provisions of the bull, and to compel obedience, through excommunication if necessary, or, failing that, through an appeal to the secular arm. Six months later, Innocent supplemented this endorsement with personal letters to Archduke Sigismund and the archbishop of Mainz, thanking them for their efforts, but also urging them to be even more active in their support of the Inquisition.[22] At the same time, Innocent wrote to the abbot of Weingarten, who had apparently assisted Institoris' campaign in Ravensburg the previous year, to say that he had urged the Archduke to protect him from the retaliation of those he had offended – some indication of just how unpopular Institoris' efforts had been.[23]

Meanwhile, Institoris had taken his campaign back to Germany, stopping first in Tyrol and the town of Innsbruck.[24] At the time, Innsbruck was a prosperous but unspectacular south German town, notable only for its proximity to Italy (the source of its prosperity) and the presence of the archduke, who had a permanent residence there since the early years of the century.[25] Tyrol was, Institoris tells us, a notorious hotbed of witches; but it is just as likely that simple convenience, combined with his haste to begin prosecutions, explains his choice of location – the diocese of Brixen, which included Innsbruck, being the first territory within his jurisdiction on the road from Rome.[26]

As was proper, Institoris first presented himself and his credentials to Golser, the bishop, in order to obtain his consent and support (although with the recent promulgation of the witch-bull, and with Innocent VIII still actively promoting his inquisitors' investigations, the bishop could hardly refuse). In mid-July Golser circulated the witch-bull throughout his diocese with an open letter to all ecclesiastical personnel, commanding them to assist Institoris' investigations and offering an indulgence of forty days to all who would step forward to denounce witches.[27] In addition, Institoris had advertisements displayed prominently about town, most likely (as he recommends in the *Malleus*) through notices on the walls of the parish church and town hall which invited anyone with any knowledge of witchcraft whatsoever to come forward and testify, under pain of severe ecclesiastical and secular penalties.[28]

Institoris knew his audience well, as the tenor of such an appeal shows. There was no talk of devils, or diabolic pacts, or intercourse with Satan; at this point in his investigation the emphasis was placed squarely upon concrete misfortunes attributed to *maleficium* and rumors of malign occult powers. Further, people were advised to come forward "if anyone knows, has seen or heard that any person is suspected of being a heretic and witch, and particularly of practicing things which do harm to people, cattle or the fruits of the earth."[29] At the same time, Institoris began a vigorous schedule of preaching, in an effort to educate his audience about the dangers of witchcraft, its signs and telltale characteristics, and to recommend permissible countermeasures. To all appearances, Institoris' campaign was immediately successful: soon he was hearing an impressive stream of testimony – an extensive melange of direct accusations, rumors, legends, and snippets of traditional witchcraft beliefs – out of which, over the next five weeks, he was to cull sufficient evidence to indict about fifty witches. At this point, however, something happened. The proceedings were delayed for three weeks, at which time Institoris produced a second, alternative list which indicted only fourteen suspects – seven from the first list and seven altogether "new" witches, prominent among whom was Helena Scheuberin.

By mid-September, Bishop Golser wrote to Institoris granting him full episcopal jurisdiction, and authorizing him to conduct trials in the bishop's name.[30] But once again Institoris' proceedings were impeded, this time by order of the archduke, who ordered Institoris to consult with a colleague – a pastor from a nearby town whom the bishop named as commissioner. It was not until October 14th that these two men, accompanied by witnesses and a notary, began to hear formal testimony concerning the suspects. Although the proceedings at Innsbruck did not conform to the neat patterns laid down in inquisitorial manuals, this was not unusual for the period. As Richard Kieckhefer has shown, in late-medieval Germany the activities of the papal Inquisition (to say nothing of episcopal inquisitions) were very much *ad hoc* affairs. Typically, inquisitors operated as independent autonomous agents; they had little supervision outside the papal curia, and their objectives and jurisdictions were only loosely defined.[31] Often enough, such institutional shortcomings led to inertia, but where motivated inquisitors actively campaigned against heresy, they led to disorganized and irregular proceedings.

Given the above, it is not altogether strange that Institoris' investigations ran into difficulties. Yet, even so, it is surprising that his investigation should have suffered so sudden and so thorough a collapse: within a month, on

November 14th, Golser wrote another two letters — the first to Institoris directly, complaining of the scandals and the dangers which his trials had generated and urging him to quit the town; the second, to a friend and priest in Innsbruck, saying that,

> if [Institoris] does not withdraw with all speed, you, father, should say to him in my place that more than enough scandals have arisen because of his bad trial, and that he should not remain in this place, lest anything worse should follow from this or happen to him.[32]

Although Golser does not specify the precise scandal he has in mind, he is probably referring to the interrogation of Helena Scheuberin with which we began. He was apparently offended by the nuts and bolts of the inquisitor's case, since he later commented to a friend that the inquisitor had "clearly demonstrated his foolishness" since "he presumed much that had not been proved."[33] Institoris for his part could not disagree more, and maintained in the *Malleus* that he would have needed an entire book to record all the instances of malign magic reported in Innsbruck alone:

> For how many of the blind, of the lame, of the withered, of those ensnared by diverse infirmities, legally swear that they strongly suspect that infirmities of this kind both in general and in particular have been caused by witches?[34]

An especially large number of alleged witches were suspected of love magic, which Institoris blamed upon the high number of bitter, betrayed women in the town.[35] Yet this connection between female sexuality and witchcraft, so obvious to the inquisitor, was decisively rejected by the investigating commission that so abruptly halted the proceedings.

Institoris, however, refused to let matters rest, and he spent the next several months hanging around Innsbruck collecting evidence, harassing witnesses, even briefly seizing a suspected witch or two on his own initiative, all in all making of himself an insufferable nuisance. This independent foray into witch-hunting, combined with the wretched outcome of the trial, induced the bishop, a man who from the outset had been less than enthusiastic about the campaign, to write his letters urging the inquisitor to quit the city and trouble its citizens no more. This one-sided correspondence grew progressively more insistent until in February 1486, his patience exhausted, the bishop wrote to Institoris for the last time. He expressed astonishment that Institoris remained in his diocese where his presence had brought errors, dissension, and scandal, and ordered him to cease molesting the citizens of Innsbruck and to return at once to his convent, lest the husbands and friends of the women whom Institoris had persecuted lay hands on him and do him injury. Further, in language

unusually blunt for correspondence among ecclesiastics, Golser informed
Institoris that he was to do nothing further in his diocese save leave it.[36] This
a disgruntled Institoris finally did, retiring to Cologne and leaving behind him
an enraged citizenry, annoyed officials, and a thoroughly perplexed archduke,
who hired two prominent doctors of law, Ulrich Molitor and Conrad Stürtzel,
to explain the whole witchcraft business to him once and for all.[37]

But by this time Institoris had also begun to write his treatise on witchcraft as a rebuttal to his critics and as a program for further action. He began
with a short manual on technical matters: a series of instructions, advisories,
and model documents for judges presiding over witchcraft prosecutions.[38]
Soon afterwards he decided to write a more substantial and ambitious work,
one in which strictly judicial matters would comprise only the final part. This
was to become the *Malleus Maleficarum*, the work that he was to "co-author"
with his fellow inquisitor, Jacob Sprenger.

Institoris' choice of Sprenger as his collaborator was both politic and
wise. Perhaps first and foremost, Jacob Sprenger was a man far more distinguished and far less contentious than Institoris; second, both as an academic
and within the Dominican Order, Sprenger's career was exemplary. Having
established himself as an outstanding scholar at an early age, by 1468 Sprenger
was already lecturing on the sentences at the University of Cologne, even as
he was still working towards his master's degree; ten years later, he was a professor of theology; and, by 1480, Sprenger had been elected dean of the theology faculty. Sprenger was also well known outside the schools as the "apostle
of the Rosary," since his ardent devotion to the Virgin had been rewarded with
a vision in which he was exhorted to spread the cult of the rosary throughout Germany. To this end, Sprenger had introduced rosarial brotherhoods
to Germany, which immediately enjoyed tremendous popularity. Finally,
Sprenger was active in Dominican politics as a champion of the Observantine
reform: he was elected prior of the prestigious convent at Cologne in 1472
while surprisingly young (probably no older than his mid-thirties), and just
two years later he won appointment as vicar to the Observant convents on the
upper Rhine; then in 1481 he also became inquisitor to the same area, principally Mainz, Trier, and Cologne. In short, Sprenger could boast of a career
as successful and as varied as any Dominican could hope for. Indeed, so
estimable were Sprenger's intellectual and spiritual attainments, that some
have questioned the actual extent of Sprenger's contribution to the *Malleus*.[39]
Although Sprenger certainly wrote the "Apologia auctoris" which prefaces the
Malleus, and did so in terms that strongly suggest his active participation in its
writing, nonetheless because the work is of one piece stylistically (and Institoris definitely wrote the third part of the text single-handedly), and because
the *Malleus* throughout reflects Institoris' known preoccupations, it is likely

that beyond lending the work the prestige of his name, Sprenger's contribution was minimal.[40]

However it came into being, by 1487 Institoris had the manuscript of the
Malleus in hand, and the same desire to produce as authoritative a text as possible that had likely led him to seek Sprenger's collaboration in the first place
now induced him to try to obtain the formal endorsement of the faculty of
Cologne.[41] Institoris' efforts resulted in two endorsements. The first, signed
by just four members of the theology faculty, allowed that the first two parts
of the text contained nothing contrary to sound philosophy and the Catholic
faith, and endorsed the third as a model for actual witchcraft prosecutions
(provided that nothing was done repugnant to canon law). The second boasted
twice as many signatories, but was also more general; not even mentioning
the *Malleus*, it simply commended the Inquisition for its zeal, acknowledged
the existence of witches, and encouraged all good Christians to assist in the
fight against this pestiferous sect.

Exactly how Institoris came by these approbations is a complex and contentious question. Hansen has suggested that the second endorsement is, in
effect, a forgery committed by Institoris with the help of a compliant notary
after the first failed to meet his expectations.[42] Schnyder, however, has recently
given new life to a simpler alternative – that the first endorsement was signed
only by those members of the faculty who could take the time to read and
review the entire book, while sympathetic but typically busy academicians
could sign the more general endorsement in good conscience.[43] In any case,
however accomplished, the result was the same: the *Malleus* was now printed
with an impressive collection of credentials, prefaced first by the papal bull,
Summis Desiderantes, then by the two approbations, uncomfortably spliced
together, and finally by letters signed by Maximilian I in 1486, placing inquisitors under his protection. In short, the text proclaimed itself to be as authoritative as the authors' ingenuity could make it.

That such a show of authority was needed demonstrates just how novel
the *Malleus* actually was. Certainly there had been witch-treatises before, but
these had either refrained from making sweeping judgments, had remained
agreeably obscure, or had avoided doctrinal pronouncements altogether. The
Malleus, on the other hand, was readily available in printed editions, addressed
thorny doctrinal problems without flinching from (or even acknowledging)
their problematic consequences, and looked at an old but always disturbing
subject in a new way. Witchcraft had for centuries remained on the periphery
of Church doctrine and, although always a grave sin and a serious concern, it
had never before been considered a cause for real alarm. In the *Malleus* though,
witchcraft was elevated to a pivotal position in the struggle between man and
the devil, and was given new responsibility for the world's ever-increasing ills.

The *Malleus*, in other words, proposed a basic shift in the way in which the Church should conceptualize evil, a shift which not all contemporaries were prepared to accept.

Institoris and Sprenger wrote the *Malleus* with several stated objectives: first, it was to refute critics who denied the reality of witchcraft and hindered the persecution of witches; second, it was to provide arguments, *exempla*, and advice for preachers who had to deal with witchcraft on the pastoral level; and third, to lend detailed assistance to judges engaged in the difficult work of combating witchcraft through legal prosecution. In broad terms, each of the book's three sections deals with one of these issues, while also addressing the two problems central to the work: "what is witchcraft?" and "who is a witch?"

Underlying this division, however, is a surprisingly sophisticated sense that categories are in part determined by the fields of discourse to which they pertain.[44] Thus, whereas a legal determination of witchcraft depends upon a sufficiency of evidence of a particular kind, derived from behavior observed and conjectured, this is a kind of determination wholly inappropriate to theological discourse. That Institoris and Sprenger understood this distinction is readily demonstrated by their consideration of who should legitimately be called a heretic: heresy, in the strict sense, was an error in understanding and of faith, ultimately discernible by God alone. For this reason, the authors submit, a theologian would never be willing to make a certain determination of heresy because, no matter what a man's behavior, it would be impossible to know if he acted out of an error of faith. For a canonist (or an inquisitor), on the other hand, a man was a heretic when he was so designated by the lawful judgment of men.[45] In other words, the definition of the category "heretic" corresponded to the kind of discourse in which the term was used.

Similarly, the seemingly utilitarian arrangement of the *Malleus* responds to more sophisticated epistemological considerations, as each section treats its subject matter with changing rules of argumentation, types of evidence and criteria for logical validity. Accordingly, the first section examines witchcraft in largely theoretical terms, through the lenses of theology and natural philosophy, by citation of authority, and by means of "scholastic" argumentation.

But, in the second section, when the authors turn to matters of practice, they begin by remarking:

> Because we are now concerned with moral issues whence there is no need to insist upon varied arguments and expositions in everything . . . therefore we pray God that the reader should not seek a demonstration of all things where

a suitable probability suffices, the truth of which follows conclusively from our own experience, seen and heard, and from the relations of witnesses worthy of belief.[46]

Thus Institoris and Sprenger call attention to the fact that their argument, which has up to this point tried to follow the rules of scholastic and theological argumentation, will now be framed in what they conceive of as moral terms; henceforth they will appeal to the rule of authority only to provide context for reliable human experience. This differentiation between kinds of discourse, however, cannot denote the presence of rigid boundaries between different realms of human experience, since it is an essential characteristic of the authors' thought that the truth theologically determined must correspond at some level with the reality of sensory experience and vice versa. Rather, this distinction is necessary to illuminate the witch in all her aspects, which indeed is the point of the *Malleus*: to take the witch constructed by learned theologians, the witch of traditional legend, folktale, and rumor, and the old woman huddled before the inquisitor's bench and to blend them into a single being – a being capable of satisfying the demands of all situations in which her existence was meaningful.

The *Malleus* was not, then, as Sprenger ingenuously stated in his "Apology," merely a compilation of materials drawn from ancient and authoritative sources; it was instead a unique assemblage of experience and authority juxtaposed in shifting ways.[47] Like all medieval academics, Institoris and Sprenger were acutely conscious of the value and importance of authorities, both to formal argumentation and to more casual discourse. Above all, they cite continuously from scripture; but in clear second place come the authors of canon and civil law: Gratian's *Decretum*, the *Decretals* of Gregory IX, the *Decretalium Liber Sextus*, Justinian's codification of civil law, and commentators on all of these. Among the *Malleus*' other frequently cited authorities (such as Isidore of Seville, Gregory I, Dionysius the Pseudo-Areopagite, Albertus Magnus, and the *Glossa Ordinaria*) there are also more recent works related to the Dominican educational background of its authors: these include Raymond of Penyafort, Peter of Palude, and, especially, Johannes Nider.[48] But there is also Institoris and Sprenger's own personal testimony; for despite our doubts as to the precise extent of their inquisitorial experience (it is not even certain that Sprenger had ever presided over a witch-trial) they both claimed extensive personal knowledge, and possessed a fund of narrative accounts taken from their own experiences or those of their informants.[49]

Institoris and Sprenger begin their text by examining witchcraft at its most abstract, from the perspective of the Dominican theological system, and the analysis which follows was intended to mimic the forms of Thomist disputation. This method, which the authors call "scholastic," begins with a series of propositional questions. Then follows the counterargument, the citation of seemingly contrary authorities, a *responsio* or solution to the problem, and finally the replies to specific objections. In capable hands, and applied to appropriate subject matter, this sort of analysis was highly persuasive and carried considerable prestige – no doubt the reason it was chosen by our authors since it was not terribly responsive to their needs. First, and perhaps foremost, it appears that Institoris and Sprenger found it difficult to subordinate their discussion to the rigid logic of the *questio*; they often embark on rambling digressions into related but not strictly relevant topics, occasionally even abandoning their chosen method entirely.[50] Second, the requirement that all objections be answered in full seems to have weighed rather heavily upon the authors. Although, to their credit, Institoris and Sprenger address difficult questions, their replies are often testy, ranging from terse, unsatisfying dismissals to lengthy and confusing bouts of jargon-filled debate.

Despite all of this, however, the main contours of their argument remain clear. The first part of the *Malleus* begins with two preliminary questions, both of which are necessary to the more detailed argument to follow. First, they ask whether the existence of witches is an essential tenet of Catholic teaching or whether witchcraft is instead imaginary, the result of some occult but natural process, the deluding phantasms of the devil, or simply the fancies of overwrought human minds.[51] The latter possibilities the authors then emphatically deny: they point out that because the devil exists and has the power to do marvelous things, witchcraft, if done through his aid and with the permission of God, could certainly be real as well. They draw a comparable conclusion from the authorities – scriptures, doctors of the Church, theologians, canon and civil law; for, they argue, if witchcraft were imaginary and witches non-existent or essentially harmless, they would surely not be so consistently and severely condemned.

Witches, in their view, are beings who are not, and could not be, imaginary, but who "can, with the help of demons, on account of the pact they have with them, and with the permission of God, bring about real harmful magical effects."[52] In the *Malleus*, witchcraft is specifically predicated upon this combination of an overtly expressed pact with the devil, the active participation of the witch in acts of *maleficium* and consequent actual, physical, harm. All else definitionally is not witchcraft and does not fall within the purview of the authors' investigation. The pact is crucial, for it articulates the relationship between the witch and Satan through which witchcraft must arise; through her pact,

> the witch has offered herself completely and has bound herself to the devil really and in truth and not fantastically and in the imagination only, and thus it ought

to be understood that she cooperates with the devil in body and in truth; for all works of witches are to this end, whether they always carry out their witchcraft through the pact, or through a glance, or through the spoken word, or through the operation of some instrument of witchcraft deposited under the threshold of a house.[53]

Since both the pact and the harm that springs from it are real, witchcraft must be real as well.

This conception of witchcraft is strikingly narrow: *maleficium* is not simply a kind of magical or occult harm, but harm wrought through a cooperative endeavor on the part of both the witch and devil, when bound together in a particular kind of contractual relationship. Such a restricted definition ˙red defense. In particular, the authors had to prove that occult harm arises ᵐ the devil and the witch in concert, since, in practical terms, ⁻torms without the help of any demon simply by drop- ɐɟ water, or if the devil in his turn could cause tem- ʰ, it would be difficult to know when to blame ⁿd when not.[54] In a long and convoluted ᵉ in effect that although devils can and ˀs, for various technical reasons they prefer not to do so. In fact, bad angels find the help of a witch so convenient when working physical harm, that they employ them as a matter of course whenever they wish to cause malicious injuries (*maleficiales*).[55] As far as the witches themselves were concerned, the matter was simpler, since if they really were witches, they must definitionally do their evil work through the devil. Although a person might employ natural agents to produce occult but still natural effects, when a witch employed any object, word, or behavior in her magic it was merely as a sign or adjunct to the power of the devil.

Institoris and Sprenger recognize that this is potentially confusing, and attempt to clarify their position using the example of *fascinatio*, the evil eye.[56] They accept as an established fact that the gaze of certain persons – menstruating women for example – has a natural power capable of bringing about physical effects, and that in some angry or disturbed old women this gaze may be sufficient to do real harm to young and impressionable minds and bodies. But the authors also insist that such old women are exactly the sort who are often witches, in which case the malice of demons inspires and assists the natural power of their eyes. The authors' point, to which they will return several times, is that the mere possibility of a natural explanation for misfortune does not mean that all misfortunes are natural. Quite the contrary, where there are witches there will be witchcraft, and so only in the absence of possible malefactors should natural agencies be considered as possible causes for harm. In this way, the *Malleus* employs the related categories of "witch" and "witchcraft" reciprocally, using the presence of one to determine the existence of the other. Where there are witches, a category that is inevitably socially defined, there must be witchcraft; where there are *maleficiales*, misfortunes that are perceived to be malicious, there must be witches. This link between moral behavior and ambiguous harm, between the perception of human malice and malicious misfortune, allows the authors to extend their conception of witchcraft to an almost limitless number of applications and makes plausible their claim that witches constitute a serious threat to Christendom.

Institoris and Sprenger believed that witchcraft was already endemic throughout much of Europe and was increasing daily. They explain that this evil had increased in recent times because of an unhappy congruence between the three necessary preconditions for witchcraft: the presence of witches (or of women ready to fill that role), the active participation of the devil, and the permission of God.[57] In this complex of interrelated variables, the necessary link between natural and supernatural realms was provided by the pact joining the witch with the devil. Looking at the problem from this perspective, the authors then begin to construct a formal definition of "witch." *Maleficium* is not a major concern here, for although witchcraft may be a highly visible and fully sufficient sign of the witch, it is not a necessary one, for a witch is a witch whether she ever casts an evil spell or not, provided only that she has entered into an express compact with the devil. This unholy allegiance does determine the witch's behavior, but her acts are those associated more with heresy than with the infliction of injury:

> Mark well, too, that among other things, [witches] have to do four deeds for the increase of that perfidy, that is, to deny the Catholic faith in whole or in part through verbal sacrilege, to devote themselves body and soul [to the devil], to offer up to the Evil One himself infants not yet baptized, and to persist in diabolic filthiness through carnal acts with incubus and succubus demons.[58]

This list is interesting not only for the lack of any mention of *maleficium*, but also for the emphasis placed upon sexuality and reproduction. Institoris and Sprenger would argue that it was the specifically sexual link between demons and witches which was responsible for the appalling growth of witchcraft in their day, serving to lure already immoral women further into sin, holding them in sexual servitude, and providing, as well, future generations of witches.

In the following three questions, the authors examine this curious state of affairs in more detail, beginning with an attempt to construct a coherent picture of the power and the nature of demons and to explain their interest in human sexuality. Logically, they should then turn to the other half of the equation and examine the role of the witch herself. But before they do so, they try to address a perceived weak point in their argument, and embark on a long and confusing *questio* on the possible influence of the stars, both as the agents of specific acts of *maleficium* and upon the growth of witchcraft in general.[59] The latter point is simplest and addressed first: again following accepted authorities, Institoris and Sprenger argue that neither "fate," nor the stars, nor the Powers that move them can determine human destinies, much less the sort of specific behavior required to become a witch, for the alternative would deny free will. Not that the human will is absolutely free, of course, else decisions would be made entirely at random: rather the will is informed by various extrinsic agents of which the stars are one. But stars affect only the body; angels, bad and good, affect the intellect; while God alone influences the will. It can happen that stars may give a person bodily appetites or physical predilections that make him more prone to witchcraft, but the catalyst for the specific sins of witchcraft will still be the temptations of the devil and not the stars, just as a choleric person, although naturally prone to anger, must be tempted in order to commit murder and is personally responsible for his actions if he does so. That the influence of the stars might lie behind specific occasions of *maleficium* is more problematic, and harks back to the unsatisfactory response to the possibility of natural causation in the second question. Ultimately, although the response is now considerably longer, it remains much the same.

> Celestial bodies cause natural effects, but the works of witches which are called malicious harms are not of this kind, in as much as they arise out of harm done to creatures contrary to the accustomed order of nature.[60]

The logical basis for this argument is the Aristotelian dictum that from the effect the cause is known; in this case the works of witchcraft are invariably harmful and unnatural and so cannot have a cause that is natural, as are the stars, or intrinsically good, as are the Powers that move them. Although not compelling, this argument allows Institoris and Sprenger to make an additional important distinction before moving on to the subject of witches and women: astrologers and magicians may employ operations that resemble the works of witchcraft, but because they utilize the natural power of the stars for their own private good, they cannot be witches.

It goes without saying that magicians and astrologers are also invariably male; that witches are most commonly female, Institoris and Sprenger accept as a simple fact, verified by their own experience and common consensus.[61] This is in part a function of simple feminine frailty, and they assemble a tiresome collection of authorities to show that women are more credulous than men, more impressionable, more superstitious, more impulsive, more prone to emotional extremes: in sum more easily ensnared by the devil due to their weaker minds and bodies. More importantly, though, just as the devil's power is greatest where human sexuality is concerned, so too is this woman's greatest weakness, for she is naturally more sexual than men, "as is made plain by her many carnal depravities."[62] Throughout the *Malleus*, women are virtually synonymous with the appetites of the flesh, and, in the minds of the authors, this carnal desire is without doubt the mainspring of contemporary witchcraft: women's lust leads them to copulate with the devil, to use magic to gain new lovers and revenge themselves against former ones, and to all manner of other sins. Thus it is no wonder, Institoris and Sprenger conclude, that witches are properly called *maleficae* and not *malefici*, for "all [witchcraft] comes from carnal lust, which is in women insatiable."[63] In this way, the spread of witchcraft in modern times is readily explicable through the increasing numbers of lustful and ambitious women who fall easily into league with the devil. Because this is the case, it is equally clear that lust, and especially lust that is manifested in some egregious sin such as adultery or fornication, is a reliable behavioral indicator of a predisposition toward witchcraft. It is not sufficient in itself, of course, as not all adulteresses are witches, but the authors' point is that many are, and so a woman's sexual behavior is a legitimate subject for inquisitorial inquiry and examination.

Witchcraft in the *Malleus* thus emerges as a phenomenon that is explicitly gendered and sexual. It arises from the insatiable sexual appetites of women; sexual intercourse with her master is the sign of a witch's servitude, and increasing the devil's progeny is one of her chief goals. Conversely, a witch's magic is especially apt to disrupt the course of benign sexual relationships and fruitful reproduction, both because the devil's power in this field is so great, and because the witch herself is predisposed toward this sort of mischief. Just how it is that witches bring about these misfortunes is the subject of the next several questions, in which Institoris and Sprenger attempt to map out the limits of witches' power and at the same time to continue to demonstrate the close relationship between witchcraft and more conventional moral turpitude.

To begin with, a witch can influence a man's passions, filling minds with excessive love or hatred.[64] The devil's ability to influence or delude the senses, and to bring fanciful images directly to mind, allows witches to do this, but it is their own desire for the chance to gratify their lusts while ruining the lives of others that makes this sort of evil so prevalent. As a rule, witches are just as repulsive physically as morally and desperately need the help of the devil to obtain the lovers whom they crave. As a result, this kind of magic is regrettably common, and the authors cannot count the number of times "adulterers inflamed with passion for the foulest of women have set aside their most beautiful wives."[65] Similarly, obstructing procreation is no trick at all for the devil, who can either interpose himself invisibly between man and woman during procreation, cause an abortion or sterility in the woman's womb, or, most common of all, cause impotence or some other sort of sexual dysfunction in men. But when this is the result of witchcraft, as is most often the case, it is further proof of the libidinous character of witches, who are eager to cast this kind of spell because they know that if men cannot perform sexually with their wives they will be more likely to submit to the witch's own adulterous embraces.[66] And so, the authors point out, "the fact that witches are more frequently adulteresses, prostitutes, and the like is shown by the evil impediment they place on the act of generative power."[67]

One of the most alarming of these impediments is a witch's ability to cause a man's penis to vanish into thin air, so that he can "see and feel nothing except his smooth body, uninterrupted by any member."[68] This is the sort of thing that chronically happens to adulterers who are not sufficiently attentive to their mistresses' needs, or worse, who abandon them entirely, thus provoking vengeance. Fortunately, as the authors reveal, the loss of one's penis is only one of the devil's illusions, and not a real transformation – although this is unlikely to be of much comfort to those afflicted, since, as they go on to say, the condition is generally permanent. Similarly, when witches change themselves or others into the shape of animals, this is just another illusion, because a real metamorphosis is beyond the devil's powers.[69] But since the deceptions of the devil seem substantially real to every test that an average person is likely to devise, as a matter of practice it will make little difference whether one is assailed by a real wolf or a witch in wolf-form, save that the latter is likely to be even more cunning and vicious.

Institoris and Sprenger conclude their tale of witches' evil deeds with an odd little digression about the abominable practices of midwife witches.[70] These creatures are the worst of all their kind, for they kill infants both in the womb and at birth, and are even in the habit of stealing, vampire-like, into homes to drink the blood of children. Worse still, even when they do not kill the children they deliver, witch-midwives devote them to the devil, dooming them to a life of evil. The *questio* is unusual both because it does not follow the normal "scholastic" method – it is a simple series of assertions, supported mainly by anecdotal evidence – and because it does not follow logically from the proceeding catalogue of kinds of supernatural harm – the question focuses completely upon the reprehensible character of the witch-midwives' crimes. In one respect, though, the question does provide a fitting conclusion to this portion of the authors' argument, for it states in the most forceful terms yet, Institoris and Sprenger's contention throughout, that although a witch may utilize the devil's power to do evil, she does it for reasons that are her own: witchcraft may be perilously tied to the demonic, but it is an entirely human sin.

This is a necessary point, for Institoris and Sprenger are about to tackle the difficult question of why, since all witchcraft is dependent upon the permission of God, God should be inclined to permit it.[71] This is an especially important problem since, as the authors observe with annoyance, certain *sapientes* among the clergy argue that witchcraft cannot be real, since God does not permit such freedom to the devil as the abominable deeds of witches would require. In order to avoid meeting this formidable objection head on, the authors make a discreet withdrawal, and treat witchcraft in this context simply as a part of the larger issue of the existence of evil. God has, of course, ordained all things, but he permits witchcraft for the same reasons that he permits any other sin. First, because an action which may appear evil from all human perspectives may in fact be the cause of much good, and thus witchcraft may provide opportunities to test, warn, or purge true Christians. And second, because if God did not permit witchcraft, he would be denying a measure of freedom to witches. He does not will witchcraft to happen, but he has created human beings with the capacity to sin, and just as God permitted Satan to fall, and Adam and Eve to sin, he is similarly compelled to allow witches to work their evil with the devil's aid. Yet these traditional explanations for the existence of sin obviously fail to answer the whole objection. For although it may be granted that God is required to allow witches to sin, it does not seem to follow necessarily that he should also give the devil leave to rain down wholesale destruction upon the innocent in the process. The permission to sin is one thing, the grant of deadly supernatural power is quite another. But Institoris and Sprenger put forth the ingenious, if rather circular argument that witchcraft is permitted precisely because the witch's sin enables the divine permission necessary for witchcraft.[72]

Here, the first section of the *Malleus* comes to an end.[73] Although the description of witchcraft that Institoris and Sprenger have built up over eighteen dense *questiones* may seem disturbingly vague and even contradictory, it has actually proceeded in reasonably ordered fashion. Each *questio* approaches witches and witchcraft from a slightly different direction, establishing the relationships between the natural and supernatural, between women and demons, superstition and sin, witchcraft and sexual sin, God and evil, and so on. Rather like a pendulum swinging back and forth between extremes, the *Malleus* has located witchcraft within a series of arcs described by devils and women along one axis, and magic and sin along the other. The length of each swing is not always regular, but as the interior of the arcs are drawn and redrawn with each subsequent *questio*, essential characteristics of the category gradually emerge.

In the second part of the book, the authors get down to actual cases; they abandon the "scholastic" method, and proceed descriptively, with evidence provided by numerous *exempla*. Institoris and Sprenger are no longer concerned with what is theoretically possible, but with what, in their experience, actually happens. The focus of their inquiry shifts accordingly, from abstract moral and theological issues to concrete questions about witches' behavior, and especially about *maleficium* and the possible remedies for it. Institoris and Sprenger begin their examination by expanding chiefly upon topics introduced in the first section, adding details, clarifications, and frequently lurid illustrative examples to the dry arguments already presented. The authors' goal is to demonstrate how their theoretical construction of witchcraft is reflected in real-world experience, and to prove that there is a "real" witch who is consistent with both:

> And lest these things [the acts of witches] be thought incredible, they have been settled in the first part of this work through questions and the solutions to arguments, to which, if it is necessary, the skeptical reader can return to investigate the truth. For the present, only those acts and deeds discovered by us or written by others in detestation of so great a crime are to be considered, in case, by any chance, the earlier questions may be difficult for anyone to understand; and from these things that are related in this second part, he who thought that there are no witches and that no witchcraft can be done in the world may take back his faith and rebound from his error.[74]

For the most part, their project is now descriptive, and several chapters are almost entirely taken up with examples alone. In places, however, they must also make some revealing adjustments to their model in order for it to remain consistent with reality as they see it.

In part one of the *Malleus*, they showed that witches can, with the devil's aid, do fantastic things; now they concede that the situation is more complicated, and that witches cannot, after all, injure or kill everyone they might wish to. In fact, witches operate under a variety of handicaps.[75] Some persons are under God's special protection; guardian angels defend saints and holy men; others may be "naturally" resistant to witchcraft due to the influence of celestial bodies and the angelic intelligences that move them; and the rites of the Church can procure similar supernatural protection for devout Christians. As the authors' observe, sacramentals and exorcisms are designed specifically to combat demonic power, and so must have the same sort of virtue against witchcraft. Institoris and Sprenger also note that men of their own class, public magistrates who bring witches to justice, are almost never bewitched. Perhaps God has sympathy for their dangerous task and shields them from harm; perhaps the devil himself provides them with incidental protection since, in order to hasten a witch's damnation, he deprives her of her powers when she is taken by the accredited agents of justice. The authors testify that, whatever the cause, they are alive and well despite the best efforts of their victims.

After this introductory digression into the limits of witches' power, Institoris and Sprenger turn to the various strategies witches employ to gain new recruits, all of which unsurprisingly exploit the immoderate physical appetites of women.[76] To recruit "honest matrons, little given to carnal vice, but who covet more earthly possessions," witches will often cause milk cows to go dry, so that the distraught women will consult some local witch for advice, adopt some superstitious and blasphemous remedy, and in this way be led down the path to damnation. With "young maidens, more given to ambition and the pleasures of the flesh," the matter is easier, and established witches need only find some pretext under which the girls can be discreetly introduced to handsome and desirable young devils.[77] Finally, women who have been abandoned by their lovers seek out the devil of their own accord, either to satisfy their lusts or to gain revenge. Of all witches, these sad women are the most common, for "just as young women of this kind are innumerable, as, alas, experience teaches, so the witches who arise from them are unnumbered."[78]

Most of the time, the devil is strangely detached from the business of finding new recruits, preferring to delegate this sordid business to the witches themselves. When the time is right, the devil appears before the assembled witches and promises them prosperity and long life in this world.[79] In return, they produce the novice witch who must abjure her former faith and perform an oath of homage to the devil, giving herself to him, body and soul, for ever. The devil then commands her to bring as many people as possible under his sway, and instructs her in the art of making a magic goo from the bodies of unbaptized children. Though some novices may balk at this, the devil is shrewd: he asks such women only to do as much as they are willing to do, leaving the most horrid acts of sacrilege for later.

Once a witch has accepted the devil, she immediately acquires the ability to fly from place to place and the regular attentions of a demon lover, both of which are well attested by current reports and traditional authorities.[80] Witches also acquire the ability to perform magic with the devil's aid, although, somewhat unexpectedly, Institoris and Sprenger admit that not all witches' magic is necessarily malign. For obscure reasons, witches are divided into three classes: those who only cause harm, those who heal as well as harm, and those who heal, but cannot bring about injuries.[81] The most formidable kind of witch, possessing the most impressive occult arsenal, is the midwife-witch, who specializes in killing and eating unbaptized children; she becomes Institoris and Sprenger's archetype, standing for all the others.

The remainder of the second part deals with *maleficium* proper, and consists of a remarkably thorough catalogue of witches' powers to do harm.[82] As mentioned before, witches can prevent procreation in various ways, turn themselves or others into animal form, or create convincing illusions of all sorts. They can also induce the devil to possess people, cause all manner of sickness in humans or beasts, raise storms, and steal milk. In short, a large proportion of life's calamities are encompassed by the witches' extensive magical repertoire.

Unfortunately for the consistency of their argument, Institoris and Sprenger recognize that some kinds of misfortune appear to be attributable solely to the devil. Lightning strikes, for instance, often occur seemingly without the participation of any witch, although it may be that the witch responsible simply remains undetected.[83] Worse, the authors are also forced to admit that *maleficium* is not quite the exclusive property of witches. Since demons are not particularly choosy about whom they aid, it is quite possible for someone who is not technically a witch to work harmful magic by virtue of a tacit pact alone, a pact forged whenever anyone uses superstitious means or rites to achieve some end.[84] Such was a traditional ecclesiastical under-standing of malign magic, but because *maleficium* is such an important part of Institoris and Sprenger's conception of what witches are it creates an annoy-ing gray area around the periphery of the authors' definition of witchcraft.

From the authors' perspective, a more helpful exception to the rule is the bizarre miscellany of male wizards which concludes their description of witches' practices.[85] Although these men are counted among those "addicted to witchcraft," it is difficult to call them witches: they do not practice con-ventional *maleficium*, have intercourse with the devil, or indulge in most other characteristically witch-like activities, and their social roles are relentlessly male. Some such men are soldiers, such as the notorious "archer wizards" (*malefici sagittarii*) who shoot their arrows into a crucifix in order to acquire diabolically enhanced accuracy. But whatever their occupation, they are not obvious social deviants, despite their grievous sins, so that "witchcraft" for men does not correspond to a readily identifiable life style. The male witch is known strictly on the basis of sacrilegious behavior. He is thus a kind of marginal "witch," who serves to define in different ways the bounds of "normal" femi-nine witchcraft.

Yet despite Institoris and Sprenger's best efforts to define witchcraft clearly, in their next topic, the possible remedies for *maleficium*, the line between witchcraft and other magical operations becomes perilously obscure. The problem is that a bewitched person looking for a cure has few options: a human curative agency is impossible, because witchcraft is the work of the devil and beyond a mortal's natural capacity to undo; divine help, though pos-sible, is extremely unlikely (given that God has permitted the initial affliction, He is not often moved to remove it); finally, although the remedies of the Church will exorcize demons and keep them at bay, they are not much use once a magical spell has taken effect in accordance with divine will. The victim

is thus in a real quandary, since the only remaining source of relief is the devil
or his agents:

> It appears besides that [the bewitched] will be freed very rarely, however much
> they may implore divine assistance and the support of saints; therefore they
> cannot be freed except by the help of demons, which, however, it is not per-
> mitted to seek.[86]

Yet despite the warning of Aquinas and the theologians that a man may not
lawfully look to cure witchcraft, certain canonists argued that the situation was
not so cut and dried, and that in the absence of viable alternatives, the works
of the devil might be legitimately destroyed through "vain and superstitious
means."[87]

The remainder of this section of the *Malleus*, Institoris and Sprenger try to reconcile these contradictory positions, and establish some guidelines by which
allowable remedies may be distinguished from condemned superstition. Their
solution is to create a narrow space for acceptable "vanities" between diabolically effective but unlawful practices on one side, and perfectly acceptable but
presumably ineffective remedies on the other. They cannot clearly define this
acceptable "space," because the nature of the operator remains much more
important in the authors' minds than the nature of the operation. It is unacceptable under any circumstances to go to a witch to have *maleficium* removed,
even if she harms nothing else in the process; on the other hand, "a remedy
which is performed with certain superstitious rites, but in which no other
person is harmed, and not done by manifest witches" may be fine.[88] No
wonder, then, that they scrupulously avoided this subject while in a theological discursive mode, for, difficult as it is to justify in practice, it would be
appallingly hard to do so in theory. In effect, Institoris and Sprenger authorize a limited amount of commerce with a passive, instrumental devil, in preference to any association with the more active moral evil of the witch. This
decision allows them to give tentative approval to a variety of obscure occult
practices which are perhaps legitimate for that reason alone.[89]

The remainder of this section of the *Malleus* examines both preventative
and curative responses to various manifestations of *maleficium*, in a manner
roughly parallel to the treatment of witchcraft itself in the previous section.[90]
Throughout, Institoris and Sprenger are concerned to separate unlawful superstition, identified by principles laid down by Aquinas and Nider, from permissible Christian countermagic. The authors consistently endorse a very
liberal application of sacramental substances and Christian charms as the best
possible preventative measures. Houses should be doused liberally with holy
water, man and beast should be festooned with written charms, and holy wax
and herbs should be placed on every threshold to ward off witches' occult

assaults. If it would curb the power of witches, Institoris and Sprenger are quite prepared to see the sacramentals of the Church, and the rite of exorcism besides, employed by pious lay men and women, and, in the event that such steps should be neglected or prove to be ineffective, the authors recommend a graduated hierarchy of responses, beginning with a regimen of prayer, confession, pilgrimage, and exorcism. Should these too fail, the patient may then turn to a broad range of possible folk remedies, which Institoris and Sprenger examine with an eye to separating the permissible wheat from the condemned chaff.

Ultimately, however, the bewitched cannot hope for an infallible remedy, for the power of witches is too strong. There is only one completely reliable way to combat witchcraft, and this is to eliminate the witches, the course of action Institoris and Sprenger endorse in one of the most impassioned passages of the *Malleus*:

> But alas, lord God, although all your judgments are just, who will free the poor people who have been bewitched, crying out in their continuous pains? Now that our sins have aroused him, the Enemy very much has the upper hand. Where are those who have the strength to dissolve those works of the devil through licit exorcisms? This single remedy seems left to us, that, by punishing through various means the witches responsible, judges restrain their outrages, whence the occasions for the sick to visit witches will be removed. But, alas, no one feels this in his heart.[91]

To aid these embattled judges, the final portion of the *Malleus* provides a detailed guide to the conduct of witch-trial. Much of this is fairly technical, taken up with sample documents and advice on how to reject troublesome appeals, but Institoris and Sprenger begin by making the more general point that witchcraft is everyone's problem and not the exclusive concern of the Inquisition alone.[92] If witchcraft were purely a matter of heresy this might not be true, but the authors make the interesting argument that a witch is a heretic in the same way as is a simoniac, only as a convenient legal fiction. Heresy, after all, is a matter of belief, and the devil does not really care if witches reject Christianity in their hearts or not; the outward show is all that really matters to him, as that is all that is needed to ensure damnation. Witches do not necessarily hold any false opinions about the faith, but are still guilty of apostasy, as well as whatever secular crimes they may have committed. Although this may seem like unnecessarily legalistic wrangling, Institoris and Sprenger were in fact entering into an important and contentious debate over the extent of the Inquisition's jurisdiction. The constitutions of Clement V had forbidden both the papal Inquisition and local episcopal courts to try cases of manifest heresy alone and without the participation of the other. Institoris and Sprenger argue that because witchcraft does not "savor of manifest heresy," it is fair game for an episcopal court alone. Further, because witchcraft is generally known by physical injuries, the witch may also be tried competently by secular courts for crimes against civil law. Particular cases might, it was true, call for the overlapping jurisdictions of the Inquisition, and of the episcopal and the secular courts, but in general witches could be tried by the episcopate without the participation of the Inquisition or, where capital punishment was not called for, by the secular arm.

With this introductory encouragement to their colleagues out of the way, Institoris and Sprenger begin a step by step guide to the conduct of a witch-trial, from the method of initiating the process and assembling accusations, to the interrogation of witnesses, the formal charging of the accused, the inter-rogation and torture of the defendant, and the final determination of guilt and assessment of the penalty. The treatise is interesting from a legal perspective, and reveals much about how the authors accumulated the experience they brought to their treatise, but it does not contribute much to the image of the witch already developed. In fact, the process is very much the other way round: Institoris and Sprenger's legal procedures would be meaningless without recourse to their already established conception of a witch. For example, the authors recommend that the accused be asked why she remains in a state of adultery or concubinage, because such women are more gravely suspected than are "honest women."[93] Similarly, a woman's guilt is known by an inability to weep during torture, since the gift of tears is a gift from God denied to witches.[94] In short, a witch-trial based upon the model in the *Malleus* is only practical if one accepts at the outset the conception of the witch and of witchcraft that it has constructed. This is, in fact, true of the *Malleus* as a whole. The book's argument is predicated upon a series of assumptions about the nature of creation, about man's relationship with God and with the devil, and about witchcraft and witches, assumptions we shall now examine.

Notes

1 For biographical accounts of Institoris and Sprenger, see Peter Segl, "Heinrich Institoris: Persönlichkeit und literarisches Werk," in Peter Segl, ed., *Der Hexenhammer* (Cologne: Böhlau Verlag, 1988), 103–26; Joseph Hansen, ed., *Quellen und Untersuchungen zur Geschichte des Hexenwahns und der Hexenverfolgung im Mittelalter* (reprint, Hildesheim: Georg Olms Verlagsbuchhandlung, 1963), 360–407; Joseph Hansen, *Zauberwahn, Inqui-sition und Hexenprozess im Mittelalter* (1900; reprint, Munich: Scientia Verlag Aalen, 1964), 474–500; Jacobus Quétif and Jacobus Echard, *Scriptores Ordinis Praedicatorum* (1719–23; reprint, New York: Burt Franklin, 1960), vol. 1, pt. 2, pp. 880–1, 896–7; Amand Danet's introduction to Henry Institoris and Jacques Sprenger, *Le Marteau des sorcières*, ed. and trans. Amand Danet (Paris: Civilisations et mentalités, 1973), 30–45. Sources for both lives are conveniently collected in André Schnyder, *Malleus Maleficarum. Kom-mentar zur Wiedergabe des Erstdrucks von 1487* (Göppingen: Kümmerle, 1993), 25–102. Henricus Institoris is simply the Latin form of the author's German name, Heinrich Krämer (that is, shop-keeper).

2 "propter senium gantz chindisch." Ammann, "Innsbrucker Hexenprocesse," 86.

3 Hansen, Quellen, 380–90.

4 For Dominican educational practice, see William A. Hinnebusch, *The History of the Dominican Order*, 2 vols. (New York: Alba House, 1973), 2:1–230, and R.F. Bennet, *The Early Dominicans* (Cambridge: Cambridge University Press, 1937), 55. Like all Dominican convents, Schlettstadt had a priory school for the humanities and, since 1400, had also supported a *studium artium*. Segl, 103.

5 Prior to being named a professor of theology, Institoris was regularly referred to as "Henricus Institoris de Sletstat, artium magister et theologiae lector." See Schnyder, *Kommentar*, docs. 5, 8, 10, 12, pp. 35–7. For Institoris' doctorate see *ibid.*, doc. 15, p. 38. It was not unusual for busy Dominicans to receive advanced degrees while in Rome on other business, for which purpose (among others) there was a *studium generale* attached to the papal court. Hinnebusch, 1:43.

6 Schnyder, *Kommentar*, doc. 4, p. 34.

7 "Sententias nostras interdicti et suspensionis divinorum per nos in oppidum Lipczk ob praesentiam Bohemorum fautorum haereticorum." *Ibid.*, doc. 5, p. 35.

8 "exercere officium inquisitionis, ubi non erit inquisitor vel ubi erit de licentia sua et beneplacito." *Ibid.*, doc. 8, 36. See also Henry Charles Lea, *A History of the Inquisition in the Middle Ages*, 3 vols. (1888; reprint, New York: The Harbor Press, 1955), 1:370.

9 "Religionis zelus, litterarum sciencia, vite integritas et fidei constancia aliaque laudabilia probitas et virtutum merita." Schnyder, *Kommentar*, doc. 11, pp. 36–7.

10 *Ibid.*, doc. 8, 36; Danet, 38.

11 Schnyder, *Kommentar*, doc. 10, p. 36.

12 *Ibid.*, doc. 13, p. 38.

13 *Ibid.*, doc. 18, p. 40.

14 *Ibid.*, doc. 19, p. 40.

15 Further conflicts arose in 1490, apparently over Institoris' conduct of an inquisition, when his Order censured him for "the many scandals which he perpetrated in the province" ("propter multa scandala, que perpetravit in provincia"); and again in 1493, when he was ordered on pain of excommunication to quit a lucrative but contested position as cathedral preacher in Salzburg (he did not, and the affair dragged on into the next year). *Ibid.*, docs. 49, 55–7, pp. 58, 60–1.

16 Institoris recalled that Reiser, in his confession prior to execution, claimed that the heretics, especially the Waldensians and Hussites, "increase daily in strength and numbers." Henricus Institoris, *Tractatus Varii* (np: 1496), sermon 2.1; Schnyder, *Kommentar*, 33, n. 1.

17 Schnyder, *Kommentar*, doc. 16, pp. 38–9.

18 See especially Institoris' sermons on eucharistic errors in *Tractatus Varii*, *passim*; and Schnyder, *Kommentar*, doc. 16, p. 38. For a full bibliography of Institoris' works, see Quétif and Echard, 897.

19 Rudolf Endres, "Heinrich Institoris, sein Hexenhammer und der Nürnberger Rat," in *Der Hexenhammer*, 207.

20 K.O. Müller, "Heinrich Institoris, der Verfasser des Hexenhammers und seine Tätigkeit als Hexeninquisitor in Ravensburg im Herbst 1484," *Württemburgerische Vierteljahreshefte für Landesgeschichte* N.F. 19 (1910): 397–417.

21 Hansen, Quellen, 24–7.

22 *Ibid.*, 27–8.

23 *Ibid.*, 29.

24 For accounts of the 1485 witch persecution in Innsbruck, see Hansen, *Quellen*, 385–6; Ammann, *passim*; and Schnyder, *Kommentar*, docs. 31–44, 48–54.

25 Dienst, 80–1.

26 *Malleus*, pt. 2, qu. 1, ch. 12, p. 136.

27 Schnyder, *Kommentar*, doc. 32, pp. 49–50. The grant of an indulgence was standard procedure for inquisitorial investigations, see Lea, *Inquisition*, 1:407.

28 *Malleus*, pt. 3, qu. 1, p. 194.

29 "Si quis scit vidit vel audivit aliquam esse personam hereticam et maleficam diffamatam vel suspectam et in speciali talia practicantem que in nocumentum hominum iumentorum aut terre frugum." *Ibid.*, pt. 3, qu. 1, p. 195.

30 Schnyder, *Kommentar*, doc. 35, p. 51. As Golser points out in his letter, by the constitution of Clement V, inquisitors were otherwise at least nominally required to conduct their business in association with episcopal authorities. See Lea, *Inquisition*, 1:387.

31 Richard Kieckhefer, *Repression of Heresy in Medieval Germany* (Philadelphia: University of Pennsylvania Press, 1979), 99–112, and *passim*.

32 Schnyder, *Kommentar*, doc. 42, p. 53. "Et si non recederet quantocius, tunc vice mea paternitas vestra sibi dicere dignetur, quod satis multa scandala sunt suborta propter malum processum suum, quod non remaneat in loco, ne deterius aliquid inde sequatur aut sibi contingat." *Ibid.*, doc. 41, p. 53.

33 "aber in practica sua apparuit fatuitas, quia multa presupposuit, que non fuerunt probata." *Ibid.*, doc. 43, p. 53.

34 "Quanti enim ceci claudi aridi et diuersis irretiti infirmitatibus iuxta formam iuris ex vehementi suspicione super maleficarum eis huiusmodi infirmitates in genere vel in specie predicentes." *Malleus*, pt. 2, qu. 1, ch. 12, p. 139.

35 *Ibid.*

36 Schnyder, *Kommentar*, doc. 54, p. 54.

37 The result of the archduke's inquiry was published by Molitor in the form of a dialogue between the two lawyers and Sigismund, in which Sigismund, interestingly enough, adopts the voice of skepticism. See Ulrich Molitor, *Tractatus de Pythonicis Mulieribus*, in Institoris and Sprenger, *Malleus Maleficarum* (Frankfurt am Main: Nicolaus Bassaeus, 1580); Lea, *Inquisition*, 3:541–3.

38 Hartmann Ammann, "Eine Vorarbeit des Heinrich Institoris für den *Malleus Maleficarum*," *Mitteilungen des Institutes für österriechischen Geschichtsforschung* 8 (1911), 461–504.

39 As early as 1496, shortly after Sprenger's death, Servatius Fanckel, a professor of theology at Cologne, wrote that Sprenger contributed nothing to, and knew nothing about the compilation of the *Malleus*: "Es [sic] quidem verum . . . quod malleus maleficarum inscribitur magistro Jacobo Sprenger pie memorie et uni altieri inquisitori sed magister Jacobus nihil apposuit aut scivit de compilatione dicti libri." Schnyder, *Kommentar*, doc. 61, p. 62.

40 Joseph Hansen has persuasively argued that Institoris was virtually the sole author of the text, and, in the main, modern scholarship has tended to confirm his view, although his evidence is almost entirely circumstantial, centered mostly around the difficulty of fitting the authorship of such a lengthy text into Sprenger's busy schedule. Hansen, *Quellen*, 404–7, and Danet, 43–5; Schnyder is more cautious, *Kommentar*, 419–22.

41 Institoris was also perhaps motivated by an order of Sixtus IV which in 1479 had given the University of Cologne the power and the obligation to censor books. Innocent VIII abrogated this order in 1487, which was perhaps just as well, because the form of Institoris' approbation bears no resemblance to the university's official *nihil obstat*. Henry Charles Lea, *Materials Toward a History of Witchcraft*, 3 vols., ed. Arthur C. Howland (1939; reprint, New York: Thomas Yoseloff, 1957), 1:337–8.

42 Joseph Hansen, "Der *Malleus Maleficarum*, seine Druckausgaben und die gefälschte Kölner Approbation vom J. 1487," *Westdeutsche Zeitschrift für Geschichte und Kunst* 17 (1898): 119–68.

43 Schnyder, *Kommentar*, 422–5. Schnyder's thesis would be more convincing were it not for the testimony of the eighteenth-century Jesuit scholar, Joseph Hartzheim, who claimed to have seen documents now lost in which two of the Cologne faculty protested against the fraudulent use of their names in the second approbation. Either Hartzheim or Institoris would seem guilty of fraud, and Institoris is usually considered the more likely suspect.

44 See Amos Funkenstein, *Theology and the Scientific Imagination: From the Middle Ages to the Seventeenth Century* (Princeton: Princeton University Press, 1986), 6.

45 See their discussion of whether the canonists or the theologians should determine whether an individual is guilty of heresy, *Malleus*, pt. 3, p. 189.

46 "Et quia in morali iam laboramus materia, unde argumentis variis et declarationibus ubique insistere opus non est . . . ideo precamur in deo lectorem ne demonstrationem in omnibus querat ubi accomodata [sic] sufficit probabilitas ea deducendo qui constat aut visus vel auditus propria experientia aut fide dignorum relationibus esse vera." *Ibid.*, pt. 2, p. 86.

47 *Malleus*, Apology, 2; see also Sydney Anglo, "Evident Authority and Authoritative Evidence: The *Malleus Maleficarum*," in Sydney Anglo, ed., *The Damned Art: Essays in the Literature of Witchcraft* (London: Routledge and Kegan Paul, 1977), 1–31.

48 For the purposes of comparison, a rough count of the number of times a given authority is cited in the *Malleus* can be obtained from the index of references in Schnyder's *Kommentar*, 288–98: the Bible (274), Thomas Aquinas (119), Augustine (75), Aristotle (34), Johannes Nider (22), Isidore of Seville (18), Gregory I (17), Dionysius the Pseudo-Areopagite (13), Henry of Seguso (13), Jerome (12), Albertus Magnus (11), William of Paris (10), Cassian (8), Raymond of Penafort (8), Vincent of Beauvais (8), Peter of Palude (6). A similar count reveals 270 references to canon and civil law, but this number may be high because it counts the citation of a particular canon as reference to all possible appropriate collections of canons since Institoris and Sprenger often did not distinguish between collections of law.

49 Of the narratives in the the *Malleus* that appear to be taken from the inquisitors' own experience, most are situated in the diocese of Constance (20 accounts, 9 from Ravensburg alone); others are taken from the dioceses of Strassburg (10), Brixen (9), Speyer (8), Basel (7), Augsburg (2), and Worms (1). There are but two accounts from lower Germany, one each from Koblenz and Cologne, while two more are from Rome.

50 In the *Malleus*, pt. 1, qu. 12, for example, when the authors set out to show the horrible crimes of witch-midwives, they simply abandon their method for flat assertions.

51 *Ibid.*, pt. 1, qu. 1, pp. 7–13.

52 "malefici sunt qui demonum auxilio propter pactum cum eis initium maleficiales reales effectus permittente deo procurare possunt." *Ibid.*, pt. 1, qu. 1, p. 10.

53 "[In quo pacto] malefica se totam obtulit et astrinxit diabolo vere et realiter et non fantastice et imaginarie solum, ita etiam oportet quod cooperetur diabolo vere et corporaliter. Nam et ad hoc sunt omnia maleficorum opera ubi super [sic: semper] aut per pactum aut per visum aut per locutionem seu per alicuius maleficii [sic] instrumenti reposito sub limine domus operatione sua maleficia exercent." *Ibid.*

54 *Ibid.*, pt. 1, qu. 2, p. 14.

55 *Ibid.*, 16.

56 *Ibid.*, 17.

57 *Ibid.*, 20.

58 "Attento etiam quod inter alios actus habent pro augmento illius perfidie quattuor exercere videlicet, fidem catholicam in toto vel in parte ore sacrilego abnegare seipsos in corpore et anima devovere, infantes nondum renatos ipsi maligno offerre, spurcitiis diabolicis per carnales actus cum incubis et succubis demonibus insistere." *Ibid.*

59 *Ibid.*, pt. 1, qu. 5, pp. 29–39.

60 "Celestia autem corpora effectus causant naturales cuiusmodi non sunt effectus maleficorum qui dicuntur maleficiales utpote in malum creaturarum preter consuetum ordinem nature prosilientes." *Ibid.*, 37. Compare Thomas Aquinas's similar proof in *Summa contra Gentiles*, bk. 3, pt. 2, ch. 114.

61 *Malleus*, pt. 1, qu. 6, pp. 39–46.

62 "[Ratio naturalis est, quia plus carnalis viro existit] ut patet in multis carnalibus spurcitiis." *Ibid.*, 42.

63 "Omnia per carnalem concupiscentiam que quia in eis est insatiabilis." *Ibid.*, 40.

64 *Ibid.*, pt. 1, qu. 7, pp. 46–52.

65 "Quot enim adulteri pulcerrimas uxores dimittentes in fetidissimas alias inardescunt." *Ibid.*, 49.

66 *Ibid.*, pt. 1, qu. 8, pp. 52–9.

67 "Scilicet quod adultere fornicarie etc. amplius existunt malefice ostenditur per impedimentum maleficiale super actum generative potente." *Ibid.*, 52.

68 "Nihil valeat videre et sentire nisi corpus planum et nullo membro interruptum." *Ibid.*, pt. 1, qu. 9, pp. 55–9, 57.

69 *Ibid.*, pt. 1, qu. 10, pp. 59–63. For the authorities, see Lea, *Materials*, 1:179–80; Hansen, *Quellen*, 39.

70 *Malleus*, pt. 1, qu. 11, pp. 63–4.

71 For reasons that are unclear, the authors arbitrarily divide this discussion into two questiones; this is a confusing development, as the solutions to the arguments presented at the beginning of question 12 are found at the end of question 13. *Ibid.*, pt. 1, qu. 12–13, pp. 64–71.

72 This is a long and at times theologically complex argument, which is made no clearer by another arbitrary division into four questions. *Ibid.*, pt. 1, qu. 14–17, pp. 71–81. See chapter 4 below.

73 The first part of the *Malleus* actually closes with a short aid to preachers, answering various common-sense objections to the reality of witchcraft sometimes brought up by troublesome laymen. The chapter is interesting but adds little to the main thrust of the book's argument. *Ibid.*, pt. 1, qu. 18, pp. 81–5.

74 "Et ne hec quasi incredibilia putarentur. Ideo in prima parte operis per questiones et argumentorum solutiones sunt decisa. Ad quas si opus sit dubius lector per investiganda veritate recurrere potest. Ad presens tantummodo acta et gesta per nos reperta sive etiam ab aliis conscripta in detestationem tanti criminis sunt deducenda ut priores questiones si fortassis alicui difficiles ad intelligendum forent. Ex his quae in hac secunda parte traduntur fidem capiat et ab errore resileat quo nullam maleficam et nullum maleficium posse fieri in mundo estimavit." *Ibid.*, pt. 2, qu. 1, ch. 5, pp. 111–12.

75 *Ibid.*, pt. 2, qu. 1, pp. 86–92.

76 *Ibid.*, pt. 2, qu. 1, ch. 1, pp. 92–5.

77 "Sed erga iuvenculas ambitioni et voluptatibus corporis magis deditas." *Ibid.*, 93.

78 "Et sicut talium iuvencularum non est numerus ut heu experientia docet, ita nec numerus maleficarum ex eis insurgentium." *Ibid.*, 94.

79 *Ibid.*, pt. 2, qu. 1, ch. 2, pp. 95–101. This account is derived principally from those found in book 5 of Johannes Nider's *Formicarius*.

80 *Malleus*, pt. 2, qu. 1, chs. 3–4, pp. 101–11.

81 *Ibid.*, pt. 2, qu. 1, ch. 2, p. 95.

82 This topic covers eleven short chapters. *Ibid.*, pt. 2, qu. 1, chs. 5–15, pp. 111–47.

83 *Ibid.*, pt. 2, qu. 1, ch. 15, p. 147.

84 For example, Institoris and Sprenger know of a magus who produced "witch-butter" without having made an express pact with the devil. *Ibid.* pt. 2, qu. 1, ch. 14, p. 143.

85 *Ibid.*, pt. 2, qu. 1, ch. 16, pp. 147–52.

86 "Apparet etiam quod rarissime liberantur quantumcumque divinum auxilium et suffragia sanctorum implorant, ergo non nisi auxilio demonum liberari possunt, quod tamen non est licitum querere." *Ibid.*, pt. 2, qu. 2, p. 152.

87 Provided, of course, that these fall well short of harmful magic and demonolatry. *Ibid.*, 153.

88 "Vero remedium quod quibusdam ceremoniis supersticiosis practicatur non tamen in nocumentum alicuius persone aut per manifestos maleficos agitatur." *Ibid.*, 156.

89 *Ibid.*, 153, 157.

90 *Ibid.*, pt. 2, qu. 2, chs. 1–8, pp. 158–84.

91 "Sed heu domine deus cum omnia iudicia tua iusta sunt quis liberabit pauperes male-
ficiatos et in continuis doloribus eiulantes, peccatis nostris exigentibus inimicus nimis
praevaluit, ubi sunt qui licitis exorcismis illa opera diaboli dissolvere valeant. Hoc
unicum ergo superesse videtur remedium ut iudices eorum [*sic*: earum] insultus adminus
refrenant [*sic*: refrenent] variis penis auctrices maleficas castigando, unde et infirmis fac-
ultas visitandi maleficas amputabitur, sed heu nemo percepit corde omnes que sua." *Ibid.*,
pt. 2, qu. 2, pp. 155–6.
92 *Ibid.*, pt. 3, pp. 184–94.
93 *Ibid.*, pt. 3, qu. 6, p. 201.
94 *Ibid.*, pt. 3, qu. 15, p. 213.

3

The inquisitors' devil

Institoris and Sprenger begin their analysis of witchcraft by observing that for witchcraft to have any effect, three things must concur: the devil, the witch, and the permission of God. For them, as for us, the devil provides a convenient starting point, because the witchcraft of the *Malleus* depends upon an unusual conception of what the infernal side of the Christian pantheon is all about. Like so many late-medieval cultural icons, the inquisitors' devil is not amenable to simple definition; nor is it easy to determine in what form and to what extent the devil was actually "present" in peoples' minds. Jeffrey Burton Russell maintains that the sinister presence of the devil was medieval man's ubiquitous companion, that "The eternal Principle of Evil walked in solid, if invisible, substance at one's side and crouched when one was quiet in the dark recesses of room and mind."[1] At the same time, however, and with equal justice, Richard Kieckhefer can point to the evidence of witchcraft prosecutions themselves, which suggest that to most people the devil was not of any particular concern, appearing instead "more as a legendary figure of folklore than as the master of a demonic cult."[2] One might plausibly maintain that these divergent views were the products of different levels of culture, one clerical and the other "popular," but the late-medieval devil was also to everyone a sort of chameleon, whose particular appearance was dictated more by circumstances and context than by anything else. Further, there was a considerable common ground between the conceptions of the diabolic held by learned inquisitors and those of their less educated informants. This partial consensus was possible because some clerics had come to accept a complicated and not wholly consistent vision of the devil, as at once a transcendent principle of evil, and at the same time as a being who was present daily in all manner of supra-normal encounters and phenomena. Certainly, the location of the transcendent in the immanent corresponds with a general tendency in late-medieval religion, but in the devil's case it also created difficult problems: where a transcendent God could manifest himself in the mundane world through a variety of mediating agents, a transcendent devil was traditionally not so well equipped.[3] While God was represented in the various manifestations of the Trinity, and had as well an array of angels and saints, to say nothing of the Church, the devil had only a multitude of demons to carry out his will on earth. Because all demons were perceived as beings of essentially the same type, not obviously distinguished from their master, the mere existence of minor demons could potentially lead to Satan's trivialization. To reconcile the apparent ubiquity of demonic power with a transcendent principle of evil, some clerics began to insist upon the necessity for human mediation of the diabolic side of the supernatural.

Such a striking dislocation of diabolic agency from the being of the devil stands in stark contrast to the thinking of earlier ages, and requires some explanation. The basic Christian devil of the Fathers had been a relatively coherent, consistent figure, who competently played out his well-defined role in God's creation. This is not to say that the conception of the devil had ever been simple, but in the earlier Middle Ages most clerics would probably have accepted as their starting point Augustine's view of a powerful but strictly limited devil.[4] This orthodox Christian demon was a fallen angel, who retained his angelic nature despite the loss of grace, and whose aerial body, superhuman intellect, and vast experience enabled him to do wonderful things. He was, however, entirely separated from the divine, and could not perform true miracles or do anything truly supernatural: a demon was simply a creature created by God, differing from the birds and beasts only in degree, and not in kind. Because the devil lacked the capacity for moral goodness, he was man's superior in neither a moral nor an absolute sense, and, despite his remarkable physical and intellectual powers, he could always be overcome, albeit with difficulty, by pious minds turned entirely toward God.[5]

Demons had a job to do, however, and that was to make life miserable for people on earth by tempting them to sin and by afflicting them with injuries. Tempting men came easily to demons, for their powers of observation revealed our weaknesses and inner characters, while their spiritual natures allowed them to beguile surreptitiously those already prone to succumb. Demons had considerable influence over such unlucky souls, and were able to persuade them to sin

> in marvelous and unseen ways, entering by means of that subtlety of their own bodies into the bodies of men who are unaware, and through certain imaginary visions mingling themselves with men's thoughts, whether they are awake or asleep.[6]

This connection between demonic activity and human sin was responsible for the prominence of the devil in Augustine's thought. Not only was man's own fall the direct result of a failure to resist the devil's lure, but the temptations of the fiend continued to inspire all manner of sins and create countless roadblocks on the way to paradise. For Augustine, "evil" was first and foremost moral evil and an expression of sin; when Augustine's devil did evil in the world, his presence was known principally by human behavior and not by mischance or misfortune.[7]

In comparison, the devil's power to cause physical harm was of almost trivial concern. It was true, Augustine admits, that the natural powers of demons enabled them to bring about physical harm – they might cause disease, for example, by rendering the air unwholesome – but, since any mundane injury was ultimately inconsequential when compared with the death of the soul, Augustine was interested in demons' capacity for physical harm only when it complemented their ability to tempt man into sin. Black magic was an important example of this kind of behavior: demons used their powers to give efficacy to magicians' spells not because they enjoyed causing suffering, but because by doing so they confirmed the efficacy of superstitious magical rites. Thus, men who longed to do evil were rewarded by God with the deception of demons. For example, when men used superstitious rites to discover the future,

> many things happen for the diviners in accordance with their divinations, so that, enmeshed in them, they are made more curious and entangle themselves more and more in the multiple snares of a most pernicious error.[8]

The same principle applied when demons impersonated pagan gods, and bestowed benefits upon their deluded worshipers: by so doing they prevented the superstitious from turning towards true religion. Similarly, demons deployed their powers to do harm and to tempt in concert to lure people to have recourse to magical remedies:

> How many wicked things [the devil] suggests, how many things through greed, how many things through fear! With these allurements he persuades you to go to the soothsayers, the astrologers, when you have got a headache. Those who abandon God and resort to the devil's amulets have been beaten by the devil. On the other hand, if the suggestion is made to someone that the devil's remedies are perhaps effective for the body – and so-and-so is said to have been cured by them because when the devil had received a sacrifice from him he left off troubling his body, having got possession of his heart; [one should say] "I would rather die than employ such remedies."[9]

Yet no matter how terrible demons might be, everything they did, whether it was to tempt or punish the evil or to test the merit of the good, was done at the express command of God and by his will:

> For [demons] can only act within the limits allowed them; and they are given
> liberty of action by the profound and just judgment of God most high, in accor-
> dance with the desserts of men, some of whom rightly endure affliction, but
> no more, at the hands of those demons, while others are, with justice, deluded
> by them, and brought under their sway.[10]

Demons remained morally culpable for the evil that they did, for they enjoyed
it and did it freely, but ultimately responsibility for their actions lay in the just
but inscrutable will of God. Under such circumstances, one should avoid the
devil and shun his works, but one need not fear provided one had faith in God.
Rather, one should say with Augustine's imaginary headache sufferer, "God
scourges me and delivers me as he wills."[11]

This Augustinian conception of the devil was never entirely displaced
during the Middle Ages, but by the twelfth century it was being amended in
the course of new learned speculation about the devil and his role in creation.[12]
Though scholastic theologians, and Thomas Aquinas in particular, added little
that could truly be called innovative to the conception of the devil, they did
alter the ways in which he and his works were perceived, in such a way that
they emerged more powerful, more independent, and more obviously present
in the quotidian world than before.[13]

Systematization was the hallmark of scholastic demonology: Aquinas's
great achievement in this field was the creation of a theoretical framework in
which the devils of Augustine, Dionysius, and the early Church could comfortably reside alongside their more contemporary kin.[14] The mere existence
of such a system, though, had an inevitable effect upon the subject being systematized. Aquinas followed Augustine in his insistence that demons were
naturally created beings, but drew the logical conclusion that both demonic
behavior and physiology were therefore legitimate objects of investigation and
analysis. As created beings, demons obeyed the same physical laws which governed the rest of the universe; from the observation of demonically inspired
effects, from knowledge gleaned from scripture and other authorities, and
from reliable accounts of encounters with devils, Aquinas had at his disposal a
body of evidence which he could interpret with reason, logic, and certainty
according to Aristotelian precepts. Consequently, it was possible to know precisely the nature of demonic bodies, demons' intellectual abilities and limitations, their speed and range of movement, the qualities of their will and
emotions, and even their sexual proclivities.[15] The ambiguity which had characterized previous descriptions of the devil was now lost: it was possible to
know exactly who and what the devil was, and how he would behave under
given circumstances. Further, Aquinas situated demons within an ordered hierarchy of creation, in which by their angelic natures they stood mid-way
between God and man.[16] For this reason, so far as Aquinas was concerned, all

demons were metaphysically superior to man just as they were man's physical and intellectual superiors; from this derived a belief in diabolic potency that was correspondingly greater and more threatening than Augustine's. This diabolic superiority was clearly expressed in the uniform insubstantiality of Aquinas's demons, since unlike most previous writers, he insisted that demons lacked any sort of corporeal body whatsoever: demons were powers and intelligences rather than beings in a physical sense.[17]

There was no room in Aquinas's universe for the ambiguously drawn demons of clerical *exempla* or the spirits of "folk-demonology," mischievous angels who had fallen to earth mid-way between heaven and hell.[18] Aquinas did not deny that trolls, fairies, incubi, and other sensible manifestations of the devil were encountered; he maintained simply that they were of the same order as the intangible beings who brought punishment and temptation. In all of their guises demons were essentially the same, fallen angels with angelic powers, whose proper dwelling place was hell, but who resided in the lower air by divine permission for the express purpose of carrying out the divine will.[19] The problem was to make evidence based upon direct observation of sensible demons square with evidence of the devil's unseen presence and with his theologically determined identity.

This is the difficulty Aquinas faced when addressing the existence of incubus demons. Although it was a necessary condition of their spiritual natures that demons could not generate human offspring, Thomas recognized that both authority and common experience reported otherwise. To reconcile this apparent contradiction, he constructed an elaborate and unconvincing scenario in which succubi received semen from their human partners and then used this as incubi to inseminate women.[20] Normally, of course, human semen lost its *calor naturalis*, and hence its potency, when removed from the body, but the superhuman speed of demonic motion was sufficient to overcome even this obstacle. But if this provided a satisfactory explanation for how demons seemed able to generate human offspring, it did not really explain why they should want to do so in the first place. For unlike Guibert of Nogent's demons, who sought intercourse with women for "sport alone," the demons of the *Summa* take no delight in carnal sins and looked only to lead men into perdition.[21]

This example illustrates how difficult it could be, even for Thomas Aquinas, to reconcile a theologically and metaphysically consistent demon with his earthly manifestations. Consequently, in scholastic demonology there is a perceptible dichotomy between the highly abstracted, impersonal, invisible devil of theory, and demons in their more concrete, personal, and sensible forms.[22] This discontinuity in the devil's nature is important, because it proved compatible with notions of witchcraft in a way that traditional conceptions of the devil were not; witches could, for some theorists, occupy this gap in the diabolic realm, mediating between the demons of theory and the world of earthly misfortune. Thus, as a general rule, the less the demons of a late-medieval treatise resembled the fallen angels of Augustine, the greater the importance, power, and danger of witches.

For example, consider the comparatively conservative views of Felix Hemmerlin, a Swiss reformer, who wrote extensively about demons in the generation prior to Institoris and Sprenger.[23] He was interested in the devil's immediate and physical appearances in the world, rather than as some abstract principle of moral evil: his devil is mainly a cause of tangible misfortune rather than of sin. But Hemmerlin's demons are in other respects quite traditional; they do not abdicate their responsibilities to their human followers, and when there is mischief to be done, they do it themselves, for their own (or God's) reasons. When Hemmerlin discusses the relationship between man and devil, it is the role of demon that is most important. For example, Hemmerlin tells us that a woman of Erfurt had a demon, who spoke fluently in German, Latin, and Czech. Institoris and Sprenger would doubtless have called her a witch for this reason alone, and made her the focus of the narrative. For Hemmerlin, however, she is of no further interest; instead, it is her demon who claims center stage: this industrious devil bragged that he was the same spirit who had seduced the Bohemians away from the true faith, and that he then destroyed with hellfire the fortifications of the invading Catholic army, because the commanding princes "did not hold God before their eyes but divided the territory of the kingdom among themselves before victory had been achieved."[24] Not only does Hemmerlin's devil act without human mediation, his activities are securely determined by a conventional moral order: he punished the Catholic army because of the sins of its leaders.

Hemmerlin also believed in magic. He knew, for instance, that peasant women brewed poisonous herbs and roots together to cause storms. When the pot was exposed to the sun, the fumes rose into the air and condensed into violent storm clouds, apparently through a process partly natural and partly diabolic.[25] He describes a "mulier strega," who could turn herself into a cat and killed many infants in their cradle before she was burned, and observes that "the world is full of this curse."[26] Yet for Hemmerlin, the devil had not been eclipsed by witches, and demons retained a well-defined role in the production of evil. Whereas misfortune in the *Malleus* is virtually the exclusive prerogative of witches, Hemmerlin's demons might still cause storms of their own accord, and were even known to make off with a penis or two.[27]

Less consistent and less traditional spirits inhabit the work of Petrus Mamoris, regent of the University of Poitiers, who wrote an interesting tract on the subject of witchcraft at the request of the bishop of Saintes around

1460.[28] In this work, the *Flagellum Maleficorum*, Mamoris tries to line up the theoretical powers of demons with the most concrete examples possible, since there are, regrettably, certain persons who will concede nothing, "unless some gross and sensible example is given them."[29] While his examples are certainly "gross and sensible," they also feature demons of unusually trivial appearance. Mamoris' demons included not only the shop-worn inhabitants of exemplary stories; they were also the products of his own extensive experience. Like Institoris, Mamoris was not a man of high birth – in his youth, he had worked as a shepherd – and his considerable first- and second-hand knowledge of demons would seem to accord with the views and experiences of most common people. He had encountered demons masquerading as ghosts and poltergeists, as well as the annoying spirits that disturbed the sleep of sheep and shepherds alike. He was also extremely credulous; not only was Mamoris prepared to accept almost any account of strange occurrences as substantially true, he also insisted upon interpreting ambiguous phenomena as demonic. In this he can be compared with another demonologist, the more traditional, and considerably more intellectually sophisticated, Johannes Nider (d. 1437).[30] Where Nider contended, following William of Paris, that humans, and not demons, go out at night and put tangles in horses' manes, Mamoris maintained that demons regularly did exactly this, and recommended giving one's horses a splash of holy water as a remedy.[31] Similarly, while Nider qualified his tales of stone-throwing devils, admitting that such things were often attributable to the frauds of wicked people, it did not occur to Mamoris to be so cautious.[32] Nor do Mamoris' narratives serve an obvious didactic purpose, as did Nider's more traditional *exempla*. They were simply intended as evidence of the devil's nature and behavior, although the two do not always exist comfortably side by side.

The most impressive ability of Mamoris' demons was their powers of local motion, for although they could not move anything in an absolute sense, as this power belonged to God alone, they could move objects relative to themselves.[33] Through this power demons could alter the weather, cause disease, carry witches through the air, and so on. As an example, Mamoris relates that he once knew a nobleman who had a familiar spirit named "Dragon." Dragon was a minor demon who had the bad luck to encounter another, stronger, demon who bound him in a ring, seemingly for no other reason than sheer malice. The stronger devil would take poor Dragon with him as he rummaged through people's houses, leaving the ring stuck behind a door or in a hole until his business was finished. From this tale, Mamoris concludes that the devil was able to manipulate both Dragon, and Dragon's tangible prison, by his powers of local motion: "For demons are of a nature superior to the rational soul which cannot move the body."[34] One cannot help but think that if little Dragon is of a nature superior to that of human beings, the exact extent of his superiority is elusive indeed. Similarly unthreatening demons populate Mamoris' accounts of stone-throwing devils, whose mischief also provided painfully direct evidence of the power of demons to move objects locally.[35]

Mamoris evidently thought in terms such as these when he envisioned the direct and unmediated influence of demons in human affairs. Demons were indeed commonly encountered, but their assaults were more likely to be annoying rather than really terrifying, of the order of broken windows rather than broken bones. He does not deny that devils can do much greater things, and readily admits that since even certain stones have the power to turn the mind to love or madness, "so much more can the devil through transmutation of the blood and humors and in another subtle way horribly produce hatred in the mind and pain in the flesh."[36] Yet it was also entirely characteristic of Mamoris to say this in reference to witchcraft rather than to any of the devil's personal endeavors. Like Institoris, Mamoris saw witchcraft as the far more frightening aspect of diabolic power: witches were the ones responsible for infertility, madness, the slaughter of infants, infestations of werewolves, and plague.

In short, in direct, worldly encounters with the authors of demonological treatises and their informants, demons often seemed insufficiently imposing to carry plausibly the responsibility for the world's ills. Nider, in his *Formicarius*, tells of a mildly troublesome demon who haunted the house of a priest living near Nuremburg,

> with hissings, whistlings, and blows, not very distinct, but audible; for sometimes he would beat on the walls of the house, and sometimes the joker would blow, as it seemed, on the various pipes of actors, and he would indulge in a lot of unrestrained behavior doing these sorts of things, that nonetheless do no harm.[37]

The worst that this demon could do was frighten those unfamiliar with its antics, and hide articles of clothing in out of the way places. Similarly, the Franciscan, Alphonso de Spina, who around 1460 devoted the long final book of his *Fortalitium Fidei* to the attacks of demons, was likewise frightened in his youth by a noisy but seemingly harmless house spirit.[38] Such demons, he says, were responsible for beating on wine casks, and pulling off one's covers at night, but could do no other harm. Many demonologists had similar experiences, and all had heard first-hand accounts of such things.

The extent to which conceptions of the devil in general were influenced by this sort of narrative depended upon the relative weight assigned to the evidence of eyewitness testimony. For Nider and Hemmerlin, although such narratives were important, they did not outweigh the importance of more traditional *exempla* in which the devil retained a more traditionally "hellish" role. In the work of Mamoris, Spina, and Institoris and Sprenger, the testimony of personal experience was given proportionally more authority, and their characterizations of demons were more apt to reflect comparatively trivial encounters with various spirits.

As appearances of the devil in late-medieval demonologies become increasingly mundane, their authors become more apt to identify as demonic all manner of supra-normal encounters, and so to assimilate demons with various traditional spirits. This was nothing new: the process of assimilation had been going on ever since Christians first identified pagan spirits and deities with the devil. But because some fifteenth-century scholastics had come to accept appearances of a very concrete and material, but not awesomely powerful devil as representative, they were also able to accept narrative accounts of encounters with such spirits, or with demons sharing many of their characteristics, as substantially real and meaningful. In this way, as the demonological conception of the devil began to approximate that of more humble folk, demonologists were able to accept as true an increasing number of traditional, "popular" narratives, thus validating their increasingly "popular" conception of the devil. Hemmerlin reported that in his day, demons "appear frequently in Denmark and Norway, and there they are called trolls, and on account of their familiarity with people they are not feared, but people make use of their obedience."[39] One could argue that later demonologists suffered from a similar problem, as their devils began to assume the contours of a variety of familiar but not overtly demonic spirits.

Ghosts are a good example of this process, since there was no necessary reason why a spirit of the dead should be anything other than what it appeared to be. Jacobus de Clusa, a fifteenth-century expert on the subject, was in fact convinced that most apparitions around monasteries, churches, cemeteries, and houses were actually the insubstantial spirits of the dead. Jacobus explained that the reason exorcisms were so often ineffectual these days, a fact which Institoris and Sprenger ascribed to witchcraft, was that rites intended to drive off demons were being wrongly applied to the Christian dead.[40]

While demonologists did not deny that ghosts existed, they believed that spirits claiming to be ghosts almost invariably turn out to be demons in disguise. Mamoris tells of a spirit which haunted a house with the usual cries and groans, claiming to the ghost of a dead lady:

> Many people heard this spirit day and night, but saw nothing. He revealed many things which had been done in the past, and these revelations were found to be true. He also used to admonish the people of the house to do many good things.[41]

Yet appearances were deceiving: the ghost interspersed certain *superstitiosa* along with his good advice, and on this basis a "wise man" was able to discover that the spirit was actually a demon. Such things, Mamoris concluded, happen all the time. By interpreting situations such as this as encounters with the devil, Mamoris and his colleagues succeeded not only in demonizing ghosts and similar apparitions, but also in giving their demons the characteristics of ghosts and nature spirits.[42]

This is most obvious where the actual appearance of the devil is concerned. The Christian devil is naturally a master of illusion, and when he was required to assume a shape for the benefit of mortal senses, the Church traditionally maintained that virtually any form was available to him. But as the character of the devil began to merge with those of other supra-normal beings, his physical appearance changed also. Like demons, traditional nature spirits could assume human form, but in their case it was customary to have some signal flaw or abnormality in their appearance so that their true nature might be known. Many European nature spirits, for instance, might appear as normal or attractive humans from the front, but were hollow when observed from behind.[43] As early as the thirteenth century, Caesarius of Heisterbach reported that when a certain woman inquired why a demon always retreated by walking backward, the devil replied: "Although we may assume human form, yet we have no backs."[44] By the fifteenth century, similar ideas about the devil's appearance were making their way into learned demonologies. Alphonso de Spina maintained that although the devil could transform himself into an angel of light, or even appear as Christ on the cross, through "diligent inspection," a tail or some similar deformity would give him away.[45] Thus for Spina, the traditional Scandinavian saying, "When the tail is seen, the troll is known," could just as easily have been applied to the devil.[46]

Thinking of the devil as he appeared on earth in these terms encouraged demonologists to construct a two-tiered model of the demonic, elaborating upon the disjunction already present in scholastic theory between the devil in his abstract and his more material forms. The most dramatic example of this exercise is found in the fifth and final book of Spina's *Fortalitium Fidei*, a lengthy discussion of the devil, his nature, origins, and works. There is a hierarchy of demons in hell, Spina tells us, and each is charged with oversight of some specific sin – Asmodeus rules lust, Mammon greed, Behemoth gluttony, and so on. There is, in addition, an army of invisible demons all around us, some responsible for specific places, others assigned to tempt particular people, and all of us can count on having at least one demon specifically charged with our own spiritual ruin. Fortunately, every demon is opposed by a particular good angel, and the two spiritual armies are constantly engaged in merciless warfare over the fate of human souls. Since the day of creation, Satan has turned all his powers toward mankind's destruction, and there is not a crime, a sin, an evil in the world, for which he is not somehow responsible.[47]

Thus far, Spina's account of demons and their works is unusual only for its elaboration. As a Franciscan, Spina looked at demons in a traditional way, more as the source of sin than of misfortune. Undoubtedly demons did cause storms and disease, but more importantly, they excited heretics and Jews against the Church, and had built up a fortress of sin in opposition to the citadel of God.[48] To delineate this earthly city of sin and its legions of heretics, Jews, and criminals arrayed against Christendom was Spina's primary objective, and occupies the first four books of the treatise. Nonetheless, Spina concludes his text with an elaborate description of demons themselves, and, one is shocked to discover, that they are unambiguously the beings of folklore.[49] They are the *duen de casa*, who break crockery, disturb sleepers and go bump in the night; they are incubi and succubi, who apart from their more direct assaults perch on sleepers' chests and send them erotic dreams; they are the *praelia*, who comprise the phantom armies that appear at times to men; they are the nightmares who oppress men in their sleep; they are fates and familiar spirits; and finally they are the *bruxae*, demons who deceive old women into thinking that they can fly through the night with Diana and do impossible things. In short, Spina demonizes a host of traditional spirits, and grafts their characteristics uncomfortably onto a very traditional conception of the devil's nature and duties. This sort of assimilation of folklore and Christian theory had been attempted before, of course, but usually in the context of exemplary stories intended to educate the unlettered about the "reality" that lay behind traditional beliefs. Spina, however, elevated this process to a formal enumeration of diabolic types, and in so doing brought into painful clarity the contrast between demons as they appeared visibly and as they operated invisibly in theory.

In the *Malleus*, this dichotomous and non-traditional conception of the devil is an integral part of the authors' argument. Whereas they discuss the devil continuously throughout the text, they usually do so in terms of his powers and motives in the abstract. These are formidable indeed. Due to the fineness of their natures, the scope of their experience, and the revelation of higher spirits, demons had knowledge far surpassing man's. Their will adhered immovably to evil, and they sinned always in pride, envy, and malice. Although they were intangible spirits, demons could nonetheless do marvelous things through the exercise of their intellect and will alone. The authors revealed to their curious readers the formidable extent of the devil's powers:

> They will discover how [the devil] knows the intentions in our hearts, how, too, he can transmute bodies, substantially and accidentally, with the assistance of a

second agent, how he can move bodies locally, and alter the inner and outer senses so that they perceive something else, and how he can, although indirectly, alter a person's mind and will.[50]

That demons used these powers tirelessly to the detriment of mankind, Institoris and Sprenger demonstrate through a catalogue of typical diabolic activities:

> Rational in mind, yet reasoning without discourse, subtle in evil, desirous of doing harm, ingenious in deceit, they alter the senses, they corrupt disposi-tions, they agitate people while they are awake, and disturb sleepers through dreams, they bring disease, they stir up storms, transform themselves into angels of light, they bear hell with them always, they usurp the worship of God to themselves through witches; through them they bring about the magic arts, they seek to rule over the good and attack them further as much as possible; to the elect they are given as a trial, and always they lie in wait for a person's ruin.[51]

This demonic agenda represents a considerable change from that assumed by earlier authors: where Augustine, for example, saw diabolic evil chiefly in terms of temptation and subsequent sinful human behavior, Institoris and Sprenger saw the work of demons rather in acts of material harm. While, to Augustine, the locus of the demonic threat was essentially interior, manifested in the impulse to sin, and resisted through the grace of God, in the *Malleus* the operation of demons is conceptually outside one's self; even when demons per-secute a sleeper through dreams, the dreams are not his own, but have been sent, like an unwelcome psychic parcel, to the recipient. This change in the locus of demonic activity allows Institoris and Sprenger to make an analogical association between demons and witches: since the harm caused by demons resembles traditional ecclesiastical definitions of *maleficium* very closely, and since demons and witches share similar goals and means, it was possible to elide the earthly presence of one in favor of the other.[52]

The devil was, of course, still the power behind the witches' magic: his was the aerial body that entered into men and inspired minds to love or hatred, his were the illusions that allowed old women to appear as cats or wolves, or that made beautiful brides look like disgusting old hags, and his was the power of motion that carried witches around on their brooms or that brought storms to damage crops and disease to injure men and animals. Yet in the *Malleus*, the devil himself is strikingly absent in all of this. When a witch dips a twig into water and then sprinkles that water into the air, rain followed automatically, without any overt sign of the devil's involvement. Similarly, when she pierces a wax image, the devil mechanically transfers the injury to the intended victim.[53] In this, the devil is merely the efficient cause of the effect; he bears no responsibility for the injury himself.[54] He did not tell the witch whom to injure or whom to spare; he was not personally present at all. In fact, magical procedures were such a reliable conduit of demonic power that the proper use of diabolic countermagic could even induce the devil to injure his own witches. In one case, when women wished to determine who was responsible for cows going dry, they hung a pail of milk over the fire and beat it with sticks; a demon then came and transferred their blows to the witch.[55] In short, the powers of the devil are utilized very much like any other natural force or property, without his overt presence being known in any way.

This view was not, of course, entirely original. Both Augustine and Thomas Aquinas accepted that the demonic component of magic was concealed, since the whole point was to trick people into sin. But in the *Malleus* this traditional perspective no longer makes sense: witches knew full well that their magic came from the devil, or else they were not really witches; instead, the devil seemed to act mechanically because either the pact or his own nature forced him to accept that role. Furthermore, magic was no longer simply a supplementary diabolic project; in the *Malleus* it has become the principal means by which demons work their harm in the world.

Incubus demons offer an illuminating specific example of Institoris and Sprenger's thinking about demons and witches. Because they define witches as such through their personal relationships with the demons, and incubi in particular, these spirits had to appear to witches regularly and directly. Furthermore, as Institoris and Sprenger strongly imply, these are the devils who, while invisible, give potency to the witches' magic. The relationship between witch and incubus, therefore, provides the point at which the theoretical powers of demons are realized in the form of the witch's diabolic magic.

Despite this, incubi are in some ways less than completely formidable creatures. The incubi and succubi of Christian tradition were originally minor spirits (almost certainly demonized forms of traditional nature spirits, poltergeists, and house spirits), and, although the association of witches with incubi was a necessary component of witchcraft in the *Malleus*, the only first-hand accounts of such associations came from the witches themselves, who confessed to such liaisons under torture or its threat.[56] Their descriptions of their demon lovers were colored by their own traditional or "popular" perceptions of supra-normal encounters, demonic and otherwise, and these, in turn, informed the inquisitors' conception of the witches' devil. The outgrowth of this dialogue was a demon that retained many characteristics of traditional spirits, and whose very lack of a forcefully diabolic nature served to emphasize the witch's own guilt and responsibility.

In the experience of Institoris and Sprenger, for example, it was rare for a demon to recruit a witch directly; more often, witches themselves acted as the devil's agents. The authors had extensive personal knowledge of this procedure, and refer to it at least four times. In one instance, they had heard the confession of a young repentant witch from Breisach, who confessed that her aunt had brought her upstairs to a room filled with fifteen young men, dressed in green, after the fashion of knights, and demanded that she take one of them as her husband. The girl was beaten until she consented, whereupon she was initiated into the society of witches.[57] Witches did not always enjoy such luck, however, and these stories could end more happily. In an analogous narrative, Institoris and Sprenger relate that in order to seduce a certain devout young virgin, a wicked old witch took her upstairs to a room full of beautiful young devils, warning her first not to make the sign of the cross. But because the girl secretly did so anyway, "the demons in that same place were unable to reveal their presence to the virgin in their assumed bodies," and she escaped with nothing worse than the witch's impotent malediction.[58]

In these narratives, the incubus plays a markedly passive role. It is the witch, and not the devil, who is responsible for luring victims to the erotic rendezvous, and it is the witch who must spell out the terms of the encounter. Nor is the devil once found very "devilish": the young knights dressed in green suggest fairies more than demons, as does their meeting place on liminal ground – in rooms above stairs or ladders. The liminal nature of the demon likewise emerges in his choice of season, for, as Institoris and Sprenger remark, these encounters typically coincide with periods of sacred time: Christmas, Easter, and Pentecost.[59] For the witch, herself a liminal figure, the devil is present at all times; for the rest of society, the devil was truly "near" only under certain special conditions, such as those arising from the person or operation of a witch. For a witch, an upstairs room on a feast day could be filled with demons, and she could bring guests into their presence; for those fortified with the sign of the cross, on the other hand, the demons were quite absent – they did not really "exist" at all.[60]

To Institoris and Sprenger, witchcraft depended upon this intimate bond between woman and demon, close even to the point of identity. In the *Malleus*, the account of Institoris' prosecutions of witches in Ravensburg describes precisely how this relationship was determined.[61] They report that about twenty-eight miles southeast of the town, a very severe hailstorm had damaged the fields and vines in a swathe a mile wide, so that for the space of three years scarcely anything would grow there. The people of the town suspected witchcraft, "and clamored for an inquisition." Institoris was duly summoned, and, after careful investigation, he seized two suspects, a bath-woman named Agnes and Anna of Mindelheim, whom he imprisoned separately. Agnes was interrogated first, but she stoutly proclaimed her innocence through "very light questioning." This clearly showed that Agnes, like many witches, was provided by the devil with *maleficium taciturnitatis*, the preternatural ability to withstand torture in silence, so it was undoubtedly due to the miraculous intervention of God that Agnes confessed, and Institoris happily recalls that when she "was suddenly freed and released from her chains, although in the place of torture, she laid bare all of the crimes which she had perpetrated."[62] Not only did she confess to works of *maleficium*, but under the questioning of an inquisitorial notary, "she publicly confessed to everything else she was asked about the renunciation of the faith and her filthy, diabolical pacts with an incubus demon."[63] In Institoris' mind, if Agnes was indeed a witch, as she manifestly was, she had also to be guilty of these crimes, for this was what witchcraft was all about. That there was no evidence that she had done these things was unsurprising, because Agnes, like all witches, had been "most secret" in her dealings with the devil; proof of her guilt, therefore, depended upon her thorough confession. But it is characteristic of the inquisitor's thought that Agnes's interrogation about the details of her liaisons with the devil had to be completed before she was questioned about her use of destructive magic.

Agnes claimed that she had been lured into the sect by another witch, who had brought her to her home to meet the devil in the guise of a young and handsome man.[64] Having been seduced sexually, Agnes was apparently unable or unwilling to do without her demon again, and had been with him for some eighteen years. When asked about the hailstorm, she confessed that one day at about noon, a demon had come to her house and asked her to bring some water out to the plain, because he wanted to make rain. As she was told, Agnes met the devil standing under a tree. There she dug a little hole in the ground and poured the water into it. She then stirred the water with her finger "in the name of the devil and all the other demons," at which point the water disappeared and the devil rose up into the air to produce the hailstorm.[65]

Under questioning, Agnes described a world filled with demons, who were her lovers, companions, and supervisors. Under their guidance and tutelage she worked her magic and evil deeds, while they rewarded her achievements and punished her failures – all of this completely invisibly to her neighbors, who suspected her simply of harmful magic. The notary had first questioned her about the charges brought against her, that she had done harm to man and beast through witchcraft, "since no one had testified against her concerning the renunciation of the faith and carnal depravity with an incubus demon."[66] To make good this lack was the inquisitor's objective.

Agnes was not, however, quite alone in this world of demons, and she implicated a confederate, Anna of Mindelheim, in her crimes. "But this was remarkable," says Institoris, that "when on the following day the other woman had been exposed for the first time to the very lightest questioning, in as much as she was hung by her thumbs scarcely clear of the ground" she freely confessed to everything without the least discrepancy between her testimony and that of Agnes.[67] There was at least one difference, however: the devil recruited Anna directly, without any intermediary. According to Institoris, the devil appeared to Anna in the guise of a man, as she went to visit her lover, "causa fornicationis," and made her a proposition:

> "I am the devil, and if you wish, I will always be ready at your good pleasure, nor shall I desert you in any necessity whatsoever."[68]

This initial unmediated intimacy with the devil was reflected in Anna's character, for, as Institoris notes, Anna was a much worse witch than Agnes, for she had been the sexual slave of the devil for longer, had done more harm, and, unlike Agnes, was unrepentant when she was burned. Of course Anna's "confession" was contingent upon that of Agnes, who had the benefit of giving her story first, and had also the comparative luxury of negotiating her confession with her interrogators. Agnes was thus able to shift her burden of moral responsibility onto the unseen and ghostly presence of her demon; the inquisitors interrogated Anna with a script ready to hand, and so it is unsurprising that her relations with the devil should be more intimate than those of her colleague.

Institoris and Sprenger are fully aware that by making the witch the focus for demonic encounters on earth, they are suggesting a new paradigm for diabolic behavior. It is true, they grant, that there had always been incubus and succubus demons to plague mankind, but their traditional role had now changed. In the past, their mode of attack and their motives were sexual: they most often persecuted those whose sins were of a particularly sexual nature, and their diabolic rape was intended to be neither pleasant nor welcome. This destructive sexuality Institoris and Sprenger now attributed to witches: whereas, "in times gone by, incubus demons infested little women against their own wills," nowadays "they subject themselves to a wretched servitude for the sake of carnal pleasure, a most disgusting thing."[69] Incubi and succubi now followed a precise order of attack, determined by the willingness of their human partners. To those women wholly willing to have them they came freely; to those who were unwilling they had to be sent – and this was the work of witches.[70]

Institoris and Sprenger illustrate this new order of demonic sexual assault with the story of a man of Coblenz, who was prone to strange and debilitating sexual fits. Although no other person seemed to be present, the man would begin to move as if copulating, until, "after enduring fits of this kind for a long time, the poor man fell to the ground, destitute of all his strength."[71] The man claimed to be completely unable to resist these spasms, and blamed a woman who had returned some offense with curses for bewitching him.

Compare this story with the roughly contemporary narrative of the Dominican theologian, Jordanes de Bergamo. Jordanes tells of a demon who assumed the likeness of a beautiful girl in order to seduce a hermit:

> When he was done and had arisen, the demon said to him, "behold what you have done, for I am not a girl or a woman but a demon," and at once he disappeared from view, while the hermit remained absolutely astonished. And because the demon, with his great power, had withdrawn a very great quantity of semen, the hermit was permanently dried up, so that he died at the end of a month's time.[72]

Although the demons in each story afflict their victims with a kind of non-productive sexual excess, the incubus of the *Malleus* acts at the behest of the witch. Jordanes' more traditional spirit both tempts and punishes sin. Jordanes' demon is tangibly present, and explains his performance to his victim; the demon of the *Malleus* is invisible, without physical presence or hint of personality, existing only as the bearer of an affliction and the instrument of a witch.

In a sense, Institoris and Sprenger's witch is Jordanes' demon transformed: an obviously feminine, insatiably sexual creature, in whom an excess of sexuality corresponds with the destruction of sexuality in others. Indeed, in the *Malleus*, at times the two are not even distinguishable. On one occasion, the authors tell us, a man was harassed by "a demon in the form of a woman," who persistently sought sexual intercourse. The creature was eventually banished with the help of the sacramentals of the Church, "Whereby," we learn, "the devil had either been present in his own person in the form of a witch, or with the actual body of a witch, since, with God's permission, he is able to do both of these things."[73] This demon, whose behavior was entirely suggestive of a succubus, thus appeared to his victim, "as a witch"; the witch, whose form or whose body the devil appropriated, was, in turn, identified in appearance and behavior with the succubus herself.[74]

Although in their confessions, witches often sought to portray themselves as tools of the devil, Institoris and Sprenger consistently rejected this possibility. The work of demons, in their view, depended upon the guiding malice of witches, and this applied not just to traditional manifestations of *maleficia*, but to other more definitively demonic behaviors, the most remarkable of which was diabolic possession. Prior to the *Malleus*, possession was an entirely characteristic occupation of the devil, having little, if anything, to do with witchcraft. Institoris and Sprenger, however, are entirely consistent in their subordination of the demons' earthly activities to the agenda of their human minions. Granted, demons were capable of possessing people any time God should require; but, Institoris and Sprenger contended, demons usually possessed their victims at the instance of witches, since God granted demons more latitude when acting through witches than otherwise.[75] Although they cited various traditional cases of demonic possession, it is clear that they considered possession through witches a relatively more serious threat.[76]

Institoris and Sprenger illustrate their understanding of demonic possession with a long story – in fact, the longest single narrative account in the *Malleus*. It is taken from Institoris' own experience: while a young man in Rome, Institoris encountered a priest possessed by a demon. Although usually lucid, the priest lost his senses whenever he wished to visit holy places or spend his time on anything divine; just as bad, he stuck out his tongue involuntarily whenever he passed a church or knelt for the salutation of the Virgin. Though such behavior was not uncommon for demoniacs, the cause of his affliction gave reason for comment: he claimed that

> a certain woman, a witch, brought this infirmity upon me; for when chastising her on account of a certain disagreement about Church rules, while I was chiding her rather harshly, because her will was stubborn, she said that after a few days I would be afflicted with these things which then befell me. But the demon dwelling in me also reports this: that a *maleficium* has been placed by the witch under a certain tree, and that unless it is removed, I cannot be freed, but he is unwilling to point out the tree.[77]

Initially, it appeared as if the demon was correct: a full battery of exorcisms in a variety of holy places fails to provide the priest with relief. Only when a pious bishop spends forty days in a continuous regimen of fasting, exorcism, and prayer is the young man delivered.

The notable thing about this saga is the way in which demonic possession becomes an aspect of witchcraft, almost wholly unrelated to the demon himself. The demon even comments in a detached way upon the priest's predicament: he has no stake in the witch's quarrel; he has nothing personally to do with the entire process. This is, in fact, a necessary part of the narrative, as it is the demon who identifies the witch and explains the completely material, and not spiritual, basis for the priest's affliction. Institoris does not even consider the demon's further remarks relevant to the proceedings, despite the fact that, as the priest was undergoing exorcism, the demon within him cried out:

> "I don't want to go out." And when asked for what reason, he responded, "On account of the Lombards." And he was asked again why he was unwilling to depart on account of the Lombards. Then he answered in the Italian tongue, although the sick priest did not know that language, saying that all of them practice such and such, naming the worst vice of lust.[78]

Under other circumstances, a young man possessed by a demon, raving presumably about sodomy, would have at least raised eyebrows. Because sin so often provided the occasion for possession, a demon's dialogue with its exorcist, and especially its commentary upon the spiritual state of the possessed and of others, was naturally of considerable interest, yet, to Institoris, the words of the demon do not pertain to the subject at hand – witchcraft. Hence he reports them merely as curiosities; the cause of possession, Institoris seems to suggest, is found buried under trees rather than buried in the soul.

For Institoris and Sprenger, witchcraft is the key to understanding the demonic, and not the other way round. The devil exists in two almost completely autonomous forms: the powerful, largely theoretical demons who invisibly moved men to sin and caused calamities on earth, and the minor spirits who haunt houses and crossroads. The witch, defined by her relationship with an incubus demon (itself mid-way between these extremes) provides a necessary intermediate term in this system, allowing the awesome power of the devil to operate on earth without the incongruous presence of decidedly unimpressive demons as agents. The witch thus becomes a human extension of the diabolic realm, at times capable of assuming the characteristics, motives, and behaviors of demons, while still retaining those of women. Further, because Institoris and Sprenger identify witches with actual women, they locate responsibility for misfortunes in the witches' own real, socially constructed, moral evil, rather than in some abstract, dualist principle of evil or in the malice of nature spirits and preternatural beings. This kind of conception of the demonic, I would suggest, corresponds closely with a level of anxiety in witch-beliefs that is at least in part responsible for sustained witch-prosecutions in the late fifteenth century: on the one hand, it accurately mirrored notions of *maleficium* and the harmful occult powers of humans found in traditional European peasant communities; on the other, it provided a context in which these beliefs could be embraced by a learned clerical elite.

As a point of contrast, let us consider the somewhat earlier work of Nicholas Jacquier, an inquisitor in France and Bohemia.[79] In his treatise, the *Flagellum Haereticorum Fascinariorum*, witchcraft is largely compatible with that of the *Malleus*, but Jacquier takes a more traditional view of the devil and his role. Jacquier conceives of witchcraft principally in terms of a heretical cult: to him it is the "abominable sect and heresy of wizards," in which demons, not witches, play the leading roles.[80] Whereas other heresies may have been instigated by the devil, with their perverse doctrines being handed down from one generation to the next by men, here, "this worst of sects and most infamous of heresies is handed down personally through demons themselves."[81] In consequence, where the *Malleus* begins with a discussion of the devil's theoretical powers, Jacquier takes as his point of departure the devil's ability to appear actually and sensibly to men.[82] Jacquier's devil is the leader of his cult: he appears visibly to men to induce them to renounce God and the Church, and to take him instead as their lord; he instructs his followers in evil, providing them with poisons and magic potions, as well as with specific instructions concerning how and where to use them; and he demands offerings from his sectaries — food and drink were acceptable, human semen was better, and the blood of innocents was the best of all.[83] In sum, the devil of the *Flagellum* is far more personally responsible for the activities of witches than is his counterpart in the *Malleus*.

Jacquier's conception of the relationship between the devil and his sect appears much influenced by a number of stories current in mid-fifteenth-century France. These accounts emphasized the devil's desire to usurp the cult of God, and hence emphasized the devotional, quasi-religious nature of the bond between witches and the devil. Most important to Jacquier was the celebrated case of William Adelmo, prior of St. Germain-en-Laye, doctor of theology, and a man whom Jacquier knew quite well. In 1453, Adelmo publicly confessed that he had renounced the faith, entered into the sect of witches, and had worshiped the devil. He further confessed that

> When he was introduced into said sect, the devil proposed that Master William might well, if he wished, be able to increase the devil's domain, and instructed the same Master William to preach that sects of this kind were nothing except illusions.[84]

The devil in Adelmo's account appears as the subtle master of a secret society whose members lurk concealed in all walks of life. In the *Flagellum Haereticorum*, it is the existence and membership of this society, which the devil so cleverly wished to keep secret, that is at issue, and not *maleficia per se*. Although the *fascinarii* are sorcerers who deploy diabolic magic by the devil's will, they derive their unique character from their personal dependence upon the devil and their membership in his cult, not from their occult powers. Indeed, Jacquier recognized that *maleficia* had nothing necessarily to do with this heretical sect; since malign magic could function regardless of whether one worshiped the devil or not, there were doubtless many *maleficii* who were not *fascinarii*.[85] Such persons must, or course, be linked with the devil by some sort of pact, either tacit or explicit, but this could easily be an individual, personal arrangement that did not imply membership in the devil's organized cult.

This posed a problem for Jacquier's conception of the *fascinarii*: since *maleficium* was not in itself direct evidence of membership, an inquisitor had to look, not for the ambiguous presence of harmful magic, but for witnesses to the Sabbat and evidence of the demonic cult itself, which, as Institoris' experience with Agnes and Anna suggests, could be very hard to come by. Direct and immediate commerce with the devil, although necessary to witchcraft, was likely to be secret and hidden, to be revealed only through torture and interrogation once suspects had already been identified on other grounds. While Institoris and Sprenger's construction of witchcraft could readily translate ideas about malign magic from a popular idiom to the more learned environment of the inquisitors, Jacquier's could not. His was a model much better suited to the testimony of a fallen doctor of theology than to a village brew-wife. Certainly, once prosecutions had begun, it was easy to extract the names of confederates from accused witches through torture, and Jacquier was at pains to defend the legal validity of such tactics, but because his conception of the witch was dependent upon heresy and the devil, initial accusations were not easy to obtain.[86]

Moreover, because Jacquier had a much more unified, conception of the devil, in whom power and personality were closely joined, he had no way to determine if the blame for any given misfortune lay with a witch or with the devil. Where Institoris and Sprenger subordinated the operation of demons on earth to the power of witches, blaming supernatural harm on witches as a matter of course, Jacquier was more cautious, noting that whatever demons did through witches, they could and would do of their own accord.[87] As a result, while many of Jacquier's ideas about witchcraft would be accepted by theorists of the following century (his notions of the diabolic Sabbat in particular), his construction of witchcraft failed to provide the consensus within the community of witch-believers – including learned theoreticians, magistrates, and inquisitors as well as unlettered peasants and townsfolk – necessary for sustained witchcraft prosecutions. For a well-defined, fully threatening witch-figure to emerge, the devil as a personality had to be divorced from the day-to-day operations of witchcraft. Such a separation would enable demonologists to accept a more remote, "god-like" conception of Satan, more in accord with current theological trends, as well as the ideas of both Protestant and Catholic writers of the next century. It was just this consensus that Institoris and Sprenger's model of the demonic would provide.

Notes

1 Jeffrey Burton Russell, *Witchcraft in the Middle Ages* (Ithaca: Cornell University Press, 1972), 102.

2 Richard Kieckhefer, *European Witch Trials* (Berkeley, University of California, 1976), 36. See also David Gentilcore, *From Bishop to Witch* (Manchester: Manchester University Press, 1992), 248.

3 For the late-medieval tendency "to grasp the transcendent by making it immanent," see Carlos M.N. Eire, *War Against the Idols: The Reformation of Worship from Erasmus to Calvin* (Cambridge: Cambridge University Press, 1986), 11 and *passim*.

4 See Valerie J. Flint, *The Rise of Magic in Early Medieval Europe* (Princeton: Princeton University Press, 1991), 146–57; Jeffrey Burton Russell, *Satan: The Early Christian Tradition* (Ithaca: Cornell University Press, 1981). St. Augustine wrote extensively on the nature of demons, but especially influential were *De Divinatione Daemonum* and *De Civitate Dei*, books 9–10.

5 Augustine, *City of God*, trans. Henry Betteson (London: Penguin, 1972), 8.15.

6 Augustine, *The Divination of Demons*, trans. R.W. Brown, in *Saint Augustine. Treatises on Marriage and Other Subjects*, ed. Roy J. Deferrari (New York: Fathers of the Church, 1951), 430.

7 For one example among many, see Augustine's sermon on John the Baptist: "The ancient enemy is always on watch against us; . . . He sets lures and traps, he insinuates evil thoughts; to goad people to ever worse kinds of fall he sets out advantages and gains, it is painful to reject his evil suggestions and willingly accept death as we know it." Augustine, *Sermons*, trans. Edmund Hill, ed. John E. Rotelle (Brooklyn: New York City Press, 1992), pt. 3, vol. 4, sermon 94A, p. 20.

8 Augustine, *On Christian Doctrine*, trans. D.W. Robertson, Jr. (Indianapolis: Bobbs-Merrill/Library of Liberal Arts, 1958), 23.35.

9 Augustine, *Sermons*, sermon on Esau and Jacob, 4:36, pp. 205–6.

10 Augustine, *City of God*, 7.35. See also 8.24.

11 Augustine, *Sermons*, 4:36, p. 206.

12 Precisely why this occurred is difficult to say, but see Russell, *Witchcraft in the Middle Ages*, 101–32, and Edward Peters, *The Magician, the Witch, and the Law* (Philadelphia: University of Pennsylvania Press, 1978), 93–8.

13 Since we are here ultimately concerned with the work of fifteenth-century Dominicans, Aquinas is unquestionably the most relevant scholastic theorist. Charles Edward Hopkin argues for the essential conservatism of Thomist demonology in his doctoral dissertation, "The Share of Thomas Aquinas in the Growth of the Witchcraft Delusion" (Philadelphia: University of Pennsylvania Press, 1940). See also Jeffrey Burton Russell, *Lucifer: The Devil in the Middle Ages* (Ithaca: Cornell University Press, 1984).

14 Hopkin, 177.

15 Thomas Aquinas, *Summa Theologiae*, ed. Institutio Studiorum Medievalium Ottaviensis (Ottowa: Studii Generalis O. Pr., 1941), pt. 1, qu. 50–64; *Postilla in Job*; *De Malo* and *De Potentia* in *Questiones Disputatae*. At the same time, a similar scholarly project defined the character and capacities of angels: "Scholastics explored with great logical rigor and tenacity the angels' intellectual and emotional capacities, their personhood, their simplicity, their problematic relationship with time and space, and even the metaphysical bases for their being. Indeed, at the university they developed what may properly be called an 'angelology,' a science of angels." David Keck, *Angels and Angelology in the Middle Ages* (Oxford: Oxford University Press, 1998), 74.

16 See, for example, *Summa Theologiae*, pt. 1, qu. 64, art. 4.

17 Dyan Elliott, *Fallen Bodies: Pollution, Sexuality, and Demonology in the Middle Ages* (Philadelphia: University of Pennsylvania Press, 1999), 129; see *Summa Theologiae*, pt. 1, qu. 50, art. 2, resp. 9.

18 In the late twelfth century, Walter Map recorded an interview with one of these lesser spirits, one of the angels who, "without assistance or consent to Lucifer's crime, were borne by foolishness to wander after the accomplices of sin" ("qui sine coadiutorio uel consensu culpe Luciferi vagi post fautores scelerum fatue ferebamur"). He and his fellows, he claimed, had no desire for the ruin of cities or the blood and souls of men; rather, they were apt to play jokes and make risible illusions with their powers. "Everything that we can, we do for laughter, and nothing for tears." ("Omne quod ad risum est possumus, nichil quod ad lacrimas"). *De Nugis Curialium*, ed. M.R. James (Oxford: Clarendon Press, 1914), dist. 4, c. 6, lines 8–17.

19 *Summa Theologiae*, pt. 1, qu. 64, art. 4.

20 *Ibid.*, pt. 1, qu. 51, art. 3; *De Potestate, Questiones Disputatae*, qu. 6, art. 8; and Hopkin, 77–9.

21 Although one may wonder how tempting such necessarily hurried couplings could possibly have been. Guibert of Nogent, *DeVita Sua, Patrologia Latina* 156, 958: "Sunt quoque quedam in nequitiis infligendis atrocia, aliqua vero solis contenta ludibriis." See also Thomas Aquinas, *Summa Theologiae*, pt. 1, qu. 63, art. 2.

22 Hans Peter Duerr, *Dreamtime*, trans. Felicitas Goodman (Oxford: Basil Blackwell, 1985), 5.

23 For dates and biography of Felix of Hemmerlin (known in Latin as Felix Malleolus), see Hansen, *Quellen*, 109.

24 "Nam dicti Principes non proposuerunt deum ante conspectum suum sed inter se diviserunt regni terminos terrarum ante Triumphum." Felix Hemmerlin, *Tractatus de Credulitate Daemonibus Adhibenda*, in Heinrich Institoris and Jacob Sprenger, *Malleus Maleficarum* (Frankfurt, 1600), 2:431.

25 Felix Hemmerlin, *Dialogus de nobilitate et rusticitate*, in Hansen, *Quellen*, 110.

26 "hac maledictione plena est terra." *Ibid.*, 110–11. The woman is Finicella, burned in Rome in 1424.

27 Hemmerlin, *Tractatus*, 429. A devil in the guise of a holy man removes a sinning priest's male member which has been the cause of all his difficulties. Naturally, it returns to view, even larger than before, at the worst possible moment.

28 See Hansen, *Quellen*, 208–9.

29 "quod numquam de talibus aliquid concederent, nisi proponeretur eis aliquod grossum exemplum sensibile." Petrus Mamoris, *Flagellum Maleficorum* (Lugdunum [Lyon], 1621), 12.

30 See Hansen, *Quellen*, 88–9.

31 Johannes Nider, *Praeceptorium Legis s. Expositio Decalogi* (Strassburg: Georg Husner, 1476), 1.11, p; Mamoris, 45.

32 Nider, *Praeceptorium*, 1.11, s; Mamoris, 19 and *passim*.

33 "Non enim coelum vel aliquod totum elementum mouere potest, quia destrueretur ordo Vniuersi, quem Deus instituit: sed potest mouere corpora sibi proportionata." *Ibid.*, 16.

34 "Sunt enim diaboli superioris naturae ad animam rationalem, quae non potest movere corpus." *Ibid.*

35 Institoris and Sprenger use a similarly trivial, not to say humorous, example of demons' powers of local motion in the *Malleus*. A priest, and a friend of one of the authors, was fortunate enough to witness a man being bodily transported through the air for some distance by a demon. The victim was a student who had been drinking beer with friends, and when an associate declined to fetch more, on account of an ominous thick cloud blocking the door, he unwisely declared that "Even if the devil were there, I will go to get a drink" ("Etsi diabolus adesset potum apportabo"). When he went outside, the devil swept him up. *Malleus*, pt. 2, qu. 1, ch. 3, p. 102.

36 "Multo plus potest daemon per transmutationem sanguinis et humorum et alio subtili modo horrorem incutere, in mente odium, et in carne dolorem." Mamoris, 32.

37 "strepitibus et sibulis [*sic*] ac pulsibus, non multum excellentibus sed manifestis; aliquando enim ad parietes percutiebat; aliquando vero ioculator varias mimorum fistulas ut videbatur flabat, et talia non nociua multum gestiebat." Johannes Nider, *Formicarius* (1480; facsimile, Graz: Akademische Druck- und Verlagsanstalt, 1971), 5.2, 200.

38 Alphonso Spina, *Fortalitium Fidei* (Lugdunum [Lyon]: Gulielmus Balsarin, 1487), book 5, consideration 10.

39 "Et his diebus taliter apparet frequenter in Dacia et Nortuvegia, et ibidem Tolli dicuntur; et propter assuetudinem ab hominibus non timentur, sed homines ipsorum obsequiis utuntur." Hemmerlin, *Tractatus*, 428.

40 Lynn Thorndike, *A History of Magic and Experimental Science* (New York: Columbia University Press, 1934), 4:289. For an overview of this problem, see André Goddu, "The Failure of Exorcism in the Middle Ages," in Albert Zimmerman, ed., *Soziale Ordnungen im Selbstverständnis des Mittelalters*, 2 vols. (Berlin: Walter de Gruyter, 1980), 2:540–77.

41 "Qui quidem spiritus audientibus multis die et nocte, et nihil tamen videntibus, multa in tempore praeterito facta revelavit, quae fuere cognita vera fuisse, et ad multa bona facienda gentes domus admonebat." Mamoris, 20.

42 A great many more examples might be given, but an interesting one is Nider's insistence that the bestial men and women sometimes encountered in the forest are not real "wild men," but demons who appear to deceive the unwary. Nider, *Praeceptorium*, k (qu. 6).

43 Reimund Kvideland and Henning K. Sehmsdorf, eds., *Scandinavian Folk Belief and Legend* (Minneapolis: University of Minnesota Press, 1988), 216–17.

44 "Licet corpora humana nobis assumamus, dorsa tamen non habemus." Caesarius of Heisterbach, *Dialogus Miraculorum*, 2 vols., ed. Joseph Strange (1851: reprint, Ridgewood New Jersey: Gregg Press, 1966), 3.6, p. 118.

45 Spina, consid. 11.

46 Katherine M. Briggs, *The Vanishing People* (London: B.T. Batsford, 1978), 76.

47 Spina, consid. 1–6.

48 *Ibid.*, consid. 6.

49 *Ibid.*, consid. 10.

50 "Invenient etiam qualiter cognoscit cogitationes cordium nostrorum qualiter etiam possit transmutare corpora adminiculo alterius agentis substantialiter et accidentaliter, qualiter etiam possit movere corpora localiter immutare etiam sensus exteriores et interiores ad aliquid cogitandum qualiter etiam possit immutare hominis intellectum et voluntatem licet indirecte." *Malleus*, pt. 1, qu. 3, p. 22.

51 "[Enim sunt humani generis inimici,] mente rationales absquam tamen discursu intelligentes, in nequicia subtiles nocendi cupidi semper in fraude novi, immutant sensus, inquinant affectus, vigilantes turbant, dormientes per somnia inquietant, morbos inferunt, tempestates concitant, in lucis angelos se transformant, semper infernum secum portant, erga maleficos divinum cultum sibi usurpant, magice artes per eos fiunt, super bonos dominari appetunt et amplius proposse infestant, electis ad exercitium dantur, semper fini hominis insidiantur." *Ibid.*, 23.

52 For example, compare Isidore of Seville's well-known definition of *malefici*: "Hi et elementa concutiunt, turbant mentes hominum, ac sine ullo veneni haustu violentia tantum carminis interimunt." Isidore of Seville, *Etymologiae*, ed. W.M. Lindsay (Oxford: Clarendon, 1911), 8.9, lines 9–10.

53 *Malleus*, pt. 2, qu. 1, ch. 11, p. 132.

54 *Ibid.*

55 *Ibid.*, pt. 2, qu. 2, p. 156. Likewise if one burns the intestines of an animal killed by witchcraft, the devil will similarly heat the witch's bowels. *Ibid.*, 158.

56 One may compare, for example, the incubus reported by Caesarius of Heisterbach, who reverted to an annoying house spirit when rebuffed, throwing things and changing food on plates to filth, or that of Gobelinus Persona, who "talked freely with all comers, played delicately on a musical instrument, played at dice, drank wine, but never allowed himself to be seen except his hands which were slender and soft." Caesarius of Heisterbach, *Dialogus Miraculorum* 3.6; Gobelinus Persona, *Cosmodromium*, aet. vi, c. 70, in Lea, *Materials*, 1:286.

57 *Malleus*, pt. 2, qu. 1, ch. 2, pp. 96–7.

58 "Demones ibidem existentes suam presentiam in assumptis corporibus illi virgini nequiebant ostendere." *Ibid.*, pt. 2, qu. 1, ch. 4, p. 110. This story also appears, with slight variations, in pt. 2, qu. 1, ch. 1, p. 94.

59 Demons do this, Institoris and Sprenger explain, so as to mock and offend God. *Ibid.*, pt. 2, qu. 1, ch. 4, p. 110.

60 Institoris and Sprenger maintain that each of us is assigned to the care of two angels, one good and one bad. For the normal run of humanity, the angels are "present" only in a highly abstract way, for example as the voice of temptation or of conscience; the witch, on other hand, will regularly eat, chat, and have sexual relations with her demon. *Ibid.*, pt. 1, qu. 3, p. 25.

61 *Ibid.*, pt. 2, qu. 1, chs. 1 and 15.

62 "subito libere et a vinculis absoluta licet in loco torture et cuncta flagitia ab ea perpetrata detexit." *Ibid.*, pt. 2, qu. 1, ch. 15, p. 146.

63 "Cetera omnia de fidei abnegatione et spurcitiis diabolicis cum incubo demone pactis interrogata publice fatebatur." *Ibid.*

64 *Ibid.*, pt. 2, qu. 1, ch. 1, p. 94.

65 Perhaps to demonstrate that he is not leading his witness, Institoris relates the exchange between Agnes and the notary as a literal interrogation. In this instance Agnes "was asked 'With what words or in what ways did you stir the water?' She replied 'I stirred it with my finger, but in the name of that devil and of all the other devils.'" ("Interrogata demum quibusne verbis aut modis aquam mouisset. Respondit digito quidem moui, sed in nomine illius diaboli et omnium aliorum demoniorum."). *Ibid.*, pt. 2, qu. 1, ch. 15, p. 146.

66 "Cum nemo testis de fidei abnegatione ac carnali spurcitia cum demone incubo aduersus eam deposuisset, [eo quod illa secretissma sint illius secte cerimonialia.]" *Ibid.*

67 "Sed et hoc mirabile cum sequenti die altera questionibus etiam leuissimis exposita primo fuisset vtpote digito vix a terra elevata post libere soluta, praefata omnia non discrepando in minimo." *Ibid.*

68 "Demon sum, et si volueris ad tuum beneplacitum semper ero paratus, nec in quibuscumque necessitatibus te deferam." *Ibid.*, pt. 2, qu. 1, ch. 1, p. 94.

69 "Incubi demones in retroactis temporibus infesti fuerunt mulierculis contra ipsarum voluntatem." "Sed sponte pro voluptate re fetidissima miserabili servituti se subiicientes." *Ibid.*, pt. 2, qu.1, pt. 4, p. 108.

70 Although men too might succumb to the wiles of an attractive succubus, Institoris and Sprenger add "not so actively of their own will," since "from the natural force of reason which is stronger in men than in women, they shrink more from such practices" ("Non ita voluntarie practicatio reperitur cum ex naturali vigore rationis quo viri mulieribus praeeminent talia plus abhorrent"). *Ibid.*, pt. 2, qu. 2, ch. 1, p. 159.

71 "Post diutinas huiusmodi vexationes pauper ille collisus in terram omnibus viribus destituit." *Ibid.*

72 "Quo facto cum surrexisset, dixit illi demon: Ecce quod egisti; non enim sum puella sive mulier, sed demon, et statim disparuit ab oculis eius; ille vero attonitus remansit. Et quia demon maximam seminis habundantiam virtute eius attraxerat, continue heremita ille desiccatus completo mense defunctus est." Jordanes de Bergamo, *Questio de Strigis*, in Hansen, *Quellen*, 198. Hansen gives a date of around 1460 for the treatise, but Lea (*Materials*, 1:301) has it composed in 1470–71. Jordanes seems otherwise unknown.

73 "Ubi diabolus per se in effigie malefice, aut cum presentia corporali malefice affuerat, cum utrumque facere deo permittente potest." *Malleus*, pt. 2, qu. 1, p. 88.

74 Similar blurrings of the lines between witch and demon can be found in German witch-trials, where *unholda* is at times used as a synonym for the devil. In one trial, cited by Hans Peter Duerr, the devil is referred to as "the old Perchtl," a word which, like *unholda*, was more often used of witches or evil spirits. Duerr, 5.

75 *Malleus*, pt. 2, qu. 1, ch. 10, p. 126.

76 As the title of their chapter makes plain: "Concerning how demons sometimes sub-

stantially inhabit people through the operations of witches" ("De modo quo demones per maleficarum operationes homines interdum substantialiter inhabitant"). *Ibid.*, 125.

77 "Mulier inquit quedam malefica hanc mihi infirmitatem contulit; briganti enim contra eam ratione cuiusdam displicentie circa regimen curie cum eam durius increpassem quia cervicose voluntatis ere dixit: quod post paucos dies haberem intendere his que mihi contingerent. Sed et demon in me habitans hoc idem refert quod maleficium sub quadam arbore positum sit a malefica, quod nisi amoveatur non potero liberari, sed nec arborem vult indicare." *Ibid.*, pt. 2, qu. 1, ch. 10, pp. 127–8.

78 "Nolo exire. Et cum interrogaret, qua de causa, respondit propter lombardos. Et interrogatus denuo, cur propter lombardos egredi nollet, tunc respondit in ytalica lingua cum tamen infirmus sacerdos illud ideoma ignoraret dicens, omnes faciunt sic et sic, nominando pessimum vitium luxurie." *Ibid.*, 128.

79 Jacquier wrote the *Flagellum* around 1458, and remained an inquisitor until his death in 1472. Hansen, *Quellen*, 133.

80 The phrase, "secta et haeresis maleficorum fascinariorum," appears repeatedly throughout the text. For a summary description of the sect's activities and organization, see Nicholas Jacquier, *Flagellum Haereticorum Fascinariorum*, ed. Ioannes Myntzenbergius (Frankfurt am Main: N. Bassaeum, 1581) ch. 7, pp. 36–51: "De differentia inter sectam et haeresin fascinariorum modernorum, et illusionem mulierum de quibus loquitur c. Episcopi."

81 "Haec pessima sectarum et haeresum nefandissima, traditur per ipsosmet Daemones." *Ibid.*, 44.

82 *Ibid.*, 7.

83 *Ibid.*, 50–2.

84 "Quod quando ipse fuit introductus ad dictam sectam, Diabolus asserebat, quod ipse Magister Guilhelmus bene posset si vellet, augmentare eiusdem Demonis dominium, praecipiendo eidem Magistro Guilhelmo praedicare, quod huiusmodi secta non erat nisi illusio." *Ibid.*, 27. Mamoris also knew Ediline, and tells substantially the same story, 67–8.

85 For example, Jacquier observes that "all witches generally, and especially the heretical *fascinarii*, are betrayers and accustomed to lying in the perpetration of their evil deeds" ("Omnes enim malefici communiter, presertim heretici fascinarii sunt proditores et fictionibus assueti in maleficiorum perpetratione."). Jacquier, 111.

86 Of course once prosecutions had begun, it was easy to extract the names of confederates from accused witches under torture, and Jacquier is at pains to defend the validity of such procedures. *Ibid.*, 173–4.

87 *Ibid.*, 117.

4

Misfortune, witchcraft, and the will of God

An obvious corollary to a belief in witches is the perception that certain kinds of recognizable injuries or misfortunes are due to witchcraft, and it is clear from the sources that many people in medieval Europe were, at times, prepared to accept certain kinds of misfortunes as the result of witchcraft or harmful magic.[1] Not everyone, however, understood the relationship between magic and its effects in the same way. For unlettered peasants and townsfolk – for everyone, in fact, but a small elite of educated men and women – the relationship between "magic" and its intended result was probably a straightforward case of cause and effect, in which the witch or sorcerer who deployed occult powers for harmful ends was as much responsible for the resulting injuries as was a person wielding a knife with murderous intent.

For the theologically more sophisticated elite, however, the relationship between a witch, her magic, and associated injuries, was fraught with difficulties of considerable complexity. From their perspective, since the witch could not be the immediate cause of magical harm, both because a demon actually effected the injury, and because the witch had no power to compel the demon to do her bidding, the extent to which witches were actually culpable for the injuries inflicted by demons in their name was questionable. The matter was further complicated by the fact that demons could act only with the permission of God. Hence, if demons acted merely in accordance with divine will, why should either the witch or the demon be blamed for the outcome? And why, too, should God have chosen to give the witch or the demon free latitude to carry out magical assaults of their own volition in the first place? To endorse witch persecution, educated Christians had to answer these questions in such a way that the witch would emerge as the efficient cause of worldly misfortune. When she was not, when either a witch's power to cause harm or her moral responsibility for it were called into question, late-medieval writers tended to dismiss the dangers posed by witchcraft. The widespread skepticism about the reality of witchcraft in the late Middle Ages responded precisely to this concern that the belief in witchcraft as, say, Institoris and Sprenger understood it, was a gross affront to both the omnipotence and justice of God. To understand the alternative explanations for magical harm and witchcraft propounded by Institoris and Sprenger and their colleagues, we need therefore first to take a more general look at medieval conceptions of magic and misfortune.

There was never a single, universally applicable explication of misfortune in the Middle Ages. Instead, circumstances dictated the conceptual model appropriate to the beliefs of the observer. In any given instance, a substantial number of interpretations were possible, witchcraft being one and never the most prevalent. Misfortune, as Rodney Needham observes, can be explained in any number of ways:

> If misfortune strikes, you can blame an inscrutable god or capricious spirits; you can concede that it is the just retribution of your sin, or else that it is the automatic consequence of some unintended fault; you can put it down to bad luck . . . , or more calculating you can ascribe it to chance.[2]

During the Middle Ages, all of these possible explanations for sudden misfortune (with the possible exception of chance) were available alongside witchcraft, making for overlapping and competing patterns of considerable complexity.

For instance, the Franciscan chronicler Salimbene de Adam reported that in 1287 a large crowd of Pisans had gathered in a square to watch a great bell being hung. Then, "just as it was being lifted off the platform, it tipped over and fell to the ground. But it injured no one, save for a young man whose foot it cut off."[3] Human life was full of such unexpected mischances, but to Salimbene, as to all knowledgeable clerics, it was misleading to call such an unfortunate accident an "evil," for God had so ordered his creation that events which were injurious or harmful from one perspective always contributed to some ultimate good. Men might be made to suffer either toward some inscrutable end known only to God, or for their own just punishment and correction as, it so happened, in the case of the maimed youth:

> For he had once kicked his father with this foot and therefore did not escape with impunity. Thus, by a misfortune of this kind, God demonstrated his justice.[4]

For Salimbene, the cause of the young man's punishment lay directly in his sin. Such an explanation did not necessarily rule out subsidiary factors – the workmen may have been careless, the platform may have been unstable, or a demon may have pushed over the bell – but it did establish why this man was harmed and no other, and explained the precise nature of his injuries.

The basis for Salimbene's understanding of this incident was provided by Augustine's thorough delineation of the problems posed by misfortune and material evil in the world. According to Augustine, divine providence dictated all the injuries suffered by man, although for a number of potentially quite different reasons. Some punishments were purificatory, intended to "discipline and correct" the sinner and to guide him along the path to salvation. All other misfortunes and injuries, Augustine believed, were

> imposed either in retribution for sins, whether past sins or sins in which the person so chastised is still living, or else to exercise and to display the virtues of the good.[5]

God did not, however, administer correction directly, but relied instead upon the agency of men and of angels, both evil and good. Through them, all were made subject to the consequences of Adam's sin; even the innocent were condemned to suffer the countless miseries of human life due simply to their own fallen natures and life in a now fallen creation. For Augustine, storms, tempests, earthquakes, fire, flood, famine – in short the entire gamut of possible calamities – were "not directed to the punishment of the wickedness and lawlessness of evil man, but are part of our common condition of wretchedness."[6] Hence, even infants newly baptized and free from any possible culpability had to suffer disease, accidents, and even the assaults of demons, because they were doomed to live in a world made dangerous by the sins of their fathers. God did not, however, harm the innocent in any absolute sense, despite the physical miseries he might inflict: true, demons were allowed to torment innocent children, but, "we must never think that these sufferings can do them real harm, even if they grow so severe as to cut off the soul from the body," since death would merely hasten the journey of blameless souls to paradise.[7]

Augustine argued that although divine providence was the ultimate cause of misfortunes and injuries, only human sin was to blame. To look outside one's self, and place responsibility for catastrophes on fallen angels or evil men, was both misguided and, at worst, a dishonest evasion of responsibility. Instead, when good Christians considered the suffering wrought by some sudden or unexpected injury,

> First, they consider in humility the sins which have moved God's indignation so that he has filled the world with dire calamities. And although they are free from criminal and godless wickedness, still they do not regard themselves as so far removed from such wrongdoing as not to deserve to suffer from temporal ills which are the recompense for sin.[8]

This did not mean, of course, that ill-doers should not be punished, still less that criminals were not culpable for their crimes, since they freely willed the evils they committed. Augustine differentiated, however, between the crimes of men and the seemingly random hazards of the world. In the case of the latter, it was pointless to rail against the angel that carried out God's will, whether evil or no, since never in the least degree could they exceed the freedom allowed them by God.

Augustine's interpretation of misfortune as the collective product of God, demons, and human sin, was echoed repeatedly during the Middle Ages. Isidore of Seville, for example, writes that "When God visits his wrath he sends apostate angels as his ministers, but limits their powers, so that they do not do the evil they wish."[9] Similarly, Gregory the Great reminds readers of his *Moralia in Job* that

> You see that one and the same spirit is both called the Lord's spirit and an evil spirit; the Lord's, that is, by the concession of just power, but evil, by the desire of an unjust will, so that he is not to be dreaded who has no power but by permission; and, therefore, that Power is the only worthy object of fear, which is when It has allowed the enemy to serve the purpose of a just judgment.[10]

And so, too, in the tenth century, Rather of Verona comments that the power to punish or correct belonged to God alone, and only "those who are deceived by this power ascribe it to the deceiver himself."[11] Thus all punishment, all misfortune, all the evils of the world were ultimately the work of God, who infuriated the devil by turning his malice to good ends: such was the traditional Christian interpretation of misfortune, until the end of the thirteenth century, when several factors conspired to modify this understanding, and to shift responsibility for misfortune away from God and towards his ministers.

Of course, monastic writings had long been filled with demons of an appearance quite different from those of the theologians and canonists. Athanasius, for example, represented the life of St. Anthony as a continuous and quite personal struggle with the devil. Temptations rose to torment the saint not as a consequence of his fallen nature, but from the machinations of the fiend, whose "commission" it was in every case to waylay pious youth.[12] When temptation failed, the devil resorted to more physical methods and assaulted the saint with blows and fearful visions of wild beasts. Yet, although Anthony lived with daily and direct intercourse with demons, Athanasius always imparts the clear sense that the saint's victory was inevitable and that the devil was powerless before God: Anthony mocks the demons that assail him, telling them that "it is a sign of your helplessness that you ape the form of brutes," and that they tire themselves needlessly, "for faith in our Lord is a seal to us and a wall of safety."[13]

Anthony's career provided a paradigm for the monastic life that was replicated faithfully many times, both in the *vitae* of saints and in the experiences

of humbler monks. Like Anthony, monks conceived of themselves as constantly
beset by temptations orchestrated by the devil, for whom the purity of their
lives acted as irresistible bait. Consistently referring to these inner struggles
in terms of combat and battle with an exterior foe, their war stories are inhabited by aggressive, formidable opponents, who, if ultimately answerable to
divine will, had to appear self-willed and independent for cogent dramatic
reasons.[14] Numerous examples reminded monks constantly that they lived in
an environment in which the power of Satan was incessantly at work, in which
any stray thought or mischance was a manifestation of the devil's immediate
presence.

It was possible, indeed easy, for this view of the world to be taken to
extremes. Peter Damian tells of a monk named Marinus, who daily encountered the devil in various forms: he appeared as an angel of light to trick
Marinus into minor sins, and, in less pleasant guise, the devil joined mock-
ingly in the celebration of *opus Dei*.[15] Still more remarkable was the case of
Ricalmus, a thirteenth-century Carthusian monk and the abbot of Schönthal,
who, by special grace, could see the normally invisible demons that swarmed
about him, and who recorded his experiences for posterity. Ricalmus' world
was filled with demons who were responsible not only for interior temptation
but also for all the other petty annoyances which distracted him from proper
concentration on the divine office:

> The devils, without a particle of respect for his character or his years used to
> call him a "dirty hairless rat;" afflicted him with bloating of the stomach and
> with diarrhea, with nausea and with giddiness; so benumbed his hands that he
> could no longer make the sign of the cross; caused him to fall asleep in the choir
> and then snored so as to make the other monks think that it was he who was
> snoring. They would speak with his voice, make him cough, force him to expec-
> torate, hide themselves in his bed and stop his nostrils and his mouth so that he
> could not breathe, compel him to urinate, or bite him like fleas; and if, endeav-
> oring to fight off drowsiness, he exposed his hands to the cold air, they would
> draw them back under the coverlet and warm them again . . . All the noises
> that proceed from the human body, all those that issue from inanimate things
> are simply the work of evil spirits, except the sound of bells, which is the work
> of good spirits. Hoarseness, toothache, partial loss of voice, errors committed
> in reading, the whims and impulses of the sick, gloomy thoughts, and the thou-
> sand petty accidents of the body and the life of the soul are due to diabolic
> powers.[16]

Admittedly, Ricalmus is an extreme case. For one thing, it is painfully apparent in his account that diabolic power has become an excuse for embarrassing
personal lapses; for another, his is an altogether dualist world, permeated by
the forces of darkness. Yet the assumptions about the role of demons in this

world that lay behind his tale were readily understood, and accepted, by his peers.

Provided that such accounts were confined to a monastic milieu, it was possible to interpret them quite traditionally, as examples of an old and respected genre of narrative. With the twelfth century, however, and especially with the expansion of preaching that followed on the heels of the Fourth Lateran Council, many of these stories were distributed in sermons further afield, where they may well have helped to disseminate the image of a powerful, self-willed, and physically concrete devil, operating with minimal divine oversight.[17] Moreover, in some of these *exempla*, which competed in sermons side by side with more edifying accounts of divine judgment, monastic demons merged with the destructive spirits of folk tradition to emphasize diabolic responsibility for misfortune at the expense of the divine.[18]

To take one example, the Dominican preacher Thomas of Cantimpré wrote in 1258 that during a demonically inspired storm, the vines of a notorious usurer were left intact, and that aerial demons were even heard to cry out, "*Cave, cave*," when an overzealous member of their company approached his lands too closely.[19] Thomas intended, of course, to illustrate that material prosperity is no sure indication of spiritual merit as well as the diabolic nature of usury, but in the process he created a group of free-wheeling demons, to all appearances acting very much of their own accord. Nor were such tales repeated only in sermons for the laity. Gerald of Wales told essentially the same anecdote but in a rather different context in his *Itinerarium Kambriae*.[20] In Gerald's version, a terrible storm had one evening destroyed the crops of a Cistercian monastery, but had spared the fields of a neighboring knight, with whom the monks had been embroiled in a protracted boundary dispute. The knight insolently and publicly proclaimed that by the just judgment of God this misfortune manifestly demonstrated that he was in the right. The abbot would have none of this, however, and replied that on the contrary the calamity was simply in accord with the usual practice of demons, who spared their friends and afflicted their enemies. The account is interesting because here we have two competing interpretations of misfortune set side by side, although, doubtless, had the situation been reversed the witty abbot would have been quick to seize the alternative explanation. Yet the ease with which demons are transformed from the scourge of sinners to the enemies of the just is striking. Nor are these demons simply straw men to be overcome by Christian faith, even that of pious monks; they are instead formidable foes, whose assaults must be endured.

Neither of these authors would have seen anything particularly incongruous in his respective *exempla*, since he would have interpreted them with a similar understanding of the relationship between God, sin, and misfortune.

Of course that is not to say that less learned folk would necessarily have grasped the unspoken consistency among them, but that while the clergy endorsed a thoroughly Augustinian demonology there was a limit to how much freedom they allowed the devil. Although demons in *exempla* might appear to act freely, their behavior was theoretically under close divine supervision. But even as the demons in ecclesiastical narratives marshaled their strength, scholastic theologians were setting about to refine and systematize their relationships with God, just as they were doing with demonic origins and nature. The result of this investigation was a marked loosening of the bonds by which the devil was confined and controlled, and a kind of theological sanction for enhanced diabolic power and responsibility.

The contribution of Thomas Aquinas to the problem of misfortune lay in two principal areas: the causes of evil and the extent of divine supervision of demons. Of these, the most basic and abstract was his discussion of the cause of evil, which was in turn based on two fundamental sets of ideas. The first, taken from Augustine and ultimately Plato, assumed that evil was a species of privation, the lack of some native or otherwise appropriate good; the second was the Aristotelian theory of fourfold causation – material, formal, efficient, and final.[21] In short, Aquinas argued that God, who was wholly good, could not be the cause of any evil of any kind whatsoever, except accidentally, because privation could only result from a deficient cause which could not be God.[22] Certainly God permitted evils to happen, because they were necessary to the goodness of his creation, but he did not in any sense cause them to happen. Even if his justice demanded that a man die, God was only the cause of justice, and not of death.[23] But since, as Aquinas clearly says, all evils must have a cause ("omne malum aliqualiter causam habeat"), whence comes evil? The answer is that one simply has to look for the last defective cause in the chain of efficient causes; to use Aquinas's example, when a boat sinks due to the carelessness of a sailor, that particular evil may be traced back only to the sailor in whom the defect lay and not to God.

This line of analysis extended to the injuries caused by demons. Certainly, everything that demons did, they did only with the permission of God, but it was much more difficult to say exactly what this permission meant, and how and why it was granted. For Aquinas, the key consideration was the difficult distinction between divine permission and divine will. Demons attacked men in two ways: first, by instigating them to sin through temptation, and, second, more directly through punishment. God ordered both kinds of attack for the higher good, but, while God's just judgments sent demons to punish certain men, temptation was sometimes permitted even though God did not will it.[24] But for this distinction to have meaning, God's permission must be a more generous form of oversight, a kind of passive adjunct to God's active will; hence Aquinas's demons appear to have had much more latitude over the manner and subjects of temptation than they did over direct punishment.

Still worse for unfortunate sinners, in Aquinas's mind, temptation could lead directly to punishment. In his discussion of the effects of Christ's passion, he explains that the devil may legitimately be said to have power over mankind:

> To the first point it should be said that the devil is not found to have had power over people to such a degree that he could harm them without God's permission, but that he was justly permitted to injure people whom by tempting he had induced to give consent.[25]

If the devil, in other words, was allowed to tempt a man of his own choosing, and if that man succumbed, the devil might also be allowed to punish him, not because God willed it, but because by sinning the man had placed himself in the devil's power. In this way, Aquinas allowed a considerable expansion of both the devil's power to make trouble and his responsibility for it. To be sure, it was not that the devil had ceased to be God's slave, or that he was no longer ultimately answerable to divine will; rather, Aquinas perceived the nature of divine oversight to be more flexible and more remote.

By the end of the thirteenth century, popular beliefs, monastic narratives, and theological speculation had thus converged around a more autonomous conception of the devil's power. Contributing to this trend, perhaps, were also anxieties felt by the Church about diabolically inspired heresy, as well as the widespread dissemination of dualist beliefs. To many people, it seemed as if God were no longer so intent on the micro-management of his demons, and that now demons held a correspondingly greater share of the responsibility for worldly misfortune.[26] Thus, especially after Aquinas had seemingly exculpated God of any share in the actual production of misfortune, late-medieval scholarly and ecclesiastical interest tended to focus on demons as the efficient cause of misfortunes in the world, and it was within this context that magic was understood.

While the devil was still constrained closely by divine will and defeated easily by Christian faith, malign magic was a relatively minor concern, for while neither Augustine nor his successors ever denied the existence of harmful magic, the restrictions they placed upon the devil's freedom of operation placed serious limitations upon its use.[27] Indeed, a battery of arguments, all of which depended ultimately upon the power and justice of God, opposed the need for serious persecution of sorcerers.

In the first place, to allow malefici to usurp the administration of divine justice would be unseemly at best. As Rather of Verona remarked irritably, if you believed that the world was full of witches flying around at night, and that misfortunes were due to their evil magic, what became of the lessons of Job?

Who I say, of people being deceived like this, seeing a man being whipped like the admirable Job . . . would urge him to say, and would believe it justly said, "The Lord gives, the Lord takes away, as the Lord pleases, so it is done?" No, he would ascribe it to wicked angels or to certain pitiable men and would urge that some controller – or "rainmaker" as he is called – be summoned and begged with gifts to deign to cure it . . . For not to mention the loss of such glory as was Job's, would they not do this about a mere trifle, a penknife or a shoelace.[28]

Since demons cannot do any harm without the Lord's direct and explicit permission, the victim of a magical attack would be better advised to spend his time searching his own conscience rather than ferreting out witches. Rather's position was simple, clear, and unmistakably Augustinian: misfortune came ultimately from God; and so, like Job, we should bear it with patience.

To most educated Christians of late antiquity, magic was a subspecies of pagan idolatry, and just as God permitted demons to impersonate pagan deities, he also occasionally allowed demons to give efficacy to magical operations. In both cases, his motive was the same: to lead the souls of superstitious operators to perdition: hence, the principal victims of magic were the magicians themselves, who, like pagans, properly could be punished, but, better still, should be converted.[29] Denigrating magicians as virtual pagans also led early theologians to be skeptical of their powers. Indeed, again according to Augustine, much of what magicians appeared to do was simply an illusion of the devil, and Augustine invariably referred to magic as a lie, a deceit, or a deception.[30] Superstitious diviners, he claims, were "subjected to illusion and deception as a reward for their desires"; the supposedly benign magic of theurgy was "all the invention of lying demons."[31]

From this perspective, all works of the devil were kinds of deceit: magic, superstition, paganism, were all, by this way of thinking, at bottom empty of substance; they were delusions. This was a tradition enshrined in a number of influential early-medieval canons, most notably the canon *Episcopi*, but also a decision of the Council of Braga that demons could not control the weather.[32] Pastoral concern to limit the scope of demonic power kept it alive. Hence early-medieval penitentials denounced those who believed that enchanters were able to summon storms, or use demons to sway the people's minds, or that some women could magically inspire love and hatred, or steal one's goods.[33] In precisely the same way, German penitentials of the late fifteenth century continue to condemn those who believe in the reality and efficacy of weather-witches, werewolves, broomstick-riders, "and other such heathen, nonsensical impostures."[34]

Although this conception of magic would have a lasting influence upon ecclesiastical thinking, it was never fully accepted. On the one hand, a popular belief in the efficacy of magic was simply too strong to be dispelled. Augustine himself, for instance, gave grudging credence to "that pernicious and abominable science by which, as the tale goes, one man's crops could be transferred to another's land."[35] On the other, most authors acknowledged that, given their natural powers, demons could do much more than work mere illusions. Thus in his little treatise, *De Magicis Artibus*, Hrabanus Maurus (d. 857) argued that magic *per se* had no power at all, unless the magician had made a pact with a demon and unless God in his wisdom permitted the demon to act in accordance with the magician's wishes.[36] This being the case, however, real effects could follow upon magical operations. When scholastics analyzed the devil's nature, irrespective of the question of divine permission, logic compelled them to enlarge considerably the range of his powers: simply by virtue of their angelic natures, demons could confound the senses, create illusions, delude the mind, cause bodily infirmity, illness and death, control the weather, move with preternatural speed, transport physical objects, and so on.[37]

Yet even so, traditionally minded writers insisted that God would never permit demons to use these powers freely. It would, for one thing, be dangerously impractical. In the thirteenth century, William of Paris allowed that harmful magic was effective occasionally because demons were permitted sometimes to chastise men in this way, but he did not permit his readers to suppose that this happened often:

> For when it has become clear to you how much care there is in the wisdom and goodness of the creator for people and human affairs, it will plainly dawn on you that he does not commit the government of them to images, or to stars, or to the luminaries, or even to the heavens, nor in any way expose them to the will of magicians or acts of harmful magic.[38]

To William, this was a matter of common sense, "For no beautiful woman would remain undefiled, no prince and no magnate would remain safe, if demons were permitted to appear and to give satisfaction to the evil will of men."[39]

William's argument reflects an ancient confidence in Christ's triumph over Satan; because magic was a tool and invention of the devil, his defeat logically gave his followers immunity. As Peter Brown puts it, "the Church was the community for whom Satan had been bound: his limitless powers had been bridled to permit the triumph of the Gospel; more immediately, the practicing Christian gained immunity from sorcery."[40] Early medieval discussions of magic regularly took such protection for granted. For example, Isidore of Seville provided the Middle Ages with its standard exposition of magic in a vastly influential and much quoted précis of Augustine's views. According to Isidore,

> Magicians are those who are commonly called *malefici* [evil-doers] on account
> of the magnitude of their crimes. These persons excite the elements, disturb
> the minds of men, and without any draught of poison, with violence only
> through their incantations, they kill . . . For having summoned demons they
> dare to boast that each destroys his enemies by the evil arts. And these men
> also make use of blood and victims, and often take the bodies of the dead . . .
> and the blood of a cadaver is scattered to arouse [demons], for demons are said
> to love blood. And so, as often as necromancy is performed, water is mixed
> with gore so that by the color of blood they are more easily excited.[41]

Although Isidore grants that sorcerers could readily effect material harm
through their magic, he makes it plain, following Augustine, that he speaks
here of pagan magicians: his sources are Lucan, Vergil, and Varro, and he nestles
"De magis" comfortably between "De Sibyllis" and "De paganis." When later
commentators quoted this passage, they modified Isidore's text to adapt his
meaning to a fully Christian society. Burchard of Worms, Ivo of Chartres, and
Gratian all included variations on Isidore's definition of magicians in their collections of canons, although mistakenly attributing it to Augustine himself.
Magicians, they reported, could excite the elements only with divine permission, and their magic could harm only those men "who have little trust in
God."[42]

Just who these faithless men were, though, was not entirely clear. While
Augustine and Isidore had conceived of magic as a kind of adjunct paganism,
a scourge afflicting those who had not yet embraced Christianity, later writers
viewed magical harm instead in more general terms as a punishment for
sinners. This made perfect sense, since if, following Aquinas, demons could
punish sinners of their own accord, they should equally have the power to
work diabolic magic. In this vein Jacques de Vitry encouraged his readers to
remember that,

> In truth, diviners and witches are unable to harm those who are confessed and
> penitent, nor are they able to delude those who place their hope in God; they
> are accustomed, however, to delude sinners, because God permits this for the
> expulsion of sins.[43]

By the late Middle Ages, then, there was a substantial and authoritative
body of opinion highly skeptical of the ability of magicians to inflict injuries
as they wished. For many, this traditional view of magic and misfortune
remained entirely sufficient: among the most spiritually inclined – those whose
attention was focused single-mindedly upon the divine – harmful magic, like
misfortune of any kind, was a matter of small concern since a man's fate lay
wholly in the hands of God. Thus Henry Suso, a fourteenth-century German
Dominican and mystic, enjoined his friends to embrace all suffering as a gift
of God:

A suffering man should remember [the martyrdom and glory of the saints] and rejoice that God has deigned, by means of suffering, to associate him with his dearest friends.[44]

Preachers, whose main concern was the spiritual welfare of laymen, likewise often took a traditionalist line, emphasizing the impotence of the devil before the omnipotence and goodness of God. Although finding forthright denials of magicians' power to harm the innocent is not so easy after 1300, still, preachers often spoke of magic in generally Augustinian terms, as a deceit or illusion and not the object of fear.[45]

Scholars trained in the *via moderna*, who in large part rejected the Thomist conception of the universe, were also generally little interested in the problem of witchcraft. Not viewing the sensible world as the lowest emanation of a unified hierarchical system, Nominalists tended to focus their investigation of physical, earthly effects on observable secondary causes.[46] Without doubt, God was the first and final cause of all things, but because material effects could not be conceived as a direct expression of rational (and so comprehensible) divine thought, it was pointless to look to heaven for causes which could be found more easily and more reliably here on earth.[47] Witchcraft, from this perspective, could never be a *necessary* cause of a given effect, because human and demonic (or angelic) realms were not deterministically linked. Nor could one of Ockham's followers ever arrive at an absolutely valid determination of witchcraft, because on purely epistemological grounds, one could admit a cause and effect relationship only if both terms were known; causation could never be determined only by effects.[48] For these reasons, most late-medieval nominalists remained comparatively unconcerned by the physical dangers posed by witchcraft and seldom wrote witch-treatises. A rare exception was Samuel de Cassini, who, in the early sixteenth century, attacked the reality of witches' flight in conventionally nominalist terms. There was no cause, Samuel maintained, which produced an effect directly, except as "naturally ordained," meaning that the agent possessed the natural and intrinsic power to carry it out.[49] Demons, furthermore, despite their powers of local motion, lacked the natural ability to move corporal bodies through the air; and, if they should by some chance happen to do so, the result, properly speaking, would be a miracle, and a miracle could never be the occasion for sin.[50] Hence, Samuel concluded, the flight of witches was merely a delusion, and those who felt otherwise offended against both the omnipotence and the justice of God.

Even among demonologists, authors who embraced this more traditional view of divine oversight, and the consequent limitations on demonic power, the persecution of witches seemed less necessary, even when they accepted the reality of a devil-worshiping sect. Ulrich Molitor, for example, admitted that witches existed, and that they were deservedly punished for giving homage to the devil, but he also stressed that whatever else they might do, witches could not be in any sense the efficient cause of misfortune. While demons could, when God permitted, bring about worldly evils, "sometimes as punishment, for the correction of the wicked, sometimes as temptation, for the increase of merit, and sometimes as a foreshadowing of a future action of grace," witches themselves had nothing to do with any of this.[51] Witches believed that they could bring about misfortune only because they were deluded by the devil. Storms, for instance, were caused by natural agencies, such as the movement of the stars or planets, or by demons if God willed it. In either case, though,

> when [the devil] knows beforehand of a future calamity of this kind, he then stirs up the minds of *Malckiesae mulieres*, sometimes by persuading them himself; sometimes on account of envy, which such wicked women bear toward a neighbor, he inspires them to a deed of vengeance, as if he were teaching the women to provoke storms of this kind and disturbances of the air.[52]

There was no reason, then, to fear old women when they brewed potions or cast water into the air, because whatever calamity ensued was destined by divine providence to happen anyway. *Maleficium* was not, to Molitor, a visible and efficient sign of the devil, but a useless and meaningless gesture, designed only to impress and delude the simple-minded.[53]

Molitor's views were shared by other learned men. Around 1475, Jean Vincent, the prior of Les Moustiers, wrote a tract in which he argued that witches were deluded into accepting the destruction caused by the devil as their own. Witches, he writes, were those who believed that they were carried to the Sabbat by a demon, while they actually slept in their beds. At the Sabbat, they burned alive children taken from their mothers' breasts. But by his knowledge of causes, the devil could predict which children would sicken, which vines would wither, and where and when storms would strike. He suggested these things to the sleeping women, who then sincerely claimed responsibility for them when they occurred.[54] More assertive yet was the famous Dominican reformer and theologian, Nicholas of Cusa. In a sermon on the pervasive belief in witches, Nicholas wondered why it was, if the devil had a free hand, that where faith in Christ and his saints was cultivated, the land was most blessed.

> Where, however, men believe those *maleficia* to be done effectually, there more witches are discovered, nor can they be extirpated with fire and sword, because the more diligently this kind of persecution is carried out, the more the delusion grows. For persecution argues that the devil is more to be feared than God,

and that he can heap up evils in the midst of evils, and so, at last, the devil, who is so feared, is sated and so his purpose is achieved.[55]

For this reason, and to spare the blood of innocents, Nicholas urged his auditors to abandon the fruitless persecution of old women and turn their minds instead to God, the real arbiter of their fate.[56]

To argue, on the contrary, that witches used their magic to cause harm freely, and that they were personally and immediately responsible for the injuries that ensued, required theorists to address the problem of divine permission. Simply to assert that all that witches did, they did with the permission of God, was insufficient. Though late-medieval demonologists seem endlessly to repeat the phrase, "with the permission of God," whenever they discussed the powers of witches and demons, almost as a polite gesture in the direction of divine omnipotence, the phrase explains nothing precisely because it could explain anything at all. As Petrus Mamoris points out, to say that something happened with divine permission is to state the patently obvious, "since there is nothing in the world which God does not permit, either good or evil."[57] Nor was God's wholesale grant of power to demons a palatable prospect: only a few authorities, such as the early-sixteenth-century witch-theorist, Vincente Dodo, went down this path.

Dodo, however, held that, with the permission of God, the devil was responsible for the flight of witches, their amazing transformations, and their malevolent magic, but that, "in consequence, divine permission is to be understood negatively."[58] That is, God permitted demons to do anything they pleased, provided he did not specifically prohibit it: Dodo maintained that God normally allowed all created beings, including demons, the free use of their natural powers, unless, as sometimes happened, he should intervene. In this, Dodo's argument was a logical extension of scholastic principles, but for most of his colleagues such a broad-ranging capitulation by the heavenly host was difficult to accept. Even in the *Malleus* God was not so passive; Institoris and Sprenger were careful to remind their readers that demons were merely agents, whom God employed to castigate sinners: "For God is accustomed to inflict the evils which are done for the exaction of our sins on earth, through demons acting as though they were his torturers."[59]

Perhaps prompted by such difficulties, by the mid-fifteenth century, theorists had begun to explore an alternative explanation of magical harm. Because God allowed demons to lend efficacy to superstitious observances in order to punish the operator, so the argument ran, divine permission depended more upon the magician's sin than that of his victim. The theory probably had its genesis in statements such as that of the early-fourteenth-century theologian, William of Ware, who declared that "magicians are unable

to disturb the minds of good men who do not believe such things, but only
the minds of infidels and evil men."[60] Although perfectly orthodox and traditional, Ware's statement could easily be misinterpreted to mean that the efficacy of magic is dependent upon belief, and this is, in fact, precisely what one
finds in a contemporary devotional treatise on the Ten Commandments,
Robert of Brunne's *Handlyng Synne*. There, a witch explains to a bewildered
bishop why he is unable to emulate her magic and animate her magic milking
bag:

> Ye beleue nat as y do:
> wold ye beleue my wordys as y,
> Hyt shulde a go, and sokun ky.[61]

In other words, if the witch is to be trusted, her *maleficium* depends upon her
own sinful belief and not presumably upon the sins of her victims.[62]

A little more than a century later, Johann Nider developed and refined
this idea in his own examination of the decalogue, the *Praeceptorium*. In a question devoted to the power of *malefici* to injure men, Nider argues that, with
the devil's aid, they can cause harm to external things – to property, person,
and reputation – but not to the soul.[63] As proof he adduces standard *exempla*
showing the power of the devil to torment Job and Anthony. Nonetheless,
Nider insists that sinners are much more afflicted by magic than the good, both
because the demons are defenseless before the power of the cross and because
the devil has greater power over sinners. For this reason, Nider adds an important qualification to his explanation of image magic: when a witch strikes a
man's image, "a demon invisibly harms the bewitched person in the same way,
with God's permission, if the guilty person merited it."[64] At the same time,
though, the sins of the witches are relevant to Nider: when he asks why witches
employ sacraments and other divine things in their magic, he responds that "as
God is more gravely offended by men . . . the greater the power he gives to
a demon over bad people."[65] It is quite possible that the *homines malos* in this
phrase are the witches themselves and not their victims, but regardless of his
intentions it was easy to read Nider otherwise, as implying that a demon's
power to do evil was at least in part a function of the magnitude of the witch's
sin.[66] If so, witchcraft was understandable as a kind of economy of effort,
whereby two sinners were punished at one time.

Writing not long after Nider, Martin of Arles developed and combined
these ideas in his tract against witchcraft and superstition. Martin argues that
just as God works miracles on account of Christian belief and faith, so false
and evil beliefs lead God to permit bad things to happen. When God recog-
nizes excessive adherence to vain observances, he allows the devil to give them
efficacy:

Just as true and Christian faith works miracles on those of good faith, so an evil and false belief, God permitting, sometimes works, or rather earns, misfortunes. For we have daily experience of people of bad faith whom God thus punishes on account of bad faith; indeed, God knows that some people adhere excessively to vain observances, permits some events to happen, and so, in consequence they are led to hold this belief even more strongly, so that their blindness becomes greater and they fall into the snare that they have made for themselves.[67]

So, the more superstitious people are, the more their superstitions seem well founded.

God, however, Martin suggests, does not restrict himself to punishing the individual sinner alone; sometimes he is so angered by sin that he punishes collectively, so that in profligate communities the good are punished along with the wicked.[68] When a community is saturated with superstitious beliefs, God permits demons to punish that community collectively through witchcraft. Thus, Martin writes that

for the worthy flagellation and punishment of these crimes, God permits so many infirmities, pestilences, and storms, sterilities of the earth and of harvests, the death of cattle and beasts of burden to happen.[69]

This notion corresponds to a general tendency in late-medieval religion to look at both sin and salvation in collective terms: just as an individual's good works redounded to the credit of his confraternity, so his sins could bring punishment upon them all.[70] And such punishment could be disturbingly severe. A popular *exemplum* in late-medieval sermons reported that after a drunken soldier knocked over the pyx with a beer pot, God's justice required that the entire region should be devastated. In the version of Johannes Herolt, a fifteenth-century Dominican preacher,

[the sea] passed beyond its bounds and flooded the land of many provinces, destroying villages and exterminating such a host of men that in all a hundred thousand perished.[71]

The destruction finally abated, though only after the specific sin responsible had been discovered and proper collective atonement had been made. If Jean Delumeau is right that "The Europeans who lived between the advent of the Black Death and the end of the religious wars had an acute sense of an accumulation of misfortune," then finding the source of such evils would be a pressing concern.[72] The sin of witchcraft was in many ways the perfect explanation: heinous enough to warrant the most awful punishment and secret enough to exist anywhere, it enabled all the calamities of the world to rest on the shoulders of socially marginal women.

Working from this established relationship between sin and retribution, late-medieval demonologists were gradually able to expand the limits of divine permission. Petrus Mamoris, like Martin of Arles, explains that the power of witchcraft depends upon the sins of the operators themselves:

> for the execrations of the devil have efficacy among those who believe or adhere to such cursed diabolical machinations, or doubt and fret in some article of the faith, or wickedly desire to test, or from some wonder or curiosity want to try or to see, these *maleficia*, or to assist those who make them: all of which is dangerous to the faith.[73]

But, whereas for Martin the efficacy of witchcraft depends only upon ignorance and superstition, Mamoris is more liberal. He argues that magical harm could stem from either excessive credulity or excessive erudition, for while the former might lead to superstition, the latter leads to skepticism.[74] Mamoris felt that not to believe in the power of witchcraft was as bad, and just as likely to incur punishment, as *vana credulitas*. Similarly, Nicholas Jacquier remarks that the devil was especially liable to injure skeptics through witchcraft:

> Whence a few ignorant people boast very foolishly, asserting that they do not fear demons or witches, nor their witchcraft, unless the witches themselves personally approach those who are boasting after this fashion and administer some poisonous substance to them in their drink or food, whence they can be harmed.[75]

To Mamoris and Jacquier, witchcraft was not a problem largely confined to the rural lower classes: anyone (hypothetically) could be a witch, and anyone could be bewitched. This was especially true, if, as Jacquier argued, defenses which might be adequate against the devil alone, failed against witch and demon combined. Although the natural power of demons was sufficient to carry out any act of witchcraft, Jacquier maintained that demons were frequently prevented from the full exercise of their power by the ministry of good angels or by spiritual defenses in human hands. In such cases, however, witches could more easily approach their victims and do them harm, since under some circumstances divine permission was more liberal with respect to witchcraft than if the devil had acted directly.[76]

Institoris and Sprenger use these ideas about the relationship between divine permission and witchcraft in their own complicated model of misfortune. Once again, the authors foreground the active role of the witch at the expense of both God and the devil: in their view, sudden misfortune is almost always the result of witchcraft, and not the work of angels or demons alone. Their explanation for this is neither logically nor literally consistent: the degree of autonomy they allow to the devil, to the witch, and even to God, varies according to context, and they can devise no rule that is not immediately contradicted by exceptions. But, no matter: what counts is that they devise an explanation for the prevalence of witchcraft in the world which is consistent with conventional orthodox assumptions.

In good scholastic fashion, Institoris and Sprenger begin by considering the nature of misfortune analytically. Injuries, they maintain, are of four kinds: *ministeriales* (beneficial misfortune), *noxiales* (merited punishment), *maleficiales* (malicious harm, or witchcraft), and *naturales* (natural harm).[77] Although these terms denote intentions or motives behind mischance, Institoris and Sprenger are really concerned with their agents: beneficial harm is the work of angels; merited injuries are carried out by demons, presumably under the supervision of God; natural injuries are due simply to natural causes, such as droughts caused by the motion of the stars and planets; and, finally, "Effects are said to arise from harmful magic when the devil works through witches and sorcerers."[78]

Maleficiales were of special interest because they were the most common and the most dangerous form of harm. Demons always prefer to work through the agency of witches, in part for the damnation of their souls, but more importantly because God permits them to do more harm through witchcraft than he would otherwise allow:

> But because they seek to work through witches of this kind, in order to insult and offend the Creator and at the same time to bring about the loss of souls, knowing that in such a way, as God is more angered so he permits them more power to rage, and because innumerable acts of witchcraft are perpetrated which the devil would not be allowed to inflict on humans if he alone were working to harm people, but which the just, hidden judgment of God permits to be done through witches, on account of their perfidy and denial of the Catholic faith, accordingly such *maleficia*, by just judgment, are imputed secondarily to [witches], however much the devil might be the primary actor.[79]

Thus, witches are directly responsible for witchcraft, because it is their sin that gives the devil his power to injure in their name. In this way, Institoris and Sprenger carry the arguments proposed by earlier theorists to their logical conclusion: if God punishes men collectively on account of sin, and if the intensity of punishment is proportional to divine anger, then the more God is offended, the more he grants the devil latitude to harm the guilty and innocent alike. There is no sin more offensive to God than witchcraft, so *maleficium* itself provokes God to grant the devil permission to make it work: "just as because of the sins of the parents the innocent are punished, so now are many innocent people damned and bewitched on account of the sins of the witches."[80] Demons could, of course, injure without the permission of the witch, but, because they were loath to do so, this happened only when they were specifically commanded by God to do so.

The mechanical nature of this conception of diabolic power is particularly evident in Institoris and Sprenger's discussion of superstitious methods of identifying a witch. Even practices which rely upon the implicit participation of the devil are reliable, they argue, because demons are prohibited from harming the innocent. Thus, if a devil is doing some witch's bidding in animal form and is wounded in process, it is the witch — and only the witch — who bears a corresponding wound.

> For it is one thing to be harmed by the devil through a witch, and another to be harmed by the devil himself, without a witch. Because when the devil in the form of an animal receives blows, he then inflicts them upon another who is joined to him through a pact . . . Accordingly, he can harm only the guilty and those joined to him through a pact, and in no way the innocent. When demons seek to do harm through witches, however, then even the innocent are often afflicted, by divine permission, in revenge of so great a crime.[81]

Oddly enough, then, the limitations of demonic power could be reliably exploited to identify guilty witches, precisely because demons themselves are mere passive agents, strictly bound by the terms of their pacts with witches and subordination to God.

Through this argument, Institoris and Sprenger aligned the causes and agencies of misfortune to give the widest possible scope to witchcraft. Unfortunately, however well this model may have reflected contemporary fifteenth-century conditions, it fits the traditional pattern of Christian beliefs quite poorly. For example, the inquisitors' argument becomes quite seriously muddled when they attempt to explain the trials of Job. The problem is that Job's afflictions were carried out by the devil in person; they were, then, *noxiales* and not *maleficiales*. But Job was also an innocent man, and when injuries happen to the innocent, they are *maleficiales* and not "merited." Some trouble-maker must have asked for an explanation, for Institoris and Sprenger reply with open annoyance:

> If, indeed, someone with too great a curiosity were to insist on knowing, just as often this material permits a strange insistence on the part of the defenders of witches, always lashing the air about the outer shells of words, and never penetrating to the marrow of truth, why Job was not persecuted by the effects of harmful magic through a demon, as he was by injuries. To these curious sorts it can be answered that Job was persecuted by the devil alone and not through the mediation of a male or female witch, either because this kind of superstition had not yet been discovered, or, if it had been discovered, then divine

providence desired that the power of the devil be made known to the world, for the glory of God, as a warning of his plot.[82]

Job, in the minds of the authors was clearly an exception: under normal circumstances, demons caused injuries only through witches, and usually had to do so if their victims were otherwise innocent.

This, then, was why witchcraft was so dangerous: God was so offended by the existence and practices of witches that he gave the devil more latitude to use his power for the affliction of men, affliction manifested in the magic of witches. This argument assumed that divine permission was a kind of sliding scale, automatically contingent upon circumstances: some actions, such as sin or the magic of witches, allowed greater applications of demonic power, others, such as prayer or Christian countermagic, allowed less. Hence, God's pervasive distaste for sex gave witches and the devil correspondingly greater power over human and animal sexuality.[83] For this reason, witches characteristically destroyed fertility because such magic was more likely to work as planned than was weather magic or demonic obsession. Similarly, some species of *maleficium* were inherently less permissible, and were only efficacious if the victim was stained with sin. For example, although witches could make the penis of a sinner appear to vanish, they could not so delude anyone in a state of grace.[84] Because God granted permission to harm according to these established rules (exactly as the devil participated in witchcraft), Institoris and Sprenger conceived of witchcraft as very much a personal duel between the witch and her victim, each trying through his or her actions to slide the scale of permission in his or her own favor.

Institoris and Sprenger held a view of the world that was both extremely mechanistic and highly anthropocentric. Because the beneficent power of God and the destructive power of the devil both functioned mechanically, the importance of the human operators who could successfully manipulate these powers was necessarily increased. Institoris and Sprenger also saw, however, that in the supernatural battle between witches and the Church, the Church was sadly overmatched: sacramental magic alone could not wipe out the scourge of witchcraft, only ameliorate its effects; to destroy witchcraft, it was necessary to destroy the witches.

Notes

1 Although it is dangerous to generalize about medieval folk-beliefs, evidence from modern and early-modern sources suggests a more or less consistent traditional European understanding of witchcraft and misfortune. See Gábor Klaniczay, "Witch-Hunting in Hungary: Social or Cultural Tensions?" in Klaniczay, *The Uses of Supernatural Power*, trans. Susan Singerman, ed. Karen Margolis (Cambridge: Polity Press, 1990), 167. For modern folk conceptions of misfortune, see Bente Gullveig Alver and Torunn

Selberg, "Folk Medicine as Part of a Larger Concept Complex," *ARV* 43 (1987), 21–44; David Rheubottom, "The Seeds of Evil Within," in David Perkin, ed., *The Anthropology of Evil* (Oxford: Basil Blackwell, 1985), 77–91.

2 Rodney Needham, *Primordial Characters* (Charlottesville: University of Virginia Press, 1978), 31.

3 Salimbene de Adam, *The Chronicle of Salimbene de Adam*, ed. and trans. Joseph L. Baird (Binghamton: Medieval and Renaissance Texts and Studies, 1986), 640–1.

4 *Ibid.*

5 Augustine, *City of God*, 21.13, 990.

6 *Ibid.*, 22.22, 1066.

7 *Ibid.*, 21.14, 992.

8 *Ibid.*, 1.9, 14–15.

9 Isidore of Seville, *Sententiae*, 1.1, c. 10, 17–18, in Lea, *Materials*, 1:69.

10 Gregory the Great, *Morals on the Book of Job*, ed. James Bliss (Oxford: John Henry Parker, 1844), 2.17.

11 Rather of Verona, *The Complete Works of Rather of Verona*, ed. and trans. Peter L.D. Reid (Binghamton: Medieval and Renaissance Texts and Studies, 1991), 1.8.

12 Athanasius, *The Life of St. Antony*, trans. Robert T. Meyer (Westminster, Maryland: The Newman Press, 1950), c. 9, p. 28.

13 *Ibid.*

14 Examples abound, but see especially Gregory the Great, *Dialogues*, trans. O.J. Zimmerman (New York: Fathers of the Church, 1959), 3.19.

15 Peter Damiani, *De Castitate*, 3.4, *Patrologia Latina* 145, 713.

16 Antonio Graf, *The Story of the Devil*, trans. Edward Noble Stone (New York: MacMillen, 1931), 97–8. See also Lea, *Inquisition*, 3:381–2; and Peter Dinzelbacher, "Der Realität des Teufels im Mittelalter," in Segl, *Der Hexenhammer*, 151–75. I have not been able to obtain the text of Ricalmus' book, the *Liber Revelationum de Insidiis et Versutiis Daemonum adversus Homines*; Dinzelbacher's reference is Bernardus Pezius, *Thesaurus Anecdotorum Novissimus*, I/2 (Augusta Vindelicorum [Augsburg], 1721), 373–472.

17 A suggestion of Edward Peters, who observes that for a monastic audience the terror of this devil was considerably mitigated by the formidable spiritual defenses which monks could deploy. For laymen and perhaps even secular clerics who were not so well fortified, the devil would then naturally appear as a relatively more threatening figure. Peters, 92–3.

18 Similarly, as the Church grew more inclusive after 1200, theological discourse began increasingly to reflect traditional popular beliefs. See Jacques Le Goff, "The Learned and Popular Dimensions of Journies in the Otherworld in the Middle Ages," in S.L. Kaplan, ed., *Understanding Popular Culture* (Berlin: Mouton, 1981), 31; and Alan Bernstein, "Theology between Heresy and Folklore: William of Auvergne on Punishment after Death," *Traditio* 38 (1982): 4–44; 5–6, and *passim*.

19 Thomas of Cantimpré, *Bonum Universale de Apibus* (NP: 1627) book 2, c. 57.3.

20 Giraldus Cambrensis, *Itinerarium Kambriae*, in *Opera*, vol. 6, ed. James F. Dimock (London: Longmans, Green, Reader, and Dyer, 1866), 1.12, p. 91.

21 For an in-depth study of Thomist theories of causation, see Francis X. Meehan, *Efficient Causality in Aristotle and Thomas Aquinas*, The Catholic University of America Philosophical Studies 56 (Washington, D.C.: The Catholic University of America Press, 1940).

22 Aquinas, *Summa Theologiae*, pt. 1, qu. 49.

23 Aquinas, *Summa. Theologiae*, pt. 1, qu. 49, art. 2.

24 "To the first point, it should be said that bad angels attack people in two ways. First, by inciting them to sin. In this they are not sent by God to attack people, but are sometimes permitted to do so according to God's just judgments. Sometimes, however, they attack men by punishing them, and in this they are sent by God." ("Ad primum ergo, dicendum quod mali angeli impugnant homines dupliciter. Uno modo, instigando ad

peccatum. Et sic non mittuntur a Deo ad impugnandum, sed aliquando permittuntur secundum Dei justa judicia. Aliquando autem impugnant homines puniendo. Et sic mittuntur a Deo.") *Ibid.*, pt. 1, qu. 114, art. 1, ad. 1.

25 "Ad primum ergo dicendum quod non dicitur sic diabolus in homines potestatum habuisse, quasi posset eis nocere, Deo non permittente; sed quia juste permittebatur nocere hominibus, quos tentando ad suum consensum perduxerat." *Ibid.*, pt. 3, qu. 49, art. 2. Lest one suppose that this situation has been somehow altered with Christ's passion, Aquinas immediately adds that, although Jesus has indeed provided a remedy to damnation, "the devil can still tempt men's souls and harrass their bodies." *Ibid.*

26 The growth of a more powerful, more terrible conception of the devil is discussed in Russell, *Lucifer*, 159–207 and *passim*; see also Russell, *Witchcraft in the Middle Ages*, 101–32, and Peters, 91–8.

27 For Augustine's own views on the powers of demons to inflict *maleficia* on a magician's behalf, see his refutation of Apuleius in *City of God*, 8.19, in which he asserts that "all the marvels of sorcery are achieved by means of the science taught by the demons and by their operations."

28 Rather of Verona, 1.10, 32–3.

29 Flint, 146–57.

30 Demons could not, for example, create real substances out of nothing or effect real transformations, although their powers over the human mind created illusions to this effect; many other marvelous things demons did by virtue of the natural characteristics of their spiritual bodies. Augustine, *City of God*, 18.18, 782–4.

31 Augustine, *De Doctrina Christiana*, 23.35; *City of God*, 10.10, 385.

32 See Lea, *Materials*, 1:143.

33 Burchard of Worms, *Corrector*, in Hanson, *Quellen*, 41.

34 Stephen of Lanskrana, provost of St. Dorothy's in Vienna, *Himmelstrasse* (1484). Quoted in Johannes Janssen, *History of the German People after the Close of the Middle Ages*, trans. A.M. Christie (New York: AMS Press, 1966), 16:231.

35 Augustine, *City of God*, 8.19, 325.

36 Hrabanus Maurus, *De Magicis Artibus, Patrologia Latina* 110, 1095–108.

37 See, for example, Thomas Aquinas, *Expositio in Job*, 1.3: "It should be understood . . . that with the permission of God demons can cause disturbances in the air, excite winds, and make fire fall from heaven" ("Considerandum est . . . quod deo permittente daemones possunt turbationem aeris inducere, ventos concitare et facere ut ignis de coelo cadat"). All this, and much more, they did through the power of local motion which was natural to both good and evil angels.

38 "Cum enim innotuerit tibi, quanta cura sit sapientiae, et bonitati creatoris de hominibus, et rebus humanis, elucescet tibi evidenter, quia nec imaginibus, nec stellis, nec luminaribus, aut etiam coelis committit gubernationem eorum, nec eos exponit ullo modo voluntatibus magorum, aut maleficiis." William of Paris, *De Universo*, pt. 1, c. 46, in *Opera Omnia* (Paris, 1674; reprint, Frankfurt am Main: Minerva, 1963), 666.

39 "Nulla enim mulier speciosa incorrupta remaneret, nullus principum, nullus magnatum incolumnis persisteret si daemones malis voluntatibus hominum adesse et satisfacere permitterentur." *Ibid.*

40 Peter Brown, "Sorcery, Demons, and the Rise of Christianity from Late Antiquity into the Middle Ages," in Mary Douglas, ed., *Witchcraft Confessions and Accusations* (London: Tavistock Publications, 1970), 15.

41 "Magi sunt, qui vulgo malefici ob facinorum magnitudinem nuncupantur. Hi [permissu Dei] elementa concutiunt, turbant mentes hominum [minus confidentium in Deo] ac sine ullo veneni haustu, violentia tantum carminis interimunt . . . Demonibus enim adcitis audent ventilare, ut quisque suos perimat malis artibus inimicos. Hi etiam sanguine utuntur et victimis, et saepe contigunt corpora mortuorum . . . Ad quos suscitandos cadaveris sanguis adjicitur. Nam amare daemones sanguinem dicitur.

Ideoque quoties necromantia fit, cruor aqua miscetur, ut colore sanguinis facilius pro-
vocentur." Isidore of Seville, *Etymologiae, De Magis*, 8.9. Ivo of Chartres, *Decreti*, "De
Incantoribus . . . ," 11.67, *Patrologia Latina* 161, 760–1.

42 "Hi permissu Dei elementa concutiunt, turbant mentes hominum minus confidentium
in Deo ac sine ullo veneni haustu, violentia tantum carminis interimunt." Ivo of
Chartres, *loc. cit.* The passage is headed "Ex dictis Augusti."

43 "Vere enim confitentibus et penitentibus nocere nequeunt malefici et divinatores, nec
illudere eis qui spem suam ponunt in Deo, peccatoribus autem illudere solent, quia
Deus, exigentibus peccatis, permittit." Jacques de Vitry, *The Exempla of Jacques de Vitry*,
ed. Thomas Frederick Crane (London : David Nutt, 1890), no. 262.

44 Henry Suso, *The Exemplar*, ed. Nicholas Heller, trans. Ann Edward (Dubuque:The Priory
Press, 1962), 5.2, p. 176. See also Richard Kieckhefer, *Unquiet Souls: Fourteenth Century
Saints and Their Religious Milieu* (Chicago: University of Chicago Press, 1984), 50–
88.

45 See Larrisa Taylor, *Soldiers of Christ: Preaching in Late Medieval and Reformation France*
(Oxford: Oxford University Press, 1992), 117–19, and as a good example, Jean Gerson,
De Erroribus circa Artem Magicam, in *Oeuvres complètes*, ed. Palemon Glorieux (Paris:
Desclee, 1969), 7:80.

46 Heiko Oberman, "The Shape of Late Medieval Thought: The Birthpangs of the Modern
Era," in Oberman, *The Dawn of the Reformation: Essays in Late Medieval and Early Reformation Thought* (Edinburgh:T. & T. Clark, 1986): 18–38; 27.

47 Gordon Leff, *The Dissolution of the Medieval Outlook* (New York: Harper and Row, 1976),
57–9; Francis Oakley, *Omnipotence, Covenant, and Order* (Ithaca: Cornell University Press,
1984), 80–1.

48 Leff, 29, 76–7.

49 "quod nulla causa agit immediate ad effectum aliquem in passo nisi naturaliter ordinata
ad illum producendum." Samuel de Cassini, *Questio Lamiarum*, in Hansen, *Quellen*, 266.

50 *Ibid.*, 267, 264.

51 "Quandoque talia permittit, in poenam correctionis peiorum, quandoque in tentationem
augmentandorum meritorum, quandoque in prodigium futurae gratiarum actionis."
Ulrich Molitor, *Tractatus de Pythonicis Mulieribus*, in Institoris and Sprenger, *Malleus Maleficarum* (Frankfurt am Main, 1580), 695, 712–13.

52 "Ita ut huiusmodi plagam praenoscit futuram, ex tunc commovet mentes huiusmodi
Malckiesarum mulierum, aliquando eisdem persuadendo: aliquando ob invidiam, quam
tales sceleratae mulieres adversus proximum gerunt, in vindictam mouendo easdem
sollicitat, quasi ipsas mulieres doceat huiusmodi tempestates, et aeris turbationes
prouocare." *Ibid.*, 698.

53 *Ibid.* Molitor was equally skeptical of Aquinas's theory that incubus demons could sire
human children with stolen semen. *Ibid.*, ch. 10.

54 Jean Vincent, *Liber adversus Magicas Artes et eos qui dicunt artibus eisdem nullam inesse
efficiam*, in Hansen, *Quellen*, 229.

55 "Vbi autem homines credunt ista maleficia effectualiter fieri: ibi reperiuntur plures malefici: nec possunt extirpari igne et gladio, quia quanto diligentius huiusmodi persecutio
fit: tanto plus crescit delusio. Nam persecutio arguit quod diabolus plus timetur quam
deus: et quod possit medio malorum mala ingerere, et demum placatur diabolus qui sic
timetur: et sic optinet intentum." Nicholas of Cusa, *Opera* (Paris, 1514; facsimile reprint,
Frankfurt am Main: Minerva, 1962), vol. 2, bk. 9, fol. 172.

56 Other skeptics had similar qualms. See for example the echoes of William of Paris in
work of the sixteenth-century Florentine Jurist, Gianfrancesco Ponzinibio, who argues
that although witches might injure men through their maleficium, their power to do
harm was strictly limited since otherwise all men might seem to be in the hands of
demons, which since the advent of the Savior was certainly not true. *Tractatus de Lamiis
et Excellentia Juris Utriusque*, in Paulus Grillandus, *Tractatus de Sortilegiis* (Frankfurt am
Main: 1592), 279.

57 "Ad quod respondent praedicti quod hoc est ex permissione divina: sed sic respondere ridiculum est, quoniam nihil fit in mundo quod Deus fieri non permittat, sive bonum sit, sive malum." Mamoris, 12.

58 "Diabolus potest de facto hominem localiter movere (permittente deo) ad maleficium perpetrandum adque obscenos actus explendos. Permissio divina in ista conclusione intelligitur negative." Vincente Dodo, *Apologia*, in Hansen, *Quellen*, 277.

59 "Mala enim que nostris exigentibus [peccatis] in mundo fiunt, deus velut per suos tortores iuste per demones solet infligere," quoting Nider, *Formicarius*, 5.4 (who supplies the missing peccatis). *Malleus*, pt. 2, qu. 1, ch. 15, p. 145. Similarly, "punishments are often brought about through the ministry of demons," (sepius tamen ista ministerio demonum exercent), pt. 1, qu. 1, p. 11.

60 "Et idcirco magi nequeunt turbare mentes bonorum qui talia non credunt, sed mentes infidelium et malorum." Guillermus Vorillongus, *Super Quatuor Libris Sententiarum*, dist. 34, in Lea, *Materials*, 1:167.

61 Robert of Brunne, *Handlyng Synne*, ed. F.J. Furnivall (London: Early English Text Society, 1901), ln. 544–6, p. 20. The treatise is an English translation of William of Wadington's *Manuel des Pechiez*; this *exemplum*, however, was an addition of Robert's own, and replaced one of Gregory the Great's tales.

62 The bishop's perfectly understandable, if illogical, response was that the witch should at once cease to believe in her magic.

63 Nider, *Praeceptorium*, 1.11, y.

64 "Invisibiliter demon maleficiatum hominem eodem modo ledit dei permissione si demeruit reus." *Ibid.*, v.

65 "Secundo ut deus sic grauiter per homines offensus . . . demoni maiorem potestatem in homines malos tribuat." *Ibid.*, z.

66 Later witch-theorists, such as Martin of Arles discussed below, certainly did so.

67 "Quod sicut vera et Christiana fides mirabilia operatur in bene credentibus, sic mala et falsa credulitas, Deo permittente, euentus malos interdum operatur, vel potius demeretur. Nam experimus quotidie in male credulis, quos ita Deus punit propter malam fidem, imodum [sic] cognoscit Dominus nimium adhaerere aliquibus vanis obseruantiis, permittit aliquos euentus contingere, et ita eos plus consequenter firmari in tali opinione, ut maior fiat caecitas eorum, et in laqueum cadant, quem sibi fecerunt." Martin of Arles, *Tractatibus de Superstitionibus*, printed in Jacquier, 437.

68 See Augustine, *City of God*, 1.9.

69 "Quod ad dignam flagellationem et punitionem horum flagitiorum permittit Deus tot infirmitates, pestilentias, et tempestates, sterilitates quoque terrae, nascentium fructuum, et interitum pecorum et iumentorum euenire." Martin of Arles, 438. Martin's views were not unique: St. Bernardino of Siena, for example, announced in a sermon that "Another sin which derives from pride is the sin in regard of charms and of divinations, and because of this God many times doth send his scourges into cities." See Bernardine of Siena, *Sermons*, ed. Nazareno Orlandi, trans. Helen Josephine Robins (Siena: Tipografie sociale, 1920), 26.2, p. 165.

70 For the importance of community to late-medieval conceptions of salvation and late-medieval religion in general, see A.N. Galpern, "The Legacy of Late Medieval Religion in Sixteenth Century Champagne," in Charles Trinkaus and Heiko A. Oberman, eds, *The Pursuit of Holiness in Late Medieval and Renaissance Religion* (Leiden: E.J. Brill, 1974), 141–76; and John Bossy, *Christianity and the West 1400–1700* (Oxford: Oxford University Press, 1985), 35–75.

71 Johannes Herolt, *Miracles of the Blessed Virgin* (1435–40), trans. C.C. Swinton Bland (London: George Routledge and Sons, 1928), c. 10, pp. 27–9; the *exemplum* is a retelling of Caesarius of Heisterbach, 7.3, although with a new moral: "From this may be seen that sometimes the whole community is punished for the fault of one."

72 Jean Delumeau, *Sin and Fear: The Emergence of a Western Guilt Culture, 13th–18th Centuries*, trans. Eric Nicholson (New York: St. Martin's Press, 1990), 302.

73 "Nam apud illos diabolicae execrationes efficaciam habent qui credunt vel adhaerent
   talibus execratis machinationibus diabolicis, vel dubitant et formidant in articulo fidei,
   vel experiri nequiter volunt, vel ex quadam admiratione seu curiositate volunt hec maleficia tentare, sive videre, vel facientibus assistere: quae omnia sunt periculosa in fide."
   Mamoris, 58.

74 *Ibid.*, 31.

75 "Unde valde stulte se iactant nonnulli ignari, asserentes, se non timere Daemones vel
   maleficos, nec eorum maleficia, nisi malefici ipsi appropinquantes personaliter huiusmodi se iactantibus aliquam rem venenatam eis ministrauerint, in potu vel cibo, unde
   laedi possint." Jacquier, 93.

76 *Ibid.*, 111, 117. Perhaps because in Jacquier's mind, a witch's maleficium resembled a
   kind of poison, against which supernatural defenses might prove unreliable.

77 *Malleus*, pt. 1, qu. 2, pp. 15–16.

78 "Et Maleficiales effectus dicuntur quando demon per maleficos et per magos operatur."
   Ibid., 16.

79 "Sed quia in contemptum et offensam creatoris simul et in perditionem animarum
   querunt huiusmodi per maleficas exercere scientes quod per talem modum sicut deus
   amplius irritatur ita et amplius permittit eis potestatem seuiendi; quia et de facto innu-
   mera malificia perpetrantur que non permitterentur diabolo inferre hominibus si per se
   solum affectaret homines ledere que tamen permittuntur iusto et occulto dei iudicio
   per maleficas propter perfidiam et catholice fidei abnegationem. Unde et eis iusto iudicio
   talia maleficia imputantur secundario quantumcunque diabolus sit actor principalis."
   Ibid., pt. 2, qu. 1, ch. 11, pp. 131–2.

80 "Unde de sicut innocentes puniuntur ex culpis parentum, ita et iam plures innoxii
   damnificantur et maleficiuntur propter peccata maleficorum." *Ibid.*, pt. 1, qu. 14, p. 71.
   This is a curious argument, and the authors admit that it is not for everyone: they advise
   preachers, for example, to explain misfortune with a simpler, if still unsatisfying proposition: "Sine culpa nisi subsit causa non est aliquis puniendus." *Ibid.*, 76.

81 "Quia aliud est a demone per maleficam ledi, et aliud per ipsum demonem absque
   malefica, quia demon per se in effigie animalis tunc verbera suscipit quando alteri sibi
   per pactum coniuncto infert. [Et quando cum eius consensu ad talem apparitionem sub
   tali forma et modo se ingessit.] Unde sic tantummodo noxios et sibi per pactum coni-
   unctos nocere potest et nullo modo innocentes. Per maleficas autem ubi demones ledere
   querunt tunc etiam innocentes permissione diuina in ultionem tanti criminis sepe affli-
   gunt." *Ibid.*, pt. 2, qu. 1, ch. 9, p. 124.

82 "Si quis vero curiosius insistaret sicut plerumque hec materia curiosas patitur a maleficarum defensoribus instantias: semper in cortice verborum aerem verberantes et medul-
   lam veritatis numquam penetrantes. Cur Job non maleficiali effectu per demonem sicut
   noxiali percussus fuit. His curios[is] etiam responderi potest quod Job fuit percussus a
   diabolo solum et non mediante malefico vel malefica. Quia hoc genus superstitionis
   vel nondum erat inuentum vel si erat inuentum diuina tamen praeuidentia voluit ut
   potestas demonis mundo ad precauendum eius insidias pro dei gloria innotesceret." *Ibid.*,
   pt. 1, qu. 2, p. 16.

83 "Plus permittit deus super hunc actum per quem primum peccatum diffunditur quam
   super alios actus humanos." *Ibid.*, pt. 2, qu. 1, ch. 6, p. 114. Although to modern readers
   this makes very little sense, Institoris and Sprenger apparently assumed that God's
   motives in this case would be so obvious as to require no further explanation.

84 This protection, however, extended only to the perception of the just of their own
   bodies: although the devil could not delude them into believing that their own bodies
   had been mutilated, he could still deceive them with illusions of absent penises in others.
   Ibid., pt. 2, qu. 1, ch. 7, p. 117.

5

Witchcraft:
the formation of belief
– part one

Ambrosius de Vignate was a well-respected magistrate and legal scholar, a doctor of both canon and civil law, who lectured at Padua, Bologna, and Turin between 1452 and 1468. On several occasions he participated in the trials of accused witches: he tells us that he had heard men and women alike confess – both freely and under torture – that they belonged to the sect of witches ("secta mascorum seu maleficorum") and that they, and others whom they implicated, had done all sorts of strange and awful things. The presiding inquisitors at these trials accepted this testimony as substantially true, and began prosecutions on this basis. Ambrosius, however, had grave doubts as to whether such bizarre crimes were plausible or even possible. In the twelfth of his twenty-one questions concerning the prosecution of heresy, he wonders

> What, therefore, do we say about women who confess that they walk at night over great distances in a moment's time, and enter the locked rooms of others, with the assistance of their diabolic masters (as they say), with whom they speak, to whom they make payment, and with whom (as they say) they have carnal intercourse, and by whose persuasion (as they say) they deny God and the Virgin Mary, and with their feet trample the holy cross, and who, with the help of demons (as they say), kill children and kill people, and make them fall into various injuries, and who say that they do many things like these, and say that they sometimes transform themselves into the form of a mouse, and sometimes, they say, the devil transforms himself into the form of a dog, or some other animal? Are these and similar things possible, or likely, or credible?[1]

In this passage, Ambrosius describes the "cumulative concept of witchcraft" as he encountered it – a combination of traditional legendary motifs, demonolatrous heresy, and maleficent magic that some of his learned colleagues considered the definitive characteristics of a very real and very dangerous sect. As aspects of a coherent and supposedly quite real whole, this particular arrangement of heterogeneous elements was new to the fifteenth century, and many people were openly skeptical. Ambrosius, for one, refused to accept the reality of the composite model of witchcraft and insisted upon treating each element individually. While men and women might indeed be guilty of working *maleficium*, their transformation into animals, he believed, was impossible. Therefore, when magistrates were faced with the confessions of accused witches, he required that they distinguish carefully between testimony which was possible and probable and that which was not.[2]

Like his counterparts in the Inquisition, Ambrosius was faced with two basic problems of belief: was witchcraft in fact real, and if so, what, precisely, was it? These two questions were intimately related: witchcraft so constituted as to be implausible either on empirical or theological grounds was more likely to be considered a delusion or an illusion than a representation of objective reality. In order for witch-beliefs to be persuasive, they first had to make sense in the context of what fifteenth-century people knew about the world. Of course, different people "knew" quite different things, and constructed their notions of witchcraft accordingly. To make sense of these diverse opinions, to understand the learned late-medieval discourse of witchcraft, we first need to comprehend the evidence and assumptions out of which categories of witchcraft were constructed, and then determine why some conceptions of witchcraft appear to have made more sense, and been more widely persuasive, than others.

Assessing the evidence

All learned theorists based their models of witchcraft upon data of similar kinds. First, there were their own personal and immediate experiences of witchcraft, meager though these usually were. Second, there were the narrative accounts of others – the testimony of witnesses, the confessions of witches, and tales of more general provenance – for most authors, but especially for inquisitors and magistrates, a much larger and more significant category. Finally there were authoritative Latin texts, the Bible above all, but also the narratives and pronouncements of a diverse assemblage of past authorities. Virtually all of this material came provided with its own interpretive frame; narratives about witchcraft were constructed in accordance with a prior understanding of the phenomenon, and reflected the beliefs of authors and narrators past and present. In this way, witch-theorists were exposed to idealized models of witchcraft of varying degrees of specificity, sophistication, and comprehensiveness. Variance between pre-existing interpretive models, or between models and evidentiary experience or accepted authority, was the driving force behind the late-medieval learned discourse on witchcraft.

Ambrosius de Vignate, for example, urged caution when descriptions of witch-craft contradicted the evidence; in turn, just such skepticism inspired Insti-toris and Sprenger to compose a rebuttal. More specifically, however, the dimensions of the category "witch" in the *Malleus* were determined by an apparent contradiction of a different sort, between notions of witchcraft authorized by learned texts, and more popular representations of witchcraft evinced by the testimony of witnesses. As Dominicans, the authors were trained to accept the authority of the text, their own sensible experience, and the testimony of reliable witnesses; any valid proposition should be verifiable by each of these means. As inquisitors, however, they found that their experi-ence in the courtroom seemed to contradict accepted authorities. Because they had no mechanism by which to discount experiential evidence, they were faced with a contradiction between two equally valid epistemological standards in a matter of considerable importance. Since such a contradiction could not be allowed to stand, they constructed new models which could reconcile the competing demands of experience and traditional authority.[3]

Institoris and Sprenger worked out this problem within an intellectual framework provided by the teaching of Aquinas, and though this debt is obvious, it must not be taken for granted. Although Aquinas was the canoni-cally accepted theologian of the Dominican Order, for the rest of Europe, and even for many Dominicans, he was not quite the dominant intellectual force of the late Middle Ages that he is sometimes thought to be.[4] Quite the con-trary, at most schools the most popular, vigorous, and influential intellectual trend of the fifteenth century was the nominalist, Franciscan, *via moderna*.[5] In many places Aquinas still suffered from his association with the extreme Aristotelianism condemned at Paris almost two hundred years before. The *Malleus*, though, was written at the University of Cologne, the most doggedly Thomist school in Europe. There the faculty did not even bother to teach the *via moderna*, and had, in fact, banned it from the curriculum in 1425. Lambertus de Monte Domini, one of Sprenger's most distinguished colleagues at Cologne, and the man whose name appears first on the faculty endorsement of the *Malleus*, even went so far as to lead an abortive drive to obtain beatifi-cation for Aristotle.[6]

This rigorously Thomist background affected Institoris and Sprenger's interpretation of witch-beliefs in ways that went well beyond the conventional association of Aquinas with the theory of the diabolic pact. The Thomist uni-verse was characterized by a strong sense of integration: there was no sharp separation between the natural and supernatural realms. For this reason it was possible to derive valid, albeit speculative, knowledge of the higher orders of creation from sense-experience, because, in Heiko Oberman's words, "in Thomas' metaphysical ontology the natural and supernatural realms are organically joined by the *Being* of God."[7] In this system, the world of sensible experience was simply one rung on a hierarchy of creation that ascended at last to God, and which, in its entirety, was an expression of God. For this reason, and particularly because the chain of cause and effect relationships extended down the hierarchy of being through various mediating agents, it was possible to apprehend, at least partially, the higher realms through the observation of earthly effects.

Such an exalted view of rational knowledge was possible in turn because of a particular kind of epistemological optimism. For Aquinas, all rational knowledge was located in this realm of the sensible: to know something rationally was invariably the result of the application of reason to sensory experience.[8] Unless one had cause to think otherwise, sensory experience had to be a reliable indicator of the actual state of the world, since it was inherently unlikely that God would have made beings who would be chronically mistaken.[9] For this reason, one might ordinarily accept a given proposition as epistemologically valid simply because it was accepted as such by large numbers of people.[10] In absolute terms, this rule was applied only to knowledge of first principles, propositions which were perceived as true the moment their terms were apprehended. Even for more complex propositions, though, the intellect was never mistaken in any absolute sense, but only "accidentally," due to errors in the formulation of a proposition (a faulty definition of "man," for example, would lead the intellect to erroneous conclusions about the nature of men). With due care, then, Thomist scholastics had every reason to believe that what large numbers of people believed about the world essentially reflected reality. Aquinas, for example, accepted the existence of minor demonic spirits, since

> Many persons report that they have had the experience, or have heard from such as have experienced it, that Satyrs and Fauns, whom the common folk call incubi, have often presented themselves before women . . . Hence it seems folly to deny it.[11]

This relationship between knowledge and experiential reality privileged the argument from personal observation and from personal experience, whether direct or based upon the testimony of reliable witnesses, over arguments based solely upon the dictates of authorities. Thus, Albert the Great remarked that "Every accepted proposition which is established by sense perception is better than that which contradicts the senses; and a conclusion which contradicts sense perception is not credible."[12] The Church, however, placed an important restriction upon such arguments. As Albert explained, although in other cases the argument from authority was weak, in theology the argument from authority was pre-eminent, since, "in theology, the argument from authority is from the inspired teaching of the Spirit of Truth."[13] The difficulty was to find out exactly where the realm of theology began and the realm of mundane experience came to an end. Since this was by no means an easy or an obvious distinction, contradictions between authority and experience inevitably arose. Late medieval theorists were faced with a problem of this kind when they considered the problem of witches, because a long line of ecclesiastical authorities had dismissed the practices of alleged witches as largely delusional.

Institoris and Sprenger addressed this problem head on: they maintained that regardless of what authorities might seem to say, regardless of the plain sense of canons, the evidence of one's own senses, of manifest experience, had to take precedence:

> Who is so stupid that he would affirm on that account that all their bewitchments and magically inspired harms are fantastic and imaginary when the contrary is apparent to everybody's senses?[14]

In this respect, the authors of the *Malleus* are nothing like the popular image of medieval scholastics, hopelessly dependent upon their authorities; they rely instead upon what they perceive as empirical evidence. What Institoris and Sprenger and other scholastic demonologists did take as a matter of faith, however, is that the universe operated according to rules, or, rather, by the natural laws of creation. Witchcraft, like the devil himself, was a part of this creation and operated only by its laws. Hence, there was nothing necessarily "supernatural" about witchcraft, and educated observers could devise a detailed, systematic, and comprehensive description of the phenomenon from a knowledge of natural law and the observation of witchcraft's material effects, even if it was not amenable to direct observation. Thomist scholastics supposed, simply, that an investigator could follow the trail of cause and effect up and down the hierarchy of being, and that theologically determined truths about the nature of creation would accurately inform his understanding of sensible, earthly events. In this way, a metaphysically higher cause could be adduced from a particular mundane effect. In the case of witchcraft, for example, reported impotence could be used as evidence for a whole range of otherwise hidden causes: the pact between the witch and the devil, diabolic powers, and the ultimate justice of divine judgments.

Thomistically oriented demonologists thus seamlessly joined the material world with higher metaphysical realms, making possible an easy move from the human to the diabolic, and, ultimately, the divine. Strangely enough, this conception of the world was remarkably compatible with that of traditional European communities. If we can visualize the former as a vertically oriented chain of being, extending upward from the material world to the supernatural, we can think of the latter as a horizontal field in which the realm of normal experience extends outward into the supranormal.[15] For peasants and inquisitors both, spirits and magic were not so much supernatural as preternatural: they exceeded the common bounds of experience, but were not in any sense beyond nature itself. For this reason, narratives informed by a traditional understanding of the supranormal world could make sense to Institoris and Sprenger provided they were reoriented to fit their hierarchically structured conception of creation.

An example of this process appears in Institoris and Sprenger's account of a town that was ravaged by the plague. There was a rumor that a woman recently buried "was gradually swallowing the shroud in which she had been buried, and that the plague could not cease until the entire shroud was swallowed and consumed in her stomach."[16] When the body was exhumed, half of the shroud was indeed found to have disappeared into the gullet of the corpse, and the horrified magistrates at once had the body decapitated, and the head thrown from the grave, at which time the plague ceased. This narrative is intensely traditional: a spirit of the dead is causing disease, which will abate only when the corpse is mutilated or destroyed.[17] Such an interpretation, however, was completely at odds with the accepted teachings of the Church, and generations of clerics had condemned such beliefs and practices as superstitious nonsense. Institoris and Sprenger accept the story nonetheless as being essentially accurate, provided that the dead woman had been a witch, and that the plague was due to divine anger over the town's earlier willingness to let her live and die unmolested, so that when her body was exhumed and mutilated, and her misdeeds exposed in the subsequent inquiry, God's wrath was allayed.[18] Although Institoris and Sprenger understand the immediate cause of the plague as the anger of a vengeful God rather than the traditional malice of a spirit, their world was as fully anthropocentric as that of traditional peasant communities: for both, just as disease could be caused by human behavior and the violation of normative social boundaries, so a cure might be effected through a ritual, communal performance. Further, as Institoris and Sprenger suggest, discrepancies between a dead person's putative social position and hidden, rumored, behaviors could result in unwanted post-mortem activity until the "secret" was brought to light and the ambiguity was resolved. Thus, the authors were able to recast an episode grounded in a traditional understanding of the relationship between the living and the dead in ways acceptable to their own understanding of creation, while keeping the underlying structures and meanings of the story intact.

Perhaps the most striking aspect of this account, though, is Institoris and Sprenger's willingness to accept a supernatural cause for an outbreak of the plague on the basis of a local "rumor." This faith in the substantial accuracy of common reports of cause and effect relationships was necessary, because if the inquisitors were not prepared to accept that particular misfortunes were caused by witchcraft, prosecutions based upon reports of *maleficium* would be impossible. Institoris and Sprenger, however, had faith not only in a deterministic model of causation that transcended all boundaries between quotidian experience and the diabolic and divine, but also in the native ability of man to recognize such relationships when they were encountered. They write that witchcraft is known by its effects, "for from the effects one arrives at knowledge of the cause."[19] The effects of witchcraft were so remarkable, so clearly not of the mundane material world, that they could not be caused by man alone:

> The power of corporal man cannot extend itself to the causation of works of this kind, which always has this quality, that the cause along with its natural effect is known naturally and without wonder.[20]

The appearance of supernatural or preternatural phenomena, then, was sufficient to warrant the assumption of a supernatural or preternatural cause; in essence, Institoris and Sprenger argue that the perception of supranormal effects indicates the real presence of the preternatural or supernatural agencies. Knowledge of witches was gained through an intuitive apprehension of what was and was not within the normal bounds of human experience: if illness or misfortunes were perceived to be "wonderful" in their scope, severity, or swiftness of onslaught, the presence of *maleficium*, and consequently of witches, was all but certain.

The assumed authority of personal perceptions, eyewitness experience, and the testimony of witnesses pervades the arguments of the *Malleus*. When the authors confidently assert that witches were more often women than men, they remark that "it is not expedient to deduce arguments to the contrary, since experience itself, in addition to verbal testimonies and the witness of trustworthy men, makes such things credible."[21] They establish that witches have frequent sexual relations with demons, because this has "been seen or heard in personal experience or by the relations of trustworthy men."[22] There can also be no doubt that some witches "work marvels over the male member," since this, too, "is established by the sight and hearing of many, and from common report itself."[23] In these, and many other instances, Institoris and Sprenger consistently privilege the argument from experience: the most persuasive arguments were those supported by the greatest weight of experiential evidence, either in terms of quantity or quality.

This reliance upon actual experience dictated in turn the forms which evidence had to take. Personal experience of witchcraft was not generally recorded in propositional statements of belief, but in narratives which related the experience itself.[24] Narratives of this kind do not normally contain explicit statements about the beliefs of the storyteller, which must be inferred by readers or auditors. When narratives circulate in fairly restricted, homogeneous communities, the underlying belief systems are easily apprehended; this is not at all the case, however, when narratives circulate more widely, and when narrator and auditor hold quite different assumptions about the nature of the world. Unlike many previous ecclesiastical commentators, who either dismissed popular narratives as fabulous or reinterpreted them beyond recognition, Institoris and Sprenger combined a trust in the substantial accuracy of such tales with an interpretive system that preserved much of their essential meaning. In this way, narrative evidence provided the basis for a conception of witchcraft that bridged traditional folk-beliefs and ecclesiastical erudition; Institoris and Sprenger created a model of witchcraft which could be expressed propositionally in scholastic style, but which rested upon their interpretation of a very large number of narrative examples. Indeed, the greater part of the evidence in the *Malleus* consists of their interpretations of narrative. André Schnyder counts 279 different *exempla* in the *Malleus*, most of which involve witchcraft or the devil.[25] Yet the *Malleus* is not precisely a collection of *exempla*, because unlike traditional medieval tale collections, such as Nider's *Formicarius*, it does not use narratives chiefly as illustrative moral examples, but as proofs sufficient in themselves.

For instance, Institoris and Sprenger advise that persons whose minds are turned toward love or hatred by witchcraft should fortify themselves with daily invocations of their guardian angel and frequent visits to the shrines of the saints. After two examples of the efficacy of these procedures, the authors are quite satisfied that they have supplied sufficient proof of their claims:

> Wherefore it deserves to be concluded that the aforesaid remedies are most certain against a disease of this kind, and thus whosoever uses these weapons is most certain to be freed.[26]

So much does the *Malleus* depend upon evidence of this kind that the logic of the inquisitors becomes at times completely indistinguishable from the logic of their stories. When they set out to prove that the regular application of sacramentals may reliably ward off the evil powers of witches, they marshal a long series of narratives as evidence.[27] In particular they mention the mayor of Wiesenthal who fortified himself every Sunday with holy water and blessed salt. One Sunday, however, in his haste to attend a wedding, he neglected this precaution and was immediately and painfully bewitched. This coincidence proved to the mayor, and to the inquisitors, the efficacy of his customary sacramental defenses and the reality of witchcraft: the mayor's malady was known to be witchcraft because it struck when he was not sacramentally protected;

the sacramentals were known to be an effective defense against witchcraft for exactly the same reason.

Although such an argument was not strictly logical because a syllogism cannot provide proof of its premise, Institoris and Sprenger accepted the logic of personal experience and its narratives as a fully sufficient arbiter of truth. In their minds, as in the narratives to which they appealed, the appearance of causal connections demonstrated their existence, and by accepting such narrative episodes as valid evidence in themselves, Institoris and Sprenger were able to elevate the discourse of village magic to the level of learned disputation.

In this discourse, the voice of collective opinion or common report was every bit as important as specific eyewitness accounts, and so Institoris and Sprenger were singularly sensitive to the value of rumor. [28] Indeed, local rumors provided such a reliable indication of the presence of witchcraft that when such rumors reached the authorities, they were sufficient in themselves to warrant an investigation. Most investigations, Institoris tells us, begin in this way, without any specific accusations.[29] His sample declaration which would formally initiate the inquisitorial process testifies to the centrality of rumor in the hunt for witches:

> It often comes to the ears of such and such official or judge, of such and such a place, borne by public gossip and produced by noisy reports, that such and such a person from such and such a place has done such and such things per- taining to *maleficia* against the faith and the common good of the state.[30]

When rumors coalesced around particular individuals, they could lead to spe- cific charges. Much of the evidence Institoris assembled against Helena Scheuberin at Innsbruck amounted to very little more than rumor. The first charge against her states that she is

> defamed particularly regarding the death of a certain knight, Spiess by name, and this not even in Innsbruck but all over the place throughout the surround- ing regions, and especially among the noble and powerful. Whether he perished by poison or witchcraft there remains some doubt. However it is generally rumored that it was from *maleficium* because the witch had been devoted to evil-doing from her youth.[31]

Having a bad reputation, *mala fama*, was almost a requirement for real witches as far as Institoris was concerned, and provided an important link between moral delinquency and maleficent magic. A bad reputation might encompass a wide range of moral failings and social deviance, and provided the necessary ground for more sinister rumors of witchcraft to take root.[32]

Rumors provided witch-hunters with the perfect narrative basis for their inquiries. It is often said that accusations of witchcraft came principally from

the lower ranks of society and not from the elite, and in a general sense this
seems to be true; but in an environment where vague rumors of *maleficia* were
swirling around, it may also be that concrete accusations were constructed by
prosecutors through the examination of rumor-bearing informants.[33] It is a
characteristic of rumor narratives that they become more detailed, more
rooted in local conditions, and more attached to specific points of reference,
as they are challenged and interrogated.[34] Further, as witnesses are required
to supply increasing levels of detail, they become increasingly amenable to the
guidance of the interrogator, and begin to look to the forms and subtext of
the examiner's questions to provide the bases for their answers.[35] The availability of rumor legends, then, may have determined the extent to which an
investigator was able to impose his own conception of witchcraft upon locally
divergent cases. If this were the case, then the activities of the inquisitor begin
to assume familiar contours: he becomes the catalyst which transforms suspicion and diverse experience into an actionable charge focused upon a single
person. In modern rural France, this role is assumed by the "unwitcher" who
occupies a crucial position between the bewitched victim and the alleged
witch.[36] As authorities agitate the community, and the level of anxiety rises,
the amount of rumor in circulation rises as well; eventually, such "hot" legends
may become reified into a set of consistent, specific accusations.[37]

From rumors, memorates, and denunciations and confessions couched
in traditional terms, Institoris and Sprenger constructed their image of witchcraft. As inquisitors and priests they were uniquely well positioned to hear an
astonishing range of opinion and narrative concerning witches, and were
equally obliged to make sense of it all. The witch-beliefs of the *Malleus* draw
heavily upon traditional beliefs and previously constituted categories which
Institoris and Sprenger reinterpreted in a manner consistent with a theologically Thomist view of the world. The success of this project was due less to
their theological sophistication and rigorous logic (neither of which is especially evident), than to their sensitivity to the world picture of their informants. They did not simply demonize popular belief, but tried instead to
reconstruct it for their own purposes. Their picture of witchcraft was successful precisely because it corresponded so closely with the ideas of the less
well educated. Other demonologists treated witchcraft as a sect, worse than,
but otherwise similar to, other heresies; because of their epistemological and
metaphysical assumptions, however, Institoris and Sprenger understood witchcraft much more as did the common man, as part of a spectrum of human
interaction with preternatural and supernatural powers. For this reason,
although the model of witchcraft in the *Malleus* is certainly a composite, constructed from several different but interrelated idea-clusters, the fit between
this model and supranormal events as they were reported was closer than the

competing models of other learned observers, and was thus more persuasive. Edwin Ardener has proposed that categories have a center of gravity, a zone most characteristic of their qualities, and that the "density gradients" of categories are related in some way to frequency of association or interaction with reality.[38] If this is the case, Institoris and Sprenger's vision of witchcraft was more successful than those of their competitors because its center of gravity was more closely aligned with the perceived reality of their contemporaries.[39]

To go beyond this sort of general statement, and to try to see exactly how Institoris and Sprenger constructed their categories of "witch" and "witchcraft" is more difficult. Like all learned witch-theorists of the late Middle Ages, they worked with reference to rules, evidence, and already extant symbols and categories: first, they accepted a set of more or less rigid assumptions about the world and its creator with which any construction of witchcraft had to be consistent; second, they had evidence, principally in narrative form, about a number of identifiable individuals whose antisocial behavior or normative boundary transgressions were defined by reference to *maleficia* and related categories; third, to make sense of this evidence, they had available a quite nebulous cluster of symbols, beliefs, and narrative structures associated with magic and supranormal beings which could be reordered in terms of any number of new categorical constructs. This is, of course, too schematic a map of the field of late-medieval witchcraft, but nevertheless an attempt to analyze late-medieval witchcraft in terms of its constituent categories and symbols seems worthwhile.[40] Not only is this a reasonably clear path to tread, but the late-medieval debate over witches centered upon just such problems of category ascription and definition. In the analysis that follows, we will look at five interrelated categories in turn, each of which appears repeatedly in late-medieval demonological discourse: the processions of spectral women, heresy and the diabolic cult, *maleficium*, superstition, and gender.

"Good women" and bad: *strigae*, *lamiae*, and the *bonae res*

Of all the beliefs out of which constructions of witchcraft were formed, the most unfamiliar to modern readers are quite probably those associated with various sorts of nocturnal female spirits. These beings inhabited the world of medieval peasants, for whom they were part of an extensive traditional lore with antecedents that reached well back into the pre-Christian past. To educated clerics of the Middle Ages, such traditions were almost as alien as they appear to the modern researcher, and so they, like us, sought out interpretations which would make sense of them, some of which were gradually assimilated with notions of *maleficium* and heresy, and ultimately provided paradigms by which the larger phenomenon of witchcraft was understood.

Scattered throughout a variety of medieval sources are tantalizing hints of a widespread tradition about the fantastic nocturnal escapades of women and female spirits. According to the disapproving accounts of churchmen, some women believed that they secretly left their homes at night to attend the court of a goddess or spirit, often identified as Diana, and rode with her on lengthy processions, traveling great distances in the blink of an eye. These ideas smacked of paganism, idolatry, or worse, and are accordingly condemned in the canon *Episcopi*, first recorded in the early tenth century in the penitential of Regino, abbot of Prüm.[41] In the following century, a well-known canonist, Burchard, bishop of Worms, repeated Regino's warnings in his confessional interrogatory, *Corrector et Medicus*:

> Have you believed or participated in that infidelity, which some wicked women, turned back after Satan, seduced by illusions and phantoms of demons, believe and confess: that with Diana, goddess of the pagans, and an innumerable multitude of women, they ride on certain beasts and traverse great distances of the earth in the silence of the dead of night, obey her commands as if she were their mistress, and on certain nights are called to her service?[42]

If anyone believes such things, and, Burchard adds, "an innumerable multitude, deceived by this false opinion, believe these things to be true," then she must do penance for two years.

Burchard, Regino, and other early-medieval ecclesiastics were all agreed that there was nothing substantial behind these tales of rustic women, and that nobody actually left their homes at night to gad about with spirits. It was rather the deceptions of the devil that were to blame: at the same time as he walked abroad at night with his fellows in the guise of Diana and her train, he sent dreams to poor ignorant women so that they would believe themselves to be traveling in the place of the demons. Nonetheless, this clerical skepticism should not be interpreted as tolerance because it was also quite clear that these beliefs were sinful, superstitious, and diabolically inspired. Insofar as these women believed themselves to go voluntarily, they participated in the demons' designs. Thus, although the nocturnal processions of spectral women were illusory, they were also quite clearly linked to the devil, a link that could be expanded in different contexts.

Exactly what constituted this traditional belief is difficult to say, since the evidence available is scattered and contradictory, and suggests a group of more or less related components rather than a single, coherent belief-system.[43] It is remotely possible that the consistent references to Diana indicate the presence of a relict pagan cult, but it seems more likely that the perception of broadly similar motifs in a variety of traditions provided the attractive force necessary to create an amalgam of beliefs, roughly centered around the nocturnal activities of women and female spirits.[44] Certainly the variety of names by whom the leader of this host was known suggests conflation of this sort, since Herodias, Abundia, Satia, Holda, Perchta, and others, all supervised processions of night-traveling women, exactly as did Diana.

Neither is it entirely certain just what these beings and their followers were wont to do on their evening rides. Some accounts suggest simply that they rode to some gathering place where they danced and feasted, and then returned home. In the thirteenth century, however, William of Paris (d. 1249), added that Domina Abundia and her ladies were believed to enter houses at night and bring abundance and riches when they found offerings prepared for them.[45] In his *Corrector*, Burchard mentioned a similar belief connected with the Fates or "the sisters," who were said to come into houses at certain times of the year and bring good luck if they found food and drink waiting for them.[46] Neither Burchard nor William identified these ladies with Diana and her train, but other authors made this connection explicit. In the *Romance of the Rose* (c. 1270), Nature remarks that since women are credulous and emotional, they are especially susceptible to illusions and phantoms:

> As a result, many people in their folly think themselves sorcerers by night, wandering with Lady Abundance. And they say that in the whole world every third child born is of such disposition that three times a week he goes just as destiny leads him; that such people push into all houses; that they fear neither keys nor bars, but enter by cracks, cat-hatches, and crevices; that their souls leave their bodies and go with good ladies into strange places and through houses.[47]

John of Frankfurt, writing in the early fifteenth century, provides a similar, albeit more detailed, warning against the dangers of these beliefs. He advises

> that a Christian should most especially flee, lest he should come to believe this, what old women report at people's births: that certain goddesses come and place a destiny of good or bad fortune upon a father's offspring and predict a death by hanging or by the sword, or great honor, or something similar which shall definitely come about . . . And certain people say that if a boy is born with a caul, that he is one of those who traverse great distances in the space of one night, vulgarly, "die farn leude" [the wayfarers]. In short, people afflicted by this insanity give the service which ought to be God's alone to those who are really demons, falsely believing them to be the dispensers of good things. So some even do on the five feast days of the four seasons and on the night preceding the ember days.[48]

Although they are scattered over several centuries, taken together these accounts suggest a reasonably consistent body of belief, closely related to the rural European "fairy cults" described by nineteenth and twentieth-century folklorists. In its medieval form, the tradition centered upon a belief in troops of spectral women, led by some specific but variously named mistress, which visited houses at certain times of the year and brought either good fortune or ill, depending upon their reception.[49] These beings might also determine a person's fate at birth, and claimed a certain number of people, sometimes up to a third of humanity, as their own.[50] Those chosen, who appear to have been mainly women, accompanied the trouping "fairies" on their rounds, paid court to their mistress, and attended their revels. According to most accounts, these women believed that they participated bodily in such activities, although some, like Jean de Meun, represent the night-travelers as entering trance-like dreams, knowing full well that they accompanied the goddess in spirit only. Like their mistress, these peripatetic female specters were known by many names — fays, fates, good women, and good sisters — but for the sake of convenience, and to avoid the anachronistic connotations of the word "fairy," I will subsequently refer to them as the *bonae res*, the "good things," a term used by the Dominican inquisitor, Stephen of Bourbon (d. 1261), in his description of the phenomenon.[51]

The full range of traditions with which the *bonae res* were associated was, however, considerably more extensive than this generalized overview would suggest. Sometimes the restless dead accompanied the *bonae res* on their nightly rounds, and both Holda and Perchta were occasionally known to lead the Furious Horde.[52] The nocturnal processions of women were also related to a set of more sinister beliefs — legends of female spirits who stole into houses to kill children and work other crimes. Such beings were often called *lamiae*, their name derived conventionally from *laniare* (to rend) and their distressing habit of tearing children into bits. In the thirteenth century, Johannes de Janua gave this etymology in his widely read *Catholicon*, and added that "old women pretend that *lamiae* enter houses through closed doors, kill infants and tear them to pieces, and afterwards restore them to life, and they have the faces of people but the bodies of beasts."[53] Such beings had clear literary antecedents in the classical Roman figure of the *strix*, the malevolent, bird-like, female monsters of Ovid and Apuleius, but medieval authors often associated *lamiae*, in less monstrous forms but with equally sinister intent, with the troupes of *bonae res*.[54] William of Paris, for example, discusses *lamiae* immediately after his account of Abundia and her ladies, and explains that both are essentially beings of the same type:

> You ought to understand in the same manner those other evil spirits which the vulgar call *stryges* and *lamiae* and which appear at night in houses in which there are nursing babes, which they seem to tear to pieces when snatched from their

cradles or to roast in the fire. They appear in the form of old women; however, they are neither true old women, nor is it possible that children are truly devoured.[55]

William states further that although these monsters appeared in the guise of old women, they were really demons who, as spirits, could not truly consume infants. They were, however, occasionally permitted to kill children to punish their parents. Demons were happy to oblige, because in so doing they inspired fear which led to superstitious idolatry – for exactly the same reason as the demon impersonating Domina Abundia provided good luck.

Several centuries earlier, Burchard had made the same connection between the monstrous *lamiae* and the more benign *bonae res*. With words identical to those he applied to the followers of the *bonae res*, he condemns the belief of women who think that they go out at night on murderous errands in spectral form:

> Have you believed what many women, turned back to Satan, believe and affirm to be true: do you believe that in the silence of the quiet night when you have gone to bed and your husband lies on your bosom, that while you remain in bodily form you can go out by closed doors and are able to cross the spaces of the world with others deceived by the same error, and without visible weapons slay persons who have been baptized and redeemed by the blood of Christ, and cook and eat their flesh, and in place of their hearts put straw or wood or something of the sort and having eaten them make them live again and give an interval of life?[56]

Quite clearly, both Burchard and William of Paris interpreted belief in *lamiae* and similar creatures under the general rubric provided by the canon *Episcopi*, and with good reason. Given the devil's well-attested power to produce nocturnal delusions and phantoms, and his desire to provoke superstitious, idolatrous belief, the canon provided a useful conceptual template through which a great many vaguely similar beliefs could be understood and condemned.

Such learned incredulity, although common, was not universal. At least a few observers found it difficult to dismiss widespread and persistent testimony as the result of diabolically inspired delusions, especially as the canon *Episcopi* did not seem to bear directly upon tales of *lamiae* and the like. Gervaise of Tilbury (d. 1235) was perhaps the most credulous of thirteenth-century writers: he declared that many women, like the women of Diana's company, claimed that they went out at night in the company of *lamiae* and flew across remote parts of the world.[57] Unlike the more benign night-travelers, however, they did not bring good luck when they entered houses at night; instead they oppressed sleepers, moved infants from place to place, drank human blood, and caused serious illness.[58] Although Gervaise acknowledged that some claimed that "these nocturnal fancies arise from timidity and melancholy, as in the insane," while others "assert that they have seen such imaginations in dreams so vividly that they seemed to be awake," he could accept neither explanation because the weight of his personal experience told against it. He knew reliable women, his neighbors, who had seen these beings abroad at night; he had heard women confess that they went out at night with the *lamiae* and molested infants; he had seen women bearing wounds which corresponded exactly with those given to nocturnal apparitions in the form of cats by vigilant watchmen. All of which told strongly against the delusional nature of such creatures, which should accordingly be combated by pious means.[59] The grounds for Gervaise's credulity should be noted: he was not simply "superstitious," but rather convinced by the weight of experiential evidence that these beings were real, an epistemological stance identical to that of later witch-hunters.

Originally, perhaps, these several different species of night-travelers, the *lamiae* and the *bonae res*, had been relatively distinct. It is also possible that both destructive *strigae* and more benign spirits were once logical counterparts within a more comprehensive system of belief, much as the *benandanti* appear to have had the *malandanti* as their perpetual foes. Among learned clerics, Stephen of Bourbon taught that while *strigae* and the *bonae res* were equally imaginary, they were otherwise well differentiated: *strigae* rode wolves at night and killed children, but the *bonae res* had less fierce steeds and were, at worst, petty vandals. The name "Holda" may also point to such a distinction, for it suggests those positive attributes associated with the words "kind," or "gracious"; indeed, the medieval Holda was so well considered as to be occasionally identified with the Virgin Mary.[60] Likewise, the common German word for witch in the Middle Ages was *unholda*, the good spirit's inverted counterpart. Unfortunately, more concrete evidence for such a system is hard to find, and the evidence provided by names is ambiguous since it is also true that words such as *holda* or *bilwis* might stand equally for fairies or for malevolent witches.[61] In any event, for most learned clerics, and probably for most common folk as well, the various spectral trains of nocturnal women had obvious similarities and were very easily conflated. John of Salisbury, writing in the mid-twelfth century, provides an early example of exactly this kind of assimilation, when he writes about those women who say that they followed "a certain woman who shines by night, or Herodias, or the mistress of the night" to assemblies and banquets. There, these women assert that

> they are employed with the tasks of various kinds of service: some are handed over for punishment, some others are elevated for their renown, each as they deserve. Moreover, infants are exposed to *lamiae*, and some having been indis-

criminately torn to pieces are added to those already thrown into the stomach by ravenous maws; while some are tossed back by the mercy of the ruler and replaced in their cradles.[62]

By the fifteenth century, this failure to discriminate between different types of night-going women had become general: instead of describing the *lamiae* and the *bonae res* as different but related components of peasant belief, learned commentators constructed a single complex, containing elements drawn from both traditions. It is this conflation of *strigae* with the more benign followers of Diana or Abundia that informs the witch debates of the late Middle Ages. Martin of Arles provides a fairly typical fifteenth-century account of the nefarious activities of these night-flying women in his catalogue of rustic superstitions. Among these, Martin describes the *Broxae*, women who claimed to fly through the air at night and transform themselves into animals. He acknowledges that these are the women whose beliefs are condemned by the canon *Episcopi*, but he goes on to emphasize the criminal nature of their imaginary excursions. Any distinction between the *bonae res* and the malevolent *striga* is completely invisible to Martin:

> Whence some little women, devoted to Satan, seduced by the illusions of the devil, believe and confess that they ride during the hours of the night with Diana, goddess of the pagans, or Venus, in company with a great multitude of women, and do other abominations, for example, tear away babes from the breasts of their mothers, carry them off and eat them, enter houses through chimneys or windows, and disturb the inhabitants in various ways, all of which happens exclusively in their imaginations.[63]

The common people greatly feared these women, and rang bells and lit fires at crossroads and in the fields on the night of St. John's day, lest witches fly overhead and cause thunder and storms. This, Martin remarks, "I have seen with my own eyes."[64]

The beliefs surrounding the troupes of night-traveling women thus occupy a somewhat paradoxical place in the late-medieval witch debate. As Norman Cohn recognized, elements drawn from this tradition were necessary, if the newly (re)constructed witch category was to be truly threatening. Without the ability to travel at preternatural speed, it was just not possible to envision hundreds or thousands of women assembling at night and carrying out their nefarious deeds without causing an obvious commotion.[65] In addition, although both heretics and *malefici* could certainly be alarming, there were recognized and effective procedures for dealing with them. Assimilation with the monstrous *striga* and *lamia* of folklore, however, resulted in hosts of newly demonic witches whose terrible occult powers and ruthlessly destructive agenda required new and more energetic measures to combat them.

The contrary, however, was also true: where this assimilation was incomplete, as was the case especially in southern Europe, *maleficae* remained well differentiated from the spectral women of the night, and "witchcraft" did not become a critical problem. It was equally the case that constructions of witchcraft in which these night-travelers were too centrally placed were not convincing, both because they ran squarely counter to the always troublesome canon *Episcopi*, and because the testimony of suspect "witches" themselves strained credulity.[66]

These difficulties are best seen in the witch-treatises themselves. At one end of the spectrum, Alphonso de Spina tried, probably harder than anyone else, to push the traditional category distinctions of the canon *Episcopi* far enough to accommodate fully diabolized witches.[67] In his opinion, the *Bruxae* or *Xorguinae* of popular superstition were demons who deceived old women in their dreams, making them think that they traveled by night, killed children, and did other evil deeds. Although these women were deceived, Alphonso makes it plain they readily participated in this evil, and would commit their crimes in reality if only they could:

> The truth of the matter, however, is that when these evil persons wish to use these most wicked fictions they consecrate themselves with words and unguents to the devil, and the devil immediately receives them in his work and takes the form and the imagination of every one of them and leads them to the places which they wish, although their bodies remain insensible and covered by the shadow of the devil so that no one can see them, and when the devil sees in their imaginations that they have completed all they wish, not withdrawing from their imaginations the diabolical fancies which they see, he leads back their imaginations, joining them with their own moving bodies.[68]

In this account, Alphonso comes very close to endorsing the very belief he purports to condemn, since the process he describes – in which the "imaginations" of women wander about with the devil – sounds suspiciously like the actual separation of body and soul. Instead of harmless delusions created by the devil, women created their own monstrous fantasies, which Satan gave the semblance of reality. He not only transported their *figura et fantasia* to remote places, he also thoughtfully concealed their dreaming bodies while he did so, so that annoying nay-sayers could not point to the obvious evidence of snoring women to discredit their stories. But, for Alphonso, these women do no real, concrete harm; instead their crime is heresy. Thus, the women of the canon *Episcopi* who assert that they follow Diana at night are not merely superstitious; rather, they are devil-worshiping heretics who are justly consigned to the stake, since their heresy consists not only of the invocation to the devil which precedes their dreams, but also of the dreams themselves, for which they are apparently fully liable. For example, Alphonso remarks that in Gascony and Dauphiné there are great numbers of these perverse women who say that they assemble at night in a deserted place "where there is a boar on a rock which is commonly called 'el Boch de Biterne,' and that they meet there with lighted candles and adore the boar, kissing him on his anus."[69] For this, he continues, many had been arrested by the inquisition and burned – there was even a painting commemorating the event in the house of the inquisitor of Toulouse, which Spina had personally admired.

Alphonso de Spina gave the delusions of night-traveling women their greatest practical significance. It was, in his view, no longer sufficient simply to condemn as superstitious those who believed that their dreams were real; the dreams themselves were criminal and deserved severe punishment. It is difficult to see, however, how such a model of witchcraft could be especially threatening to the populace at large, since no matter how much these heretics were responsible for their fantasies, they were still just fantasies, and not the cause of real harm. Furthermore, witchcraft so defined could neither be separated from notions about nor the persons of the women who believed that they rode with the *bonae res*, and there is no indication that medieval people in general found either particularly threatening or bothersome.

The experience of Nicholas of Cusa, the great reformer and theologian, provides a case in point. In 1457, while traveling through the French Alps, he met two old women who had been imprisoned for witchcraft and threatened with the stake. They told him that they were in the service of Domina Abundia, and went with her to revels where there was laughing, dancing, and celebrations, and where hairy wild men devoured unbaptized children. By their own admission these women were apostate Christians, since they had vowed themselves to "Richella" in return for good fortune and had promised to abstain from all Christian observances. Nicholas at once recognized that these women had been deceived by the devil in their dreams, and that, although grievous sinners, they were not *maleficae*. In the Lenten sermon in which he gives this account, he concludes that sometimes the devil

> deludes some old and infatuated woman, and leads her on so that she is captured and tortured as a witch, and God permits this on account of her sins, and then very great evils follow, because of the death of an innocent. Therefore beware, lest wanting so much to be rid of evil, yet more evil is garnered.[70]

Accordingly, Nicholas arranged for these "decrepit and delirious" women to receive penances and be released. Their dreams, no matter how bizarre, did no real harm; the women were not, therefore, *maleficae*, and so their persecution was both pointless and wrong. It is true that they had made an unholy bargain with the devil, but they had been tricked into doing so, and were, in

any case, less than fully culpable by reason of their age, poverty, gross ignorance, and failing mental health.

Despite their differences, Alphonso de Spina and Nicholas of Cusa both
accepted an essentially conservative and traditional view of witchcraft, in
which the experiences of women who followed the *bonae res* were basically
imaginary. For others, this kind of faith in ecclesiastical tradition seemed no
longer possible. Alonso de Madrigal, bishop of Ávila, was one prominent
churchman whose initial stance of traditional skepticism was shaken, and
finally demolished, by the weight of circumstantial evidence. In his *Commentary on Genesis* (c. 1436), Alonso had remarked that in his region of Spain there
were women who through certain superstitious observances and unguents
believed themselves transported to sumptuous feasts in distant places.[71] Upon
investigation, however, it was determined that while these women thought
they were abroad, they were really lying motionless in a stupor, completely
insensible of their actual surroundings and conscious of neither words, nor
heavy blows, nor even burns. Thus, their journeys were nothing but the deceits
of the devil. Several years later, in his *Commentary on Matthew* (c. 1440), Alonso
had completely changed his mind. He now maintained

> that what is said of certain women who run about through many places at night
> is true. For this has often been discovered and judicially punished. And some,
> wanting to imitate their infamous ceremonies, have incurred great distress. Nor
> can it be said that this happens in sleep, since not only those who have them-
> selves undergone this, but many others, too, have testified to this thing. Nor is
> there any reason that this should be doubted, though it is true that among the
> simple much that is false has been mixed up with some truth, because demons
> desire to do harm not only to morals, but also to faith.[72]

In this passage, Alonso tries explicitly to convince his readers that his dramatic
about face was justified, and that women really do fly through the air at night.
Like Gervaise of Tilbury, his newfound credulity rested upon the value of testimony and personal experience, which had finally become too compelling for
him to dismiss. For example, although he acknowledges that there are theological arguments to the contrary, he argues that demons have the power to
carry people from place to place since "this is so manifest, that it would be
imprudent to deny it, when we have met a thousand witnesses who have been
made aware of this."[73] Rather than dismiss the unanimous verdict of so many
witnesses, it was now easier for Alonso to revise the meaning of the canon
itself, such that it now forbade only the belief that women rode with Diana
and similar spirits, and not belief in the night ride itself.

For many other witch-theorists, such a deliberate misreading of the
canon was just as unacceptable as was complete skepticism, which created a

serious problem for those more inclined to consider arguments on both sides of the issue. Around 1460, in a treatise dedicated to Francesco Sforza, the Dominican theologian Girolamo Visconti took time to ponder whether "lamias, which the vulgar call strias" go to the *ludus* in fact or in imagination only.[74] As he had encountered it, witchcraft was a composite of beliefs drawn from popular traditions, *maleficia*, and demonic heresy, although the various parts of this whole were so poorly integrated in his mind that he never quite convinces himself, or his readers, of its objective reality. Witches go to their assemblies, or *ludi*, riding on broomsticks or demons in the shape of wolves; they do this for base, material motives, in order to gain money, revenge, or success in love; once there, they adore the "lady of the game" as a goddess, kill baptized infants, work black magic, and feast upon oxen which their mistress then magically restores to life.[75] To determine how much of this is real, Visconti marshals evidence and arguments, both for and against. On one side there is the testimony of the accused witches themselves and of witnesses who have seen these women abroad, the evidence of undeniable magical harm, and the undoubted power of the devil to do marvelous things. On the other, there is the testimony of canonical authorities and numerous respected churchmen, the fact that the women can be seen sleeping even while they claim to be riding at night, and the incredible nature of their claims.

Visconti's solution is interesting. The evidence of authority, and of the physical bodies of sleeping women, is irrefutable, and such "witches" do not really go to the *ludus*, rather, they, and those who think that they see them, are deceived by the devil. At the same time, because demons have the power to transport people from place to place at fantastic speeds, and because theologians are agreed that incubi and succubi are real, it is *possible* that women might attend these nocturnal assemblies and mingle physically with demons, "because, following logic, many things are possible, which are nonetheless false."[76] This is an extremely half-hearted endorsement of the canon *Episcopi*, but Visconti will not go further. He does not seem able to reject the validity of the canon out of hand, because his understanding of witchcraft is so firmly rooted in testimony and narratives concerning the *bonae res* and their followers, as his "witches" are still recognizably the same as the women condemned by the canon. Nonetheless, despite Girolamo's reluctance to do away with the canon completely, he provides the intellectual basis for that move, for once the reality of the Sabbat was accepted as a possibility, a sufficient quantity of circumstantial evidence would establish it as fact.

The crux of the problem was the power of the devil: did he give substance to the claims of alleged night-travelers, or merely defraud their minds and senses? Confusion on this score was nothing new. Back in the thirteenth century, in another of Stephen of Bourbon's stories, a priest was invited out for a ride with the *bonae res*, and rode a wooden beam to a great feast attended by many beautiful people. When he made the sign of the cross, the glorious party vanished, and the naked priest was discovered in the wine cellar of a local lord and narrowly avoided being hanged as a thief.[77] Stephen's expressed purpose was to mock superstitious belief, but this same *exemplum* could also demonstrate the real power of the devil to transport people invisibly into locked rooms while at the same time deceiving their senses. In other words, Stephen's narrative made exactly the same point as did Girolamo Visconti: such things are possible, even if they do not usually happen.[78]

Around 1470 the Dominican theologian Jordanes de Bergamo took Girolamo's argument to its logical conclusion in his *Questio de Strigis*.[79] "*Strigae* or *strigones*,", he writes, are "men and women who run about at night over long distances or enter houses by the power of demons, who also are said to bewitch children."[80] Once again, this conception of witchcraft centers around the companies of night-traveling women, and so, like Girolamo, Jordanes must address the problem of the canon *Episcopi* head on. His solution is simple: where the canon specifically forbids belief, in animal transformations for example, the devil accomplishes this through illusions; in all other cases, witches may do things in reality or in their dreams, depending upon the mood of the devil. Thus, when baleful *strigae* suck the blood of children at night, this may be the devil acting in some woman's stead, or it may be the woman herself, transported and otherwise abetted by Satan.

This "half-a-loaf" approach to witchcraft, in which, as Jordanes remarks, "some things pertaining to witches should be rejected from the hearts of the faithful, while some, in fact, should be firmly held," satisfied apparently no one else.[81] In particular the issue of *maleficium* proper was entirely peripheral to the subject of *strigae*, and for this reason his witches continued to resemble evil, heretical, fairies – the *lamiae* of Gervaise of Tilbury's and Stephen of Bourbon's *exempla* made real – more than they did the maleficial witches of the *Malleus*.

Elsewhere, definitions of witchcraft took rather different directions and the whole issue of the *bonae res* and the canon remained of secondary importance. North of the Alps, especially, writers were on the whole disinclined to attach the label "witch" to the woman who rode with the *bonae res*, and accordingly interpreted their beliefs in a more traditional manner. Nider's *Formicarius*, for example, a text which would remain one of the definitive sources for information about witchcraft throughout the fifteenth century, treated the women who believed they rode with Diana traditionally. One of his teachers, Nider recalls, had told him of a woman who could not be cured of her superstitious beliefs until a Dominican persuaded her to let him, along with several others, witness her flight.[82] When the moment came, she put a large bowl on a table, seated herself in it, and began to apply a salve to her body while saying an evil charm. She fell at once into a deep sleep, in which she thrashed so violently that she fell from the table and hit her head. When she awoke she claimed to have been out with Venus, but the protestations of the witnesses finally convinced her of her error. Nider complements this account with other details of medieval traditional lore. He tells the well-known incident from the life of St. Germanus, in which the saint found lodging at a house where peasants had set out a feast in expectation of a visit by the Good Women of the night. Germanus stayed up to keep watch, and was not surprised when a horde of demons in the likeness of women entered the house, sat down at the table, and began to eat.[83] Through these stories, Nider makes the point that while demons are responsible for belief in Diana, Venus, and the Good Women, those who believe in these things are not themselves demonic, merely superstitious, stupid, and rather silly. They do not kill babies, cause storms, ride on wolves or assume animal form; instead, these are all characteristics that Nider associates with heretical *malefici*.

Institoris and Sprenger generally concurred. In the *Malleus*, they argue that it is necessary to distinguish clearly between the women described in the canon *Episcopi* and "real witches," who committed real crimes and knowingly devoted themselves to the devil.[84] Where, however, Nicholas of Cusa and his like could use this distinction to exculpate accused witches, for Institoris and Sprenger the canon *Episcopi* describes a virtually empty set: they have no personal experience of such women, and seem to feel it rather unlikely that they would ever meet them. If a woman was found who superficially resembled those discussed in the canon, she would doubtless fall within their expansive parameters of witch proper.

Nonetheless, Institoris and Sprenger incorporated many of the characteristics of the malign cousins of the less savory night spirits into their own conception of witches. Night flight, for example, was one of the definitive characteristics of both the *lamiae* and the *bonae res*, and does not seem to have been much associated with traditional representations of *malefici*. The *Malleus*, however, routinely describes witches as having the power of flight. The authors explain that when witches want to fly, they take an unguent made from the limbs of slaughtered children and smear it over a chair or some other piece of wood, at which signal an invisible devil will come and bear them away.[85] Sometimes, Institoris and Sprenger admit, the devil actually appeared in the form of an animal to carry the witch, but he far preferred her to fly by means of the magical salve so that more children might be killed before baptism. In this way, the authors brought the witch's infanticide – another of the *lamia*'s most obvious characteristics – alongside her powers of flight to form a new, logical whole. They created a fusion of the *lamiae* with the *malefica* which effectively replaced earlier conceptions of malign female spirits while remaining fully compatible with them.

For this reason, Institoris and Sprenger can support this interpretation with narratives that closely resemble those that had been told about *lamiae* and their kin. They relate that in the same year that their book was begun, in the city of Speyer, a pair of women had words which escalated, *more muliercularum*, into an abusive quarrel.[86] Since one of the women was rumored to be a witch, the other went home fearing for her newborn child and scattered blessed herbs, consecrated salt, and holy water around his cradle. Her fears were warranted, because in the middle of the night she heard her son whimpering, and when she went to comfort him, she found his cradle empty. Weeping for the loss of her son, the poor woman lit a candle, and was relieved to find the baby under a table in a corner, sniffling but unharmed. That the witch was unable to do more than this, Institoris and Sprenger attribute to the mother's good sense and prompt deployment of sacramental defenses. It is impossible to tell whether the authors have reworked this very traditional account of the depredations of *lamiae* to fit their ideas about witchcraft, or whether such stories were beginning to influence the discourse of village magic.[87] In either case, the story illustrates how a clear occasion for *maleficia* – a mundane quarrel between two women, one with reputed malign occult powers – could evoke a much more monstrous and diabolical conception of witchcraft.

Similarly, Institoris and Sprenger incorporated the trance-like dream state of women who ride with the *bonae res* into their image of the witch. They had once asked a women whether witches could travel in their imaginations, through illusion, or bodily, and she had replied that both ways were possible. When they wanted to go to the assembly of witches, either a devil could transport them, or, if that were inconvenient, they could invoke the devil and go to sleep; a bluish vapor would then proceed from their mouths by which they were clearly aware of everything that was done there.[88] Again, this narrative does not appear grounded in learned conventions (the mist issuing from a sleeper's mouth is too obviously suggestive of the soul leaving the body), but in a more popular representation of the dream trance. Nonetheless, it fits Institoris and Sprenger's purposes well, since it makes clear that it is the witch herself, more than any devil, who is responsible for her dreams. In the *Malleus*, when a witch dreams of the Sabbat, she does so accurately, as a valid, if still inferior, substitute for her actual presence at the event.

In this way, Institoris and Sprenger transformed the motifs of folk traditions into substantial truths about witchcraft. All that the canon *Episcopi* and Burchard of Worms held to be delusions, they found to be the awful truth. All evidence to the contrary was either irrelevant, because it did not apply to witches, or it was erroneous. Sometimes it was both. For example, the popular stories of obviously slumbering women who claimed to fly at night might either refer to stupid, deluded women who were not witches, or to witches who were actually abroad at night, while demons assumed their forms in their husbands' beds.[89] Thus, where Alphonso de Spina's devil made dreaming women invisible in order that his deceits might appear more real, the devil in the *Malleus* used his illusions to conceal the reality of their absence. Similarly, perceptions of the *bonae res* merely masked the real presence of demons or witches:

> There was an error arising from the demons of the night or, as old women say, *die seligen* [the fairies], but who are witches or demons in the form of witches, have to consume everything so that afterwards they may give back more abundantly.[90]

This substitution of witches for demons blurred the stark division between the diabolic fantasies of the canon and the diabolic "realities" of the *Malleus* such that fairy beliefs could be interpreted as just one more manifestation of witchcraft. Institoris and Sprenger could do this because they embraced a concept of the witch that was simultaneously concrete and diabolic, able to incorporate both dreaming old women and the devils from whom their dreams came. In this way, Institoris and Sprenger functionally legislated the superstitious women of the canon, along with their fantasies, out of existence, to be replaced in their entirety by the shockingly real presence of the witch.

Notes

1 "Quid ergo dicimus de mulieribus, quae confitentur nocturno tempore ambulare per longa locorum intervalla in momento temporis, et intrare cameras alienas clausas, coadiuvantibus earum magistris daemonibus (ut dicunt), cum quibus loquuntur, quibus praestant censum, et cum quibus (ut dicunt) habent copulam carnalem, et quibus persuadentibus (ut dicunt) abnegant deum et virginem Mariam, et cum pedibus conculcant sanctam crucem, et quae daemonibus coadiuvantibus (ut dicunt) interficiunt pueros et interficiunt homines, et faciunt eos cadere in infirmitates diversas, et quae dicunt se multa his similia facere, et aliquando se transformare in formam muscipulae, et diabolum dicunt se aliquando transformare in formam canis, vel alterius animalis? An haec et his similia sint possibilia, vel versimilia, vel credenda?" Ambrosius de Vignati, *Tractatus de Haereticis*, in Hansen, *Quellen*, 216.

2 *Ibid.*, 225.

3 See Clifford Geertz, "Religion as a Cultural System," in Geertz, *The Interpretation of Cultures* (New York: Basic Books, 1973), 100–1.

4 The Dominican Order accepted St. Thomas as their definitive theologian in 1329. Hinnebusch, 2:159.

5 Heiko Oberman, "*Via Antiqua and Via Moderna*: Late Medieval Prolegomena to Reformation Thought," *Journal of the History of Ideas* 48 (1987): 23–40.

6 *Ibid.*, 28.

7 Author's italics. Heiko Oberman, "Fourteenth Century Religious Thought: A Premature Profile," in Oberman, *The Dawn of the Reformation*, 6.

8 Thomas Aquinas, *Summa Theologiae*, qu. 87, arts. 6 and 8.

9 See Scot MacDonald, "Theory of Knowledge," in Norman Kretzmann and Eleanor Stump, eds., *The Cambridge Companion to Aquinas* (Cambridge: Cambridge University Press, 1993), 160–95; 185.

10 *Ibid.*, 170–85; see also Aquinas, *Summa Theologiae*, qu. 85, art. 6.

11 Aquinas, *Summa Theologiae*, pt. 1, qu. 51, art. 3, quoting Augustine, *City of God*, 15.23. See also the *Malleus*, pt. 1, qu. 3.

12 "Omnis enim acceptio, quae firmatur sensu, melior est quam illa quae sensui contradicit, et conclusio, quae sensui contradicit, est incredibilis." Albertus Magnus, *Physica*, lib. 8, tract. 2, c. 2, in *Opera Omnia*, ed. Paulus Hossfeld (Aschendorf: Monasterium Westfalorum, 1993), vol. 4, pt. 2, p. 587; cf. Hinnebusch, 2:127.

13 "Ad quartum dicendum, quod in theologia locus ab auctoritate est locus ab inspiratione spiritus veritatis. Unde Augustinus . . . In aliis autem scientiis locus ab auctoritate infirmus est et infirmior ceteris, quia perspicacitati humani ingenii innititur, quae fallibilis est." Albertus Magnus, *Summa Theologiae* tract. 1, qu. 5, ch. 2, in *Opera Omnia*, ed. Dionysius Siedler *et al.* (Aschendorf: Monasterium Westfalorum, 1978), 18; cf. Hinnebusch, 2:127.

14 "Quis tam stolidus vt propterea omnia eorum maleficia et nocumenta esse fantastica et imaginaria affirmaret cum ad sensum omnibus appareat contrarium." *Malleus*, pt. 2, qu. 1, ch. 3, p. 105.

15 Kvideland and Sehmsdorf, 9.

16 "ubi fama volabat quod quedam mulier sepulta lintheamen in quo sepulta erat successiue deglutiret et quod pestis cessare non posset nisi ex integro lintheamen deglutiendo ad ventrem consumpsisset." *Malleus*, pt. 1, qu. 15, p. 75.

17 Similar stories were told by Saxo Grammaticus and William of Newburgh; for discussion of the medieval ghost in folk and clerical traditions, see Claude Lecouteux, *Geschichte der Gespenster und Wiedergänger im Mittelalter* (Cologne: Böhlau Verlag, 1987), and Jean-Claude Schmitt, *Les Revenants* (Paris: Gallimard, 1994).

18 Women with reputations for malign occult powers were notoriously restless after death; for the best known example see the tale of the witch of Berkeley in William of Malmesbury, *De Gestis Regum Anglorum*, ed. William Stubbs (London: Longmans, Green, Reader and Dyer, 1887–89), 1:253–5.

19 "Nam ex effectibus deuenit in cognitionem cause." *Malleus*, pt. 1, qu. 5, p. 36.

20 "[Ex quibus elicitur quod] virtus corporalis hominis ad huiusmodi opera causanda non se extendere potest que semper hoc habet ut causa cum suo effectu naturali nota sit naturaliter absque admiratione." *Ibid.* In a fine example of the application of scholastic exclusionary categories to practical problems, Institoris and Sprenger explain that if a man could be found who did have the power to create such marvels, he could not really be called a "man" at all. Of course, if this being were not a man, he must necessarily be either a devil or an angel, since these are the only rational beings in creation. See *ibid.*, pt. 2, qu. 2, ch. 8, p. 183.

21 "et quidem in contrarium in argumenta deducere non expedit cum ipsa experientia preter verborum et fidedignorum testimonia talia facit credibilia." *Ibid.*, pt. 1, qu. 6, p. 40.

22 "Constant ergo omnia aut visus vel auditus propria experientia aut fide dignorum relatibus." *Ibid.*, pt. 2, qu. 1, ch. 4, p. 108.

23 "Nulli dubium quin malefice quedam mira operantur circa membra virilia vt ex visis et auditis plurimorum imo et ex ipsa publica fama constat." *Ibid.*, pt. 1, qu. 9, p. 56.

24 As is true of all supra-normal encounters. See Lauri Honko, "Memorates and the Study of Folk Belief," in Reimund Kvideland and Henning K. Sehmsdorf, eds., *Nordic Folklore* (Bloomington: Indiana University Press, 1989), 100–9.

25 *Kommentar*, 351–408. Although approximately four fifths of these are drawn from literary sources, in comparison with contemporary texts using comparable numbers of

exempla, Institoris and Sprenger include an extraordinarily high number of narratives drawn from their personal experience.

26 "Quare et merito concluditur praefata remedia contra huiusmodi morbum esse certissima ita quod certissime ita liberantur quicumque his armis vtuntur. *Malleus*, pt. 2, qu. 2, ch. 3, p. 165.

27 *Ibid.*, pt. 2, qu. 1, p. 88.

28 Similarly in the nineteenth century, J. Lecœur reported that when peasants in the Bocage began to suspect that their misfortunes were due to witchcraft, "They worry, they mull it over, and look at what is happening around them with distrust. The talk continues; soon one name is mysteriously on everyone's lips." *Esquisses du bocage normand* (Condé-sur-Noireau, 1887), 2:38; cited in Judith Devlin, *The Superstitious Mind: French Peasants and the Supernatural in the Nineteenth Century* (New Haven: Yale University Press, 1987), 102.

29 This procedure, the *diffamatio*, was not unique to inquisitorial investigations of witchcraft. When an inquisitor suspected the presence of heretics but denunciations were not forthcoming, he could require persons generally acknowledged to be respectable and trustworthy to denounce those who failed to live as good Catholics. A.S. Turberville, *Medieval Heresy and the Inquisition* (1920; reprint, London: Archon Books, 1964), 142–3, 190–1.

30 "Ad aures talis officialis aut iudicis talis loci pervenit pluries fama publica referente ac clamosa insinuatione producente quod talis de tali loco dixit vel fecit talia ad maleficia pertinentia contra fidem ac communem vtilitatem reipublice." *Malleus*, pt. 3, qu. 1, p. 196.

31 "diffamata insuper plurimum super mortem cuiusdam militis Spiess et hoc nedum in Ysbruck sed et circumquaque per vicinas terras et presertim apud nobiles et potentes. An autem toxico vel maleficio ipsum interemit, manet sub dubio, communiter tamen famatur, quod maleficio eo quod a iuventute maleficiis servivit." Ammann, 39.

32 See David Gentilcore, 243–4.

33 For example Robin Briggs, *Witches and Neighbors: The Social and Cultural Context of European Witchcraft* (New York: Viking, 1996), 398.

34 Georgina Boyce, "Belief and Disbelief: An Examination of Reactions to the Presentation of Rumor Legends," in Paul Smith, ed., *Perspectives on Contemporary Legend* (Sheffield: CECTAL Conference Papers Series no. 4, 1984), 64–78; 75.

35 Gorden W. Allport and Leo Postman, *The Psychology of Rumor* (New York: Henry Holt, 1947), 52.

36 Jeanne Favret-Saada, *Deadly Words: Witchcraft in the Bocage*, trans. Catherine Cullen (Cambridge: Cambridge University Press, 1980), 9 and *passim*. Modern American Satanism "experts" offer a similar and in many ways more exact parallel. See Linda Dégh, "Satanic Child Abuse in a Blue House," in Linda Dégh, *Narratives in Society: A Performance-Centered Study of Narration*, Folklore Fellows Communication 255 (Helsinki: Academia Scientiarum Fennica, 1995), 358–68.

37 Dégh, 360–3. See also Allport and Postman, 34 and 36.

38 Edwin Ardener, "Social Anthropology, Language and Reality," in *Semantic Anthropology*, ASA monograph 22 (London: Academic Press, 1982): 1–14; 8.

39 See also Donald P. Spence, "The Mythic Properties of Popular Explanations," in Joseph de Rivera and Theodore Sarbin, eds., *Believed-In Imaginings: The Narrative Construction of Reality* (Washington, D.C.: APA, 1998): 217–28.

40 Neither this method nor this insight is my own, and the following discussion owes an obvious debt especially to Norman Cohn and Joseph Hansen. See also Cohn, *Europe's Inner Demons* (New York: Basic Books, 1975), Richard Kieckhefer, *Magic in the Middle Ages* (Cambridge: Cambridge University Press, 1989), and Andreas Blauert, *Frühe Hexenverfolgungen* (Hamburg: Junius, 1989).

41 Regino of Prüm, *De Ecclesiasticis Disciplinis*, ii, c. 364, *Patrologia Latina* 132, 352.

42 Burchard of Worms, *Decreta*, xix, *Patrologia Latina* 140, 963. For English translation see John T. McNeill and Helena M. Gamer, trans., *Medieval Handbooks of Penance* (New York: Columbia University Press, 1938).

43 Contra Carlo Ginzburg, who posits the existence of an inclusive "mythic complex," based loosely upon the models provided by Eurasian shamanism. See Ginzburg, "Deciphering the Sabbath," trans. Paul Falla, in Bengt Ankarloo and Gustav Henningsen, eds., *Early Modern European Witchcraft* (Oxford: Clarendon, 1990): 121–37; however, see also Robert Muchembled, "Satanic Myths and Cultural Reality," in Ankarloo and Henningsen, 139–60; Wolfgang Behringer, *Chonrad Stoekhlin und die Nachtschar* (Munich: Piper, 1994); and Claude Lecouteux, *Fées, sorcières et loups-garous au Moyen Âge: histoire du double* (Paris: Imago, 1992).

44 A genuinely persuasive interpretation of the evidence for a medieval cult of Diana (or whomever) is difficult to find; see, however, Flint, 122–5; Duerr, 15; Carlo Ginzburg, *The Night Battles*, trans. John and Anne Tedeschi (Baltimore: The Johns Hopkins University Press, 1992), 40–50, and *Ecstasies: Deciphering the Witches' Sabbath*, trans. Raymond Rosenthal (New York: Pantheon Books, 1991), 89–121; Cohn, *Europe's Inner Demons*, 210–24.

45 William of Paris, 1066.

46 Burchard of Worms, 971.

47 Guillaume de Lorris and Jean de Meun, *The Romance of the Rose*, trans. Charles Dahlberg (Hanover: University Press of New England, 1971), lines 18411–60, 305–6.

48 "[Sequitur quinto,] quod christiano permaxime fugiendum est, ne fidem adhibeat huic, quod vetule referunt in nativitatibus hominum quasdam deas venire et necessitatem geniti proli imponere fortunium aut infortunium, suspendium, occisionem gladialem aut dignitatem magnificam vel consimile prenunciare, que necessario eveniant. [Unde eciam si quis submergatur aut suspendatur, dicunt consolatorie se exhortantes tales necessario tamquam prenunciatum evenisse.] Et quidem si puer nascitur in pellicula, dicunt ipsum esse de illis, qui magna spacia in una nocte per transeunt, vulgariter 'die farn leude' etc. Denique homines in hanc labuntur demenciam, ut cultum soli deo debitum ipsis, qui vere demones sunt, exhibeant quosque largitores bonorum false existimant. Sic eciam quidam faciunt in quintis feriis Quatuor temporum et in nocte precedenti quarte ferie Cinerum." John of Frankfurt, *Questio, utrum potestas cohercendi demones . . .* in Hansen, *Quellen*, 76.

49 For the medieval cult of the fairies, see Gustav Henningsen, " 'The Ladies from the Outside': An Archaic Pattern of the Witches' Sabbath," in Ankarloo and Henningsen, 191–215; for the European fairy cult generally, see Éva Pócs, *Fairies and Witches at the Boundary of South-Eastern and Central Europe*, Folklore Fellows Communication 243 (Helsinki: Academia Scientiarum Fennica, 1989), and Briggs, *The Vanishing People*.

50 This belief is also found in Burchard, who refers to the women concerned simply as "Fates" (*parcae*). *Corrector, Patrologia Latina* 140, 971.

51 Étienne de Bourbon, *Anecdotes historiques*, ed. A. Lecoy de la Marche (Paris: Librairie Renouard, 1877), *exempla* 368–9. Stephen uses the word to distinguish the good women of the night from the evil *strigae*.

52 Ginzburg, *The Night Battles*, 44–55.

53 Cited in Lea, *Materials*, 1:112; the etymology is from Isidore; Gregory the Great describes the *lamia* with a human face and a bestial body as a metaphor for heresy and for hypocrites (*Magna Moralia*, in Lea, 1:110–11). It is worth noting that Johannes' contemporary, Albertus Magnus, gave a far more prosaic description of the *lamia*: "an enormous fierce animal which emerges from the forest at night and skulks into orchards where it slashes and uproots trees." Albertus Magnus, *De Animalibus*, trans. James J. Scanlan (Binghamton: Medieval and Renaissance Texts and Studies, 1987), 22.112, p. 155.

54 For a discussion of Roman literary witches, see Eugene Tavenner, "Canidia and Other Witches," reprinted in *Witchcraft in the Ancient World and Middle Ages*, ed. Brian Levack (New York: Garland Publishers, 1992), 2:14–39; and Baroja, *The World of the Witches*, 17–40.

55 "Idem et eodem modo sentiendum est tibi de aliis malignis spiritibus, quas vulgus stryges et lamias vocant, et apparent de nocte in domidus in quibus parvuli notriuntur, eosque de cunabulis raptos laniare, vel igne assare videntur. Apparent autem in specie vetularum videlicet, quae nec vere vetulae sunt, nec vere pueros devorare."William of Paris, 1066.

56 "Credidisti quod multae mulieres retro Satanam conversae credunt et affirmant verum esse, ut credas inquietae noctis silentio cum te collocaveris in lecto tuo, et marito tuo in sinu tuo jacente, te dum corporea sis januis clausis exire posse, et terrarum spacia cum aliis simili errore deceptis pertransire valere, et homines baptizatos, et Christi sanguine redemptos, sine armis visibilibus et interficere, et decoctis carnibus eorum vos comedere, et in loco cordis eorum stramen aut lignum, aut aliquod huiusmodi ponere, et commestis, iterum vivos facere, et inducias vivendi dare?" Burchard, 973. See also Katharine Morris, *Sorceress or Witch? The Image of Gender in Medieval Iceland and Northern Europe* (Lanham: University Press of America, 1991), 160–2.

57 Gervaise ofTilbury, *Otia Imperialia*, ed. Felix Liebrecht (Hanover: Carl Rümpler, 1856), c. 93, p. 45.

58 *Ibid.*, c. 86, pp. 39–40.

59 *Ibid.*, c. 93, pp. 45–46.

60 See Edgar A. List, "Holda and the Venusberg," *Journal of American Folklore* 73 (1960): 307–11 and "Is Frau Holda the Virgin Mary?" *German Quarterly* 32 (1953): 80–4.

61 Duerr, 169, n. 29, citing the *Handwörterbuch des deutschen Aberglaubens*, c. 1314. The gloss on the *Lex Salica* gives *fara* or "the one who goes" for *striga*, which may also suggest an early association of nocturnal witches with night-traveling women.

62 "Quare est quod noticulam quamdam vel Herodiadem vel praesidem noctis dominam concilia et conventus de nocte asserunt convocare, varia celebrari convivia, ministeriorum species diversis occupationibus exerceri, et nunc istos ad poenam trahi promeritis, nunc illos ad gloriam sublimari. Praeterea infantes exponi lamiis, et nunc frustatim discerptos, edaci ingluvie in ventrem trajectos congeri, nunc praesidentis miseratione rejectos in cunas reponi." John of Salisbury, *Polycraticus, sive de Nugis Curialium et Vestigiis Philosophorum*, 2.17, cited in Lea, *Materials*, 1:172–3. John firmly believed that no educated person should give credence to such "empty and senseless falsehoods."

63 "Unde quaedam mulierculae inseruientes Satanae, daemonum illusionibus seductae, credunt et profitentur nocturnis horis cum Diana Paganorum Dea, vel Venere, in magna mulierum multitudine equitare, et alia nephanda agere, puta paruulos a lacte matris auellere, assare, et comedere, domus per caminos seu fenestras intrare, et habitantes variis modis inquietare, quae omnia et consimilia solum fantastice accidunt eis." Martin of Arles, 363.

64 *Ibid.*

65 Cohn, *Europe's Inner Demons*, 205. One must admit, though, that there is an element of circular reasoning in this argument since the notion that women assembled in vast throngs at night was surely drawn from the traditions of the *bona res* and company to begin with.

66 Compare the experiences of Nicholas of Cusa, below.

67 Alphonso de Spina (c. 1420–91) was a baptized Jew who became a Franciscan theologian at Salamanca, the confessor of King John II of Castile, and bishop of Orense. Compare Hansen, *Quellen*, 145.

68 "Veritas autem huius facti est quod quando iste male persone volunt uti his pessimis fictionibus consecrate se cum verbis et unctioribus diabolo, et statim dyabolos recipit eos in opere suo et accipit figuram earum et fantasiam cuiuslibet earum ducitque illas per

illa loca per que desiderabant corpora vero earum remanent sine aliqua sensibilitate et cooperit illa dyabolus umbra sua ita quod nullus illa videre possit, et cum dyabolus videt in fantasiis earum quod impleuerant que volebant non amouendo ad [*sic*] earum fantasiis diabolicas fantasias que viderunt reducit illas imaginationes coniungens cum suis propriis motibus et corporibus." Alphonso de Spina, consid. 10.

69 "ubi est aper quidam in rupe qui vulgariter dicitur el boch de biterne et quod ibi conueniunt cum candelis accensis et adorant illum aprum osculantes eum in ano suo." *Ibid.*

70 "Et ideo infatuatam mulierem aliquam vetulam deludit, et ducit ut quasi malefica capiatur et trucidetur, et deus permittit ob peccata ista, et tunc sequuntur maxima mala ob mortem innocentis sanguinis. Ideo cauendum est valde ne volendo malum eiicere: malum accumuletur." Nicholas of Cusa, IX, fol. clxxii, "Haec omnia tibi dabo."

71 Alphons Madrigal Tostatus, *Commentary on Genesis*, Hansen, *Quellen*, 109, n. 1.

72 "Quod dicitur de mulieribus, quae per noctem discurrunt per diversa loca, etiam verum est. Nam saepe hoc inventum est et iudicialiter punitum. Et aliqui volentes imitari earum nefandas caeremonias, magna incommoda incurrerunt. Nec potest dici illud per somnium accidere, cum non solum ipsi, qui passi sunt, sed etiam plures alii huius rei testes erant. Nec est aliqua causa de his dubitandi. Verum est autem, quod apud simplices aliquibus veris multa falsa circa haec admixta sunt, quia daemones non solum in moribus, sed etiam in fide nocere cupiunt." *Commentary on Matthew*, qu. 47, Hansen, *Quellen*, 107.

73 "Et istud ita manifestum est, quod imprudentia sit, illud negare, cum mille nobis testes occurrant, qui sibi horum conscii sunt." Hansen, *Quellen*, 106.

74 "Utrum lamie que uulgari nomine strie nuncupantur vere et non fantastice siue apparenter ad ludum eant." Girolamo Visconti, *Lamiarum sive Striarum Opuscula* (Milan: Leonardo Pachel, 1490), a ii. Visconti was a professor of logic at the University of Milan, and later Domincan Provincial of Lombardy, a position he probably held until his death in 1477. See Hansen, *Quellen*, 200–1.

75 Girolamo Visconti is unusual in his insistence that the devil and his allies killed only baptized infants. His conclusion, which is very typical of his thinking, is that divine justice normally allows only baptized Christians to be killed because such children are led immediately to heaven. When, on occasion, an unbaptized child is slain, then doubtless he was destined for a life of sin, in which case the limbo of children is a better alternative to hell. Visconti, b. iii.

76 "Quia secundum logicos multa sunt possibilia, que tamen sunt falsa." *Ibid.*, a viii.

77 Étienne de Bourbon, 97. The same principle lies behind a story of William of Paris, in which a man thinks that he is attending a feast in glorious castle, attended by beautiful women, but awakes to find himself in a puddle embracing mud. William of Paris, 1065.

78 Because Stephen is writing moral *exempla*, and not a theoretical treatise, logical contradictions trouble him little, if at all. In later stories, he states the contrary position, that women cannot magically enter locked rooms at night, and one suspects that this would be his considered opinion. Étienne de Bourbon, 368 and 369.

79 Hansen, *Quellen*, 195–200.

80 "Apud fere omnes per strigas sive strigones intelliguntur mulieres aut viri, qui de nocte sive domos aut per longa spatia virtute demonis discurrunt, qui etiam parvulos fascinare dicuntur." *Ibid.*, 196.

81 "Aliqua quidem abicienda sunt de ipsis strigis a cordibus fidelium, nonnulla vero firmiter sunt tenenda." *Ibid.*, 200.

82 Nider, *Formicarius*, 2.4, 71.

83 *Ibid.*, 72.

84 *Malleus*, pt. 1, qu. 1, p. 10. This is also the tack chosen by Ulrich Molitor, who devotes the ninth chapter of his witch-treatise to the problem of whether women really go to the feast at night, or whether this occurs only in dreams. He cites the usual authorities

and pronounces the whole affair nothing but a delusion of the devil. As in the *Formicar-ius*, though, these beliefs are not really central to his concept of witchcraft. See Molitor, 705–8.

85 *Malleus*, pt. 2, qu. 1, ch. 3, p. 104.

86 *Ibid.*, pt. 2, qu. 1, p. 88.

87 Gervaise of Tilbury, for example, had told an almost identical story about lamiae over two hundred years earlier; see 3.86, 40. The tale can also be found in modern German folklore: see no. 89, "Watching Out for the Child," in Jacob Grimm, *The German Legends of the Brothers Grimm*, ed. and trans. Donald Ward, 2 vols. (Philadelphia: Institute for the Study of Human Issues, 1981), 1:99.

88 "Ex tunc quasi vapor quidam glaucus ex eius ore praecederet, unde singula que ibi agerentur perlucide consideraret." *Malleus*, pt. 2, qu. 1.3, p. 105.

89 *Ibid.*

90 "Error erat vt venientes de nocte demonibus aut vt vetule dicunt die seligen sed sunt malefice vel demones in earum effigiis debent omnia consumere vt post abundantius tribuant." *Ibid.*, pt. 2, qu. 2, ch. 8, p. 183.

6

Witchcraft:
the formation of belief
– part two

In the previous chapter we examined how motifs drawn from traditional beliefs
about spectral night-traveling women informed the construction of learned
witch categories in the late Middle Ages. Although the precise manner in which
these motifs were utilized differed between authorities, two general mental
habits set off fifteenth-century witch-theorists from earlier writers. First, they
elided the distinctions between previously discrete sets of beliefs to create a
substantially new category ("witch," variously defined), with which to carry
out subsequent analysis. Second, they increasingly insisted upon the objective
reality of their conceptions of witchcraft. In this chapter we take up a rather
different set of ideas, all of which, from the clerical perspective, revolved
around the idea of direct or indirect commerce with the devil: heresy, black
magic, and superstition. Nonetheless, here again the processes of assimilation
and reification strongly influenced how these concepts impinged upon categories of witchcraft.

Heresy and the diabolic cult

Informed opinion in the late Middle Ages was in unusual agreement that
witches, no matter how they were defined, were heretics, and that their activities were the legitimate subjects of inquisitorial inquiry.[1] The history of this
consensus has been thoroughly examined, and need not long concern us here.[2]
Instead, let us examine how the witch-theorists of the fifteenth century used
ideas associated with heresy and heretics to construct their image of witches.
This is a problem of several dimensions, involving both the legal and theological approaches to heresy and to magic, and the related but broader question
of why heretics were conflated with magicians, malefici, and night-travelers in
the first place.

Part of the solution to this problem is related to the idea of the demonic pact. Magic, from a very early point in Christian history, was closely related to idolatry: magicians received their powers in return for their worship of pagan idols, who were, of course, really devils. So Pharaoh's magicians were able to work their wonders. With paganism dead or dying, demons could, at times, afford to eliminate their now extraneous idols, and insist that they receive service directly in return for their magical gifts. In the endlessly popular story of Theophilus, the devil required the unfortunate man to produce a written pact in which he explicitly repudiated the Christian God. Like Theophilus, a given magician might come by his power either through an explicit pact, or, like the sorcerers of Pharaoh, through some pagan observance in which the devil was not directly named. This distinction, between an open or manifest pact, in which the operator made an explicit bargain with the devil, and a tacit pact, in which the participation of the devil was concealed, was important, but in either case the devil was always involved.

Augustine himself had strongly suggested that any accommodation between man and devil implied some kind of pact and the denial of God. In *De Doctrina Christiana*, he concludes a lengthy denunciation of various magical and superstitious observances with a passage critical to the medieval understanding of magic:

> Therefore all arts pertaining to this kind of trifling or noxious superstition constituted on the basis of a pestiferous association of men and demons as if through a pact of faithless and deceitful friendship should be completely repudiated and avoided by the Christian, "not that the idol is anything," as the Apostle says, but because "the things which heathens sacrifice they sacrifice to devils, and not to God."[3]

The practice of magic, then, was very close to apostasy in Augustine's opinion, as it would be for most churchmen throughout the Middle Ages. There were exceptions, but not many: in Aquinas's view all magic accomplished through "invocations, conjurations, sacrifices, fumigations, and adorations" implied a pact with the devil and apostasy.[4] Such a stance left a tenuous opening for legitimate natural magic which relied upon the occult properties of heavenly bodies, herbs, and stones, but, as Aquinas noted, even such seemingly legitimate practices all too often simply disguised the presence of demons.[5]

Because magic depended upon a diabolic pact inconsistent with Christian faith, the practice of magic was always potentially heretical, and this identification became more common over time. In 1257, for example, Pope Alexander IV specifically prohibited inquisitors from prosecuting simple sorcery unless it savored of manifest heresy, yet by 1400 the papacy was prepared to admit that manifest heresy was present in virtually all sorcery, and that the inquisition ought to be involved when it was discovered.[6] Ritual magic, practiced by more or less learned men and involving the explicit invocation of demons, was the first target of the Church's campaign against magic, because both the practitioners themselves and their errors of faith were more visible than were those of less erudite magicians. In theory, however, all were guilty of similar offenses, and so workers of *maleficium* were increasingly identified as heretics from the thirteenth century onwards. *Maleficium* was classified as a form of heresy in the laws of Frederick II, for example, because it depended upon a pact with demons.[7] Even more influential for churchmen was the common gloss on Exodus 22:18, "You shall not suffer witches [*maleficos*] to live":

> Understand that witches who work deceptions of the magic art and diabolical illusions are heretics, who should be excommunicated from the company of the faithful, who truly live, until the *maleficium* of their error shall die in them.[8]

Although in the thirteenth century, this biblical injunction was not taken literally, the gloss made clear to every literate cleric that malign magic was heresy and had to be treated accordingly. Hence, by the early fifteenth century, virtually any form of magic, including comparatively benign medicinal spells, could technically be used as evidence of heretical belief.

At the same time, heresy itself acquired new and increasingly sinister connotations. In the late twelfth century, Walter Map warns that the ancient heresy of the Publicans and Paterines has recently won many adherents. These heretics assemble at night and wait for a huge black cat, descending on a rope suspended in mid-air, to appear in their midst. At this time they extinguish all lights and adore the beast with kisses on its feet, anus, and genitals, as a prelude to an indiscriminate orgy.[9] This story gives an early version of the Sabbat, the diabolic assembly which would become closely associated with the late-medieval witch. The Sabbat was an enormously popular and successful piece of slanderous propaganda, which, in its most elaborate form, contained six basic elements: (1) On the appointed night, the sectaries assembled at a remote or concealed site, often flying or riding demonic animals; (2) once there, they summoned the devil in one of his many forms, and worshiped him in disgusting or humiliating ways, most characteristically by the obscene kiss; (3) at the devil's command, they renounced Christ in graphic fashion, trampling on or otherwise abusing the host; (4) they slaughtered infants or children, who were brought along for this purpose, and put their flesh to some foul and often magical use; (5) they indulged in a high-spirited revel, eating, drinking, and dancing, until the evening's festivities were concluded with an orgy (6), in which they violated as many sexual conventions as the fertile imagination of the narrator could devise.[10]

As heretics became progressively more demonized, the diabolic cult and the Sabbat became an increasingly important part of the general understanding of what heretics were. When these aspects of heresy came to overshadow doctrinal errors, when a close association with the devil, not specific errors of faith, determined the presence of heresy, the category "heretic" could be disassociated from the persons of "real" heretics. That is, if attendance at the Sabbat, infanticide, and the obscene kiss were the principal determining characteristics of heresy, then the average Waldensian resembled a "heretic" no more than anyone else.[11] Heretics, magicians, malevolent *lamiae*, and the *bonae res*, all belonged to ill-defined categories that shared a close association with demonic power, and so it is unsurprising that their boundaries might blur, and aspects of one spill over into the others.

In an interesting example, Stephen of Bourbon tells of some suspected heretics that he was summoned to investigate.[12] One of the prisoners confessed that she and many others had assembled at night in a subterranean place, gathered around a basin of water in which a lance had been placed upright, and there summoned Lucifer by his beard. At the adjuration, a huge cat descended the lance, and after a few additional preliminaries, the lights were again extinguished for the promiscuous orgy. Although, in general terms, Stephen corroborates Walter's account, he is openly skeptical, and suggests that the woman's entire testimony is based upon a delusion, sent to her in a dream by the devil. "To this error, which arises in sleep," he continues, "pertains the error of those women who say that during the night they walk and ride on certain beasts with Diana and Herodias and other persons they call the *bonae res*."[13] At the same time, and for no clear reason, he calls the suspects *malefici*, illustrating how tangled and intertwined these categories could become, even in the mind of learned inquisitor.[14]

Similarly, around 1435, an anonymous inquisitor wrote a short tract describing his encounter with heretics, which he called *The Errors of the Gazarii or of those who are shown to ride on a staff or a broomstick.*[15] Now *gazarii* is simply an Italianate variant of "Cathars," as the author surely knew, but what is interesting is that he identifies these heretics in the second place by their magical flight on wooden beams, a mode of locomotion that had, in the past, been a monopoly of the women who went out with the *bonae res*. Furthermore, this sect had no visible resemblance to conventional Cathars at all. Initiates to the sect were presented to the devil, who appeared either as a black cat, or as a misshapen man. They were required to make a detailed oath of allegiance, consisting of seven points: they swore to keep faith with the master and with the entire society, to recruit as many new members as possible, to reveal none of the society's secrets even till death, to kill all the children of up to three years of age that they could and to bring the bodies to their meetings, to hasten to the assembly whenever called, to impede all marriages through magic and *maleficium*, and, finally, to avenge any injuries done to the sect or its members. At their meetings, or *synagoga*, the sectaries gave the devil the obscene kiss on the buttocks or anus (depending upon his chosen form) in token of homage, after which they enjoyed a banquet of roasted children. An orgy in darkness followed, in which "one man joins carnally with one woman, or a man with another man, and sometimes father with daughter, son with mother, brother with sister, and every law of nature is violated."[16] Finally, everyone ritually defecated into a cask in despite of the Eucharist and then returned home. The author learned all of this from the confessions of the sectaries themselves, who were seduced into this evil either by their carnal lusts, their abject poverty, or their fear of powerful enemies.

These were heretics defined not by their intellectual errors but by their membership in a secret society, by their demonolatry, and by their explicit pact with the devil.[17] They won converts not by seductive arguments and preaching, but by the promise of occult powers. Black magic was an integral part of their program. At their meetings, the devil gave each member a variety of magical pharmaceuticals: a flying ointment made from boiled children, a venomous goo which caused death when touched, and powders which caused disease or sterility when scattered in the air. Sometimes the devil even led his followers on field trips to the mountains where each malefactor gathered up a load of ice to drop from the air upon unsuspecting farms. Their oath of allegiance highlighted the importance of magic to the sect, since, for no obvious reason, initiates were required to swear to use their magical powers to "impede" marriage. Nor was it any accident that this is precisely the kind of magic most often associated with village wizards: impotence, sterility, and marital discord were all caused by the magic of envious and hostile sorcerers, whose identities were seldom totally mysterious. In these ways, although in other respects the existence of the sect was a closely guarded secret, magic made the identification of the heretics possible. As the inquisitor comments, the heretics were always careful to appear as good Christians, and that, "those of the sect seem to be better than the other faithful, and they commonly hear mass, and confess often during the year; and they frequently take sacred communion."[18] Their obsession with malign magic, however, provided a potential weakness in their carefully constructed identities that an inquisitor could exploit.

A similar grounding in popular culture was possible through the assimilation of motifs drawn from traditional beliefs about night flying women and the demonolatrous sect of *malefici*. An early and interesting example appears around 1436 in the account of a magistrate in the Dauphiné, Claude Tholasan. Tholosan had been involved in a series of trials, which began around 1425 and would continue for almost twenty years, in which authorities made extensive use of models of witchcraft patterned closely after conceptions of the diabolic cult.[19] He reports that he had encountered witches having exactly the same cannibalistic tendencies as more "conventional" heretics. When these witches successfully summoned the devil,

> they place their knees to the ground, and kiss the devil, who commonly appears to them in the form of a man and of many kinds of animals, and they kiss him on the mouth, giving their own body and soul and one of their children, especially their first born, whom they burn and sacrifice; on bended knees they hold it naked under the arms and shoulders and, at last, kill it, and afterwards exhume the remains and with that, and with other things described below, they make a powder.[20]

This powder the witches used as the basic ingredient in their various poisons with which they worked their malign magic.

Tholosan's witches themselves, however, told a rather different story. They claimed (he says) that they went out at night, usually on Thursday, in the company of devils, and strangled children or visited them with some sickness. From these children they drew out food which they boiled and ate.[21] They would then fly upon brooms smeared with the fat of their victims to a banquet presided over by a devil, where they could eat and drink as much as they wished without ever diminishing anything. But all this, Tholasan tells us, was an illusion of the devil; the reality – although scarcely more plausible – was the conventional diabolic Sabbat. What we seem to have here, then, is a remarkably straightforward instance of a learned magistrate deliberately "making sense" of testimony grounded ultimately in traditional belief by imposing the roughly similar conceptual template provided by accounts of diabolic heresy.

As Tholosan's testimony reveals, the witch's proclivity for infanticide was an important element of her definition. This was an especially "unthinkable" aspect of her persona but one on which most commentators were in unusual agreement; on the other hand, the precise manner in which the witch's anthrophagy was understood varied widely. As we have already observed, authors such as Girolamo Visconti, who constructed witchcraft largely on the basis of traditional representations of *lamiae* and *strigae*, logically interpreted the witch's cannibalism on that basis. Men like Tholosan, however, who viewed witchcraft as a kind of diabolic sect, looked to quite different sources for their understanding of child-murder. For, as Norman Cohn has pointed out, accusations of ritual infanticide had a lengthy history as part of a traditional derogatory stereotype, one which may be used to demonize almost any allegedly subversive group.[22] By the late Middle Ages, heretics had been accused of cannibalistic practices for years. As early as the late eleventh century, a Benedictine monk of Chartres described in elaborate detail the disgusting rites of a heretical cult in terms which would have been immediately familiar to witch-hunters four centuries later. When the celebrants had all assembled, he writes,

> like merry-makers they chanted the names of demons until suddenly they saw descend among them a demon in the likeness of some sort of little beast. As soon as the apparition was visible to everyone, all the lights were forthwith extinguished and each, with the least possible delay, seized the woman who first came to hand, to abuse her without thought of sin.[23]

If a child was produced during one of these blasphemous couplings, the heretics murdered it and burned its corpse to ashes. Although this account accords perfectly with other stereotypical relations of the Sabbat, its author uses an accusation of cannibalistic infanticide as much more than simply a useful defamatory topos: here, the cannibalism of the heretics was expressly a diabolic parody of the Eucharist. The heretics carefully gathered the child's ashes and preserved them "with as great veneration as Christian reverence is wont to guard the body of Christ" and gave them as a viaticum to the dying. Nor was their rite devoid of efficacy, for, as our author relates,

> such power of devilish fraud was in these ashes that whoever had been imbued with the aforesaid heresy and had partaken of no matter how small a portion of them was scarcely ever afterward able to direct the course of his thought from this heresy to the path of truth.[24]

From the ashes of dead children the heretics received their diabolic grace.

With minor variations, fifteenth-century witch-theorists utilized this same motif in their elaboration of the diabolic Sabbat. Peter of Bern reported to Nider that certain *malefici* in Lausanne cooked and ate their own children, and in Bern, thirteen children were devoured by witches. One female witch in particular testified to practices which vividly recall to mind the description of heretical infanticide reported at Chartres over three centuries before:

> We attack unbaptized children, and even baptized ones, especially if they are not guarded with the sign of the cross and with prayers. With our ceremonies we kill infants in their cradles or by the side of their parents, who are then thought to have been smothered or killed by another cause. We secretly steal their bodies from their graves, boil them in a cauldron until their whole flesh is separated from the bones and rendered suckable and drinkable. Of the solid matter we make an ointment which accomplishes our desires, our art, and our transformations; with the liquid or fluid we fill a flask or skin bottle, and he who drinks it, with a few ceremonies, at once understands and is a master of our sect.[25]

A captured male witch confirmed this account, testifying that whoever partakes of this abominable potion, "he feels at once within him that he understands and retains the image of our art and the principal rites of this sect."[26]

It is not necessary to assume that this similarity between quite disparate sources depended completely upon a well-known stereotype inherited from lurid tales of heresies past; it is equally possible that this is another indication that the categories "witch" and "heretic" occupied very similar conceptual spaces in the minds of clerical authorities. Cannibalism is, of course, a devastating inversion of social norms, and the witch, like the heretic, was constructed to be the embodiment of anti-social vice and deviance: "Hence the inverted witch stereotype includes all manner of sexual perversion, incest, and the ultimate denial of human sociability and commensality – cannibalism."[27] But cannibalism is also a powerful sign, and an indicator of contact with the supernatural: the image of "cannibalism," provides, "a device through which the unthinkable (eating people) gives form to the otherwise inconceivable substance of the relationship to oneself and to the supernatural."[28] For this reason, any discussion of cannibalism in late-medieval Europe evoked disturbingly anomalous images of the eucharistic feast and of diabolical infanticide and anthropophagous orgies. In each case the consumption of human flesh was the sign of an effective relationship with the supernatural, and of participation in a community composed of both corporeal and spiritual beings. It made sense, then, that the most powerful witches described in the *Malleus* were those who, "contrary to the inclinations of human nature, indeed, contrary to the nature of every wild beast . . . , [were] accustomed to greedily devour and eat children of their own kind."[29] Accusations of cannibalism and child-murder, then, became a powerful and evocative symbol in the hands of witch-theorists, a symbol of the witch's identity with the devil, her spiritual depravity, and her responsibility for a particularly awful form of concrete social harm. More than this, however, because infanticide had become a recognized complement to the denial of the faith, a trait shared by all the diabolized enemies of Christendom, accusations of child-murder served to create (or reinforce) the conceptual links between notions of heresy and witchcraft.[30] When categories are collapsed into symbolic representations of the "demonized other," it becomes difficult, if not pointless, to distinguish between various "others."[31]

The effects of this category collapse upon the development of witchcraft become clear when we compare the account of the Sabbat in the *Malleus* with that in its source, Nider's *Formicarius*. Institoris and Sprenger are in fact surprisingly unfamiliar with the conventional details of the witch's Sabbat – they seem completely unaware of the prosecutions in France and the Savoy in which the Sabbat occupied such a prominent place – and instead depend almost entirely upon Nider's account of Swiss witches for their knowledge of their

regular conclaves. As a typical example, they recount the confession of a pen-
itent witch examined by Peter of Bern. The initiate, they say, enters an un-
occupied church with the leaders of the diabolical congregation,

> and in their presence he denies Christ, his faith, baptism, and the universal
> Church. Then he pays homage to the *magisterulus*, that is, the little master, for
> thus and not otherwise they call the devil . . . Afterwards he drinks from the
> skin mentioned earlier.[32]

Their narrative is almost Nider verbatim, but the exception is interesting: in
the ellipsis they explain that it makes no difference to the oath of homage
whether the devil is actually present at the ceremony. Sometimes the devil is
worried that the initiate might be (understandably) alarmed by the real presence of a demon during his abnegation of the faith, and so he simply fails to
appear. When this happens, the other witches refer to the devil *in absentia* in
gentle and benign terms as the "little master" to allay fears and suspicion. In
either case, the pact is fully valid and binding. This addition is significant, since
where Nider clearly felt that the material presence of the devil was a necessary prerequisite for the ceremony, Institoris and Sprenger are prepared
to elide him entirely from the proceedings. Because the devil is unnecessary
to the Sabbat, in the *Malleus* the Sabbat is an entirely unnecessary adjunct to
witchcraft.

It seems unreasonable to suppose that Institoris and Sprenger were completely ignorant of the alternative constructions of witchcraft current at the
time. Both were men of wide experience within the Dominican order, and
surely had at least heard oral reports of the diabolic Sabbat so graphically
described by their French colleagues. Further, the calculated reservations
which circumscribe their own account of the sect of witches suggest a deliberate attempt to step back from Nider's more restrained notions of witches'
conclaves and devil worship. There are several possible explanations for why
the authors should want to do this, beginning with the reciprocal relationship
between theoretical notions of witchcraft and the persons actually identified
as witches.

When the cult of the devil was the most important element of witchcraft, it was invariably composed of both men and women. In fact, Jacquier
made the point explicitly that while the canon *Episcopi* spoke of women alone
deluded by the devil, "In this sect or synagogue of sorcerers, not only women
but men also assemble, and what is worse, ecclesiastics and religious, who
stand and talk perceptibly with demons."[33] Institoris and Sprenger, on the other
hand, were convinced that witchcraft was a vice restricted almost entirely to
women, and especially women of the lower class. Clergy, in their view, were
never potential witches. Along similar lines, most authors seem to have been

fully aware that heretical communities tended by their very nature to be text-based, and descriptions of heretical cults routinely included references to their texts and writings. Thus, notions of witchcraft centered upon the image of the diabolic cult easily accommodated literate, educated witches. Jacquier, for example, recalled that "around twenty years ago, a certain great baron of France secretly strangled around twenty children, so that he might write a book in honor of the devil with their blood."[34] Institoris and Sprenger, however, argue that "this kind of superstition [witchcraft] is not practiced in books or by the learned but entirely by the ignorant."[35] Their conception of witchcraft, in other words, was not centered upon an assemblage of motifs derived from images of heresy, so much as upon actual women. However they defined what witchcraft was, it had to remain consistent with the women whom they had identified as witches in the course of their own witch-hunting experience.

Furthermore, although Institoris and Sprenger may have had a very restricted notion of who were potential witches, their conception of witch-craft was very expansive. Because witchcraft in the *Flagellum Haereticorum* and the *Errores Gazariorum* was so tightly focused on the Sabbat and diabolical heresy, these works excluded the plain, garden variety of *malefici* from consideration. Institoris and Sprenger developed an inherently more useful category through the simple determination that *malefica* and witch were precisely the same thing. To make this identification, however, they admitted an astonishingly wide array of practices and behaviors: magic of almost any kind, rumors of animal transformation, stories of fairies or changelings, magical flight, the evil eye, all could be interpreted as direct evidence of witchcraft. Because the *fascinarii* and *gazarii* were theoretically defined by their participation in a non-existent cult, their identification in practical terms tended to be quite arbitrary. In contrast, Institoris and Sprenger were able to build upon already existing social mechanisms to identify witches "accurately." Witchcraft in the *Malleus* was thus much more centered upon the witch herself than were competing notions centered upon the Sabbat. For this reason, the witch in the *Malleus* always retained her own unique social identity, and did not become submerged into a diabolic collective dominated by the person of the devil.

Maleficium

Far more important to witchcraft in the *Malleus* than notions derived from heresy were ideas associated with *maleficium* – although what exactly that word meant is difficult to explain. The primary meaning of *maleficium* had once been "evil deed," but as early as Tacitus, it had also been used to mean sorcery and malign magic; while *maleficus*, as a synonym for black magician, was in use by the sixth-century *Codex Justinianeus*.[36] During the Middle Ages, the term retained both meanings, although in demonological texts and witchcraft treatises *maleficium* usually referred to harmful sorcery, and, more precisely, to its effects – impotence, for example, was a common instance of medieval *maleficium*. Sometimes, however, *maleficium* might also refer to magical practices themselves, as in the often quoted canon *Si per Sortiarias* which stated that *maleficium* may cause impotence.[37] Finally, *maleficium* sometimes denoted the material object in which malign magical force resides; Duns Scotus used the term in this sense when he addressed the question of whether it was licit to cure a person bewitched by finding and destroying the sorcerer's *maleficium*.[38] In all these cases, however, the key notion was harm: unlike *sortilegium* or other forms of divination or magic, *maleficium* was known not by its practitioners' procedures, but by those procedures' unfortunate results. For this reason, the relationship between *maleficium* and other forms of magic was always ambiguous, since a whole series of operations could theoretically be turned to harmful ends.

The range of harmful effects potentially classed as *maleficium* was extensive, but not unlimited. Malign sorcery was blamed for interference with human and animal sexuality (love magic, magically induced impotence, infertility, and abortions), the theft of milk, crops, wine, and other products, harmful weather magic, and, most seriously, for causing death, disease, or bodily infirmity in man and beast. All of these kinds of harm were once again conveniently enumerated in that catalogue of condemned belief, Burchard's *Corrector*. Burchard castigates those women who believed that by their glance or word they could kill young poultry or pigs, or the fetus of any animal; worse were those who believed that through their incantations or enchantments they could transfer their neighbor's milk or honey to themselves.[39] Burchard also railed against the use of ligatures (binding magic, often practiced sympathetically by tying knots in physical objects): women, he says, are accustomed to use ligatures to cause impotence in men; men of the viler sort, however, also make ligatures out of grass or other materials and hide them in trees or at crossroads, so that any illness or injury will be transferred from their animals to those of another which pass by.[40] There were enchanters who claimed to cause destructive storms or to alter the minds of men, women who thought that their magic could ensure another's love, and evil women who gave their husbands or lovers lethal or debilitating potions. These and other kinds of *maleficium* condemned in the *Corrector* are found in other sources scattered throughout the Middle Ages, and they approximate to what we may call the traditional and popular assessment of *maleficium*.[41]

The magical techniques available to do all this were similarly varied. Some, like ligatures and image magic, were almost invariably interpreted as indicative of *maleficium*. The use of poison, a similarly secretive and horrible kind of harm, was also closely identified in the medieval mind with *maleficium*. Indeed, the words *veneficium* and *maleficium* were frequently synonymous: Gregory of Tours accused Queen Fredegund of both malign sorcery and poisoning, while later witch-theorists would make absolutely no distinction between a witch's use of poison and what we would consider more properly "magic."[42] Other magical practices could cause harm or not, since cures that transferred an injury to an unsuspecting third party and most love magic might be judged harmful or beneficial depending entirely upon one's perspective.

All of this meant that the person of the *maleficus* was correspondingly ill-defined: there was no clear stereotype associated with this word until several were invented at the close of the Middle Ages. In early-medieval texts, *malefici* are found in close company with a varied assortment of sorcerous types: *praecantores, sortilegi, divini, magi, tempestarii, incantores*, and others.[43] All made use of condemned magical operations, but the *malefici* were especially attacked because of the harmful nature of their spells. For the most part, early-medieval sources represent *malefici* as men and women of no great social status and little education, marked out simply by perceptions of magical power and malevolence. Of course, the same person might be regarded as a *maleficus* by some, and as a kindly *herbarius* or *medicus* by others, depending upon their perspective and the result of treatment. Likewise, because magical power did not necessarily depend upon special knowledge, but could result from heredity, disposition, or individual aptitude, anyone with a generally bad reputation could, under the right circumstances, be suspected of causing *maleficium*.

At the same time, though, this emphasis upon magical harm separated conceptions of *malefici* from those of *strigae* and the *bonae res*, and until the late Middle Ages, texts usually kept these categories reasonably distinct. In the ninth century, Hincmar of Rheims took a close look at the various magical practitioners loosely associated with the court of Lothar II, since *maleficium*, he suggested, was endangering the royal marriage. Hincmar gives a thorough catalogue of the magical specialists he encountered – *magi, malefici, arioli, necromantii, hydromantii, incantatores, aruspices, augures, pythonissae*, and *praestigiatores* – but does not include *strigae* in the list; instead, *strigae, lamiae*, and *dusii* he describes elsewhere as beings whose magical attacks afflict the unwary and incautious.[44] The canon *Episcopi* likewise drew a clear line between sorcerers who perpetrated their crimes while fully awake and the women who dreamed that they rode at night. The canon admonishes that

> Bishops and their officials must labor with all their strength to uproot thoroughly from their parishes the pernicious art of sorcery and malefice invented

by the devil, and, if they find a man or woman follower of this wickedness, to eject them foully disgraced from their parishes.[45]

It is this command which leads the author to explore the beliefs of the night-traveling women, almost as an afterthought. Similarly, none of those writers who subsequently discussed the cannibalistic habits of *lamiae* described them as instances of *maleficium*.[46]

By the later Middle Ages, however, like other kinds of magical practitioners, *malefici* were gradually identified as a species of heretic, and, as the heretical component of their alleged practices assumed greater and greater importance in the minds of clerical authorities, the distinctions between different kinds of magical operations gradually collapsed. Although ritual magic dealt with demons directly, all who knew their Aquinas were aware that all magic involved at least an implicit or tacit pact with the devil and had to be similarly condemned. Due to this kind of reasoning, by the fifteenth century, theologians and canonists found little to distinguish *maleficium* from other, more overtly diabolical, sorts of magic.[47] Thus, *malefici* were in turn conflated with the diabolic necromancers of learned traditions on the one hand, and the *bonae res, lamiae,* and the other products of diabolically inspired dreams and illusions on the other.

For example, in the fifteenth century, Fray Lope de Barrientos, bishop of Cuenca, denounced the superstitions of women in his diocese, and especially their belief in

> the women called witches who are said and believed to accompany the Pagan Goddess Diana at night, together with many other women who ride on beasts and travel through many towns and places, and are said to be able to harm animals or make use of them.[48]

These women were all perfectly imaginary, and, he adds, "to believe the contrary is to be lacking in common sense." "Consequently," he concludes, "women should pay heed to their animals and watch over them, and if they die through lack of care let them not blame it on witches who come through crannies to kill them." Fray Lope's account is interesting because the followers of Diana, nocturnal witches, and charges of conventional *maleficia* are combined into a single, well-defined image. There is no reason to think that the bishop was ill-informed about the beliefs he describes or was writing in response to growing fears of heretical, *maleficium*-wielding devil worshipers; rather, it seems much safer to assume that he has accurately described local beliefs as he understood them. If such is indeed the case, Fray Lope had met a version of the *bonae res* who, although traditionally the bearers of good luck, were here also held responsible for certain kinds of misfortune.

Yet there is a difficulty here which harks back to the reason why this particular kind of witch was unacceptable to more traditionally minded clergy. Although Fray Lope's perfectly rational explanation for the apparent effects of malign magical powers could logically be extended to skepticism about *maleficium* in general, in the late Middle Ages such a view was theologically untenable; but if a witch's *maleficium* was real, it was reasonable to suppose that she was likewise not merely a delusion. This is precisely the problem that Martin of Arles was unable to face squarely in his discussion of the *broxae*, malign women who were believed to cause storms, damage crops, and kill children, as well as to ride about at night with Diana.[49] Quite conventionally, Martin condemned these beliefs as false, and delusions of devil. For the Latin equivalent of *broxae*, however, Martin gave *maleficae et sortilegae*, words which, in another context, he used to refer to women who had quite real powers to work material evils – summoning storms and damaging fields among them.[50]

Once Martin had accepted that the ability to cause occult harm was part of the image of night-flying women, it became difficult for him to separate them from more substantial *maleficae*. Since, like Fray Lope, Martin insisted that his was an accurate account of popular beliefs he had encountered, it is again reasonable to suppose that this confusion of categories reflected simply the ambiguity inherent in the beliefs of his informants. This is not in itself cause for surprise, since there is no reason to expect that traditional beliefs should be systematized in a way which corresponds to theologically ordered categories. What is surprising, however, is that neither Martin nor Fray Lope completely subordinated their description of peasant belief to readily available orthodox paradigms, but allowed their concern to represent peasant belief realistically to override absolute logical consistency.

This concern to understand accurately the content of popular belief and practice underlies much of the late-medieval witch debate; many late-medieval clerics were unwilling to adopt a stance of "blind skepticism," and insisted upon examining the logical basis behind the claim that so much of what people said they did was merely diabolically inspired fantasy. As authors began to take common perceptions more seriously, and to accord them a higher epistemological value, educated opinion changed in response and began to consider the possibility that much that had once been dismissed as illusion or fantasy had some more material basis. Once it was admitted that these phenomena were not entirely imaginary, the basis for distinguishing between them and *maleficae* or diabolic heretics promptly disappeared.

An instructive example of this conflation of categories occurs in the *Questio de Strigis* (c. 1470) of the Dominican theologian Jordanes de Bergamo. Jordanes writes that

> Among nearly everybody, by *strigae* or *strigones* are understood women or men
> who by night dash either about their homes or over long distances by the power
> of the devil, who are also said to bewitch children . . . Women of this kind are
> accustomed to be called *maliarde* from the evil deeds that they do: among others
> they are called *herbarie* from operations of the same kind, *fascinatrices* because
> they bewitch children; in French, *fastineres* or *festurieres*; *pixidarie*, [from their
> boxes] in which they place unguents; *bacularie*, because they are borne on sticks
> by the power of the devil.[51]

Jordanes' approach to the problem of witchcraft is striking: he distinguishes
carefully between a large number of terms, many of them in the vernacular,
almost all of which designate various kinds of magicians known for their acts
of *maleficia*. But, he insists that these are all simply specific manifestations of
the *striga*, a witch which he has constructed based upon conventional stereo-
types of child-eating monsters. The common understanding of *maleficium* and
of *maleficae*, then, are all but entirely subsumed into Jordanes' broader notion
of witchcraft, which becomes an umbrella category that by its very nature
erases the distinctions previously made.

   Jordanes then tries, but ultimately fails, to reconcile the skepticism of
the canon *Episcopi* with the reality of occult harm. Some, he says, believe that

> by the power of the devil *strigae* can be changed into cats, and by means of oint-
> ments and sticks cross over many places and long distances, and by the power
> of words and signs the *strigae* themselves can produce hail and rain and things
> of this kind, all of which are false and such persons are in danger of weakening
> their faith.[52]

Yet, Jordanes insists, with the aid of demons witches do kill children, cause
storms and do similar things: the illusion to which the canon refers simply
masks the intervention of the devil, making the witches believe that they do
these things of their own power.

   Not all witch-theorists, however, were prepared to admit that *malefici*
were substantially the same as *strigae* and *lamiae*, and that the reality of occult
harm necessarily implied the reality of "witches". Girolamo Visconti, for
example, wondered whether because Thomas Aquinas and Albertus Magnus
agreed that *maleficium* was real "so were those things that were done at [the
witches' assembly] since all were done by that art and the wiles of the devil."[53]
Ultimately, however, he was forced to admit that there was no clear relationship between the two, and that just because *maleficium* caused real harm there
was no reason to think that magicians went to the witches' Sabbat or did other
such things. The evidence of magic, he thought, was especially tenuous because sterility and impotence were not necessarily the product of *maleficium*:
quite the contrary, both conditions could have perfectly natural causes.[54] For

Visconti it was hard enough to prove the linkage between harmful sorcery and some particular misfortune let alone to prove that sorcerers went out at night to the Sabbat.

Witch-theorists who grounded their conceptions of witchcraft in notions of heresy had fewer difficulties incorporating *malefici/ae* into their models, because magic was an accepted indication of heretical depravity. For Nicholas Jacquier the link between *maleficium* and witchcraft was much closer than for Girolamo or Jordanes, since black magic was characteristic of witches and evidence of their pact with Satan. Witches, he writes,

> bring on or procure infirmities, weaknesses, frenzies, marital impediments, death to both people and beasts, abortions and impediments to conception, and the destruction of crops and many worldly goods. Therefore, since the aforesaid *maleficia* are real, and dependent on the invocation and patronage of demons, and the evil fruits of the aforesaid sect and heresy of evil-doing enchanters, it is clear that the aforesaid heretical enchanters are really and not in fantasy conjoined with demons and that they worship and obey them.[55]

By eliding in this place the more fantastic notions of the Sabbat, and concentrating upon the admitted link between sorcerer and demon, Jacquier makes Girolamo's argument much more persuasive: the effects of magic are real, witches are real, and, hence, their pact with the devil is real. Jacquier's witches, however, use an unusual and quite specific procedure to work their nefarious ends. Rather than employing the traditional hodge-podge of practices attributed to *malefici*, they do their harm with the aid of magical substances given to them by the devil or manufactured under his guidance. Witches secretly introduced these substances, which often combined poisons and venom with the bodies of murdered children, into their victim's food or drink, as did the other traditional enemies of Christendom – Muslims, lepers, and Jews.[56] During the thirteenth and fourteenth centuries, France had been rocked by rumors of conspiracies involving each of these groups and their plots to poison wells and water-supplies with diabolic powders.[57] By emphasizing poison as the agent of *maleficium*, Jacquier and similar authors reinforced their image of an aggressive but insidiously covert antisociety, and, once again, foregrounded the role of the devil.

The net effect of this picture of *maleficium*, though, was to distance Jacquier's heretics from the image of more conventional *malefici*. Jacquier never claimed that his witches had a monopoly on black magic, and he distinguished between traditional sorts of *malefici* and the heretical *fascinarii*.[58] To Jacquier this was perfectly reasonable, because he found the existence of the cult more alarming than its magic, the effectiveness of which was ultimately in the hands of God. The problem, however, was how to identify the *fascinarii* if harmful sorcery was not a sufficient indicator in itself. Because Jacquier's construction of witchcraft was so dependent upon motifs which had no apparent basis in popular perceptions of reality, it was difficult to know who was and was not a witch. In part, this is Jacquier's point: anyone could be a witch, even a respected master of theology such as William Adelmo, prior of St. Germain-en-Laye.[59] But at the same time, the cult's pervasive secrecy made effective persecution quite difficult.

For witch-theorists who simply equated *maleficium* with witchcraft, however, the presence of *maleficium* alone constituted direct evidence of witchcraft. One such scholar was Petrus Mamoris, who was unusual among French authors in that he viewed witchcraft as a kind of baleful occult knowledge more than as a heretical sect. Magical practices, he believed, had arrived in France during the Hundred Years War, carried by the strange foreigners employed as mercenaries by both sides.[60] These men had corrupted some of the French, and taught them *sortelegia vel maleficium*, which hitherto had been unknown. Some "especially dim persons" continued to disbelieve in magic, while others claimed that it was all an illusion; learned people, however, conversant with scripture, "with firm reason affirm that the said *maleficia* can be done."[61] The knowledge of *maleficium* carried with it membership in the diabolic cult, and implied devil worship and participation at the Sabbat. Mamoris was not particularly interested in this aspect of witchcraft, however, and his perfunctory description of the Sabbat is interesting principally because it indifferently combines so many motifs from so many different traditions. Mamoris writes that witches had confessed that

> Some of them are carried at night, or during the day, by a demon to places near and far, and there they can dance and worship the devil, men can have intercourse with women, and demons can replace the women; they can eat and drink in reality or in appearance, cause death and disease to others, that they can enter cellars and drag out the wine and carry it off to distant places, put people to sleep, take children from their mothers' arms and roast them, divine some events of the future, stir up thunder and hailstorms, strike down and kill with lightning, destroy crops, and perpetrate many other evils with the help of demons.[62]

This is a Sabbat grab-bag, in which diabolic heresy, *maleficium*, and motifs culled from stories of *lamiae* and the *bonae res* are piled indiscriminately one atop the other. Mamoris does not want to exclude anyone through omission, and because the details of the Sabbat are not especially important to him, he can afford to generalize.

But was all this real or was it simply an illusion? For Mamoris, it seems a difficult question. One of the strangest things about the *Flagellum Malefico-*

rum is a long passage appearing almost halfway through the treatise. Here, contrary to all expectation, Mamoris asserts that the Sabbat and all of its trappings are imaginary, that everything witches are said to do — their devil worship, their feasts and orgies, their nocturnal flight, and their visits to wine cellars — are merely phantoms sent into the minds of old women by the power of the devil.[63] He then proceeds calmly and, from our perspective, rationally, to answer the objections to his startling claim. If witches confess to these things, one should reply that "the number of fools is infinite," and that confession itself does not make a thing true.[64] If witnesses claim many times to have observed the Sabbat, Mamoris invokes the devil's power to deceive the senses. If men claim that witches have robbed their cellars, and that wine has truly disappeared, Mamoris advises them to blame instead poorly sealed and leaky casks. And, finally, if people point to innumerable injuries caused daily through witchcraft, Mamoris responds that all of this comes not from witches but from natural causes,

> and that a child gets sick, a cow dies, cancer afflicts the face, a storm destroys crops and kills people . . . and the devil puts the illusions of all these things into their fantasies, with the result that they think that they have done the things that they saw in the illusions, and on that account such persons manifestly cannot be accused of those crimes, nor can they be discovered to have made a pact with the devil in silence or secret.[65]

Yet, after this refutation of arguments in favor of the reality of witches, Mamoris changes his mind: as his discussion of *maleficium* progresses, he arrives at the physical existence of magical paraphernalia — "the powders, liquors, hairs, nails, toads, and similar things" — through which witches did their magic. The combination of the undeniable presence of such objects, manifest real harm, and the unambiguous testimony of witches and their victims alike overcomes his skepticism, and he now concludes that "they really are guilty of witchcraft, of which they are accused, and they should be subjected to legal punishment.[66]

This odd train of thought provides an unusually transparent illustration of the lines that separated different kinds of late-medieval witch-beliefs. First, Mamoris' argument shows the importance of definitions, for if Mamoris had thought of "witchcraft" in terms of separable, discrete parts, as did Visconti and Nicholas of Cusa, then his analysis of the reality of the Sabbat would not have led necessarily to his questioning of the reality of *maleficium*. Nor would an admission that one element of the whole was real have determined the real existence of the rest. Second, unlike Ulrich Molitor, Mamoris was unable simply to dismiss an increasingly formidable mass of circumstantial evidence by an appeal to the devil's powers. At some point he found the weight of empir-

ical evidence and testimony too great to be denied.[67] It was this precise con-
junction of category definition with analytical perceptions of reality that made
this image of witchcraft so persuasive.

But if a witch is understood to be exactly the same thing as a *maleficus*,
and if *maleficium* is direct evidence of the witch, the question then becomes
how to define *maleficium*. Mamoris' approach was straightforward: *maleficium*
proceeded from materially harmful magic. Magic, he informs his reader,
comes in thirty varieties, all inventions of the devil. *Maleficium*, however, can
result only from nine types that cause injuries at the prompting of demons.[68]
These Mamoris categorizes by the procedures or operations through which
they supposedly work: *fascinatio* (by glance), incantation (by spoken word),
breviaria (by brief inscriptions), *ligatura* (by knots and weaving), *veneficium*
(by poison), *caracteria* (by pouring molten lead into cold water and then either
inspecting the resulting mass with an eye toward divination, or using it for
image magic), *imaginaria* (by manipulating images of wax, metal, or stone),
mandragora (by use of the mandrake root as a kind of charm), and *praestigium*
(in which the devil appears in the sight, hearing, or interior senses of the
operator in order to reveal the future).[69] There are other kinds of magic, too
– necromancy, the notary art, astrology, and all kinds of divination – and these
also require the cooperation of the devil, though not necessarily membership
in the sect of witches. Mamoris does not distinguish between learned magic
and *maleficium*: a witch might as easily be an educated sorcerer as an illiterate
village wizard. While some witches tied knots or mutilated dolls, and others
drew magic circles and used herbs and stones to compel demons to respond
to their commands, all were witches just the same.[70]

Institoris and Sprenger chose a quite different path. Their more traditional enumeration of learned magical practices comprises fourteen different
types, divided into three headings depending upon the operator's degree of
complicity with the devil.[71] The most condemned magic involved the open
invocation of the devil, and included *praestigium*, geomancy, necromancy, false
prophecy, and other kinds of divination. None of these, however, were properly witchcraft:

> Although all of these are done through the express invocation of demons, yet
> none is comparable to the *maleficia* of witches, since they are never directly
> intended for the harm of men, animals, or the fruits of the earth.[72]

Learned magicians used their magic to obtain some "private good" and not,
like witches, solely to cause injury.[73]

Institoris and Sprenger did not mean to imply that witchcraft could be
distinguished by intentionality (except insofar as everything that witches do is
motivated by malice), but rather that the magic of illiterate female witches

was of an altogether different kind from the learned sorcery of male magicians. The authors understood the *maleficium* of witches theoretically as the maleficent effect of demonic power; but they conceived of *maleficium* practically as a discursive process, operating within localized communal bounds. *Maleficium* was seldom simply a matter of a witch, out of pure malice, causing hail to fall on random farms. Instead, magical harm grew out of, and was inseparable from, certain kinds of social relations and the person of the witch herself. *Maleficium* began almost invariably with hostility between acquaintances. Witches were not strangers or anonymous monsters, they were neighbors, lovers, and relatives. Nor did they cause injuries capriciously or randomly, but because they felt injured or aggrieved; witchcraft stemmed directly from the personal motivation of the witch – her jealousies, hatreds, loves, and fears. Her *maleficium* took the form most appropriate to circumstances: spinsters prevented brides from consummating their unions, barren old women caused abortions, and paupers made the wealthy poor.[74] When Institoris and Sprenger write that it is beyond the devil's power to produce something out of nothing, they simply repeat what every peasant already knew: that they lived in a world of limited resources, where one person's success turned upon another person's failure – when a witch's crops flourished and her butter churns were full, a neighbor inevitably suffered.[75]

In the *Malleus*, witchcraft sometimes begins when a person who is conscious of his good fortune, but not yet secure in his enjoyment of it, links an injury with the malicious jealousy of others. Thus a "very wealthy man" who loses forty cattle in a single year blames the hostility of witches. Likewise, Institoris and Sprenger tell us, witches habitually kill only the "best horses and the fattest cattle" of the region.[76] Because of their poverty, beggars were always suspected of witchcraft, and the authors conscientiously warned their readers to refuse any alms to suspected witches, because such charity was all too often repaid with witchcraft.[77]

More often, however, witchcraft begins when envy or jealousy combines with a sense of personal insult or injury. Unsatisfactory love affairs provide fertile ground for this combination of feelings: it comes as no surprise, then, that Institoris finds that, when men abandoned their lovers, they, or their new loves, become frequent targets of *maleficium*.[78] A count of Westreich, for example, who left his mistress to marry a noblewoman, became impotent for three years, because the spurned lady had sought out a witch to work her revenge.[79] Even worse, a young man of Ravensburg "lost his virile member" when he wished to forsake his girlfriend.[80]

In still other cases, witchcraft followed upon quarrels over money, vandalism, or slander. Witches were naturally sensitive about their reputations, and strongly disliked people drawing attention to their illicit pursuits. To call a known witch a witch to her face was thus an invitation to disaster. Animosity itself, of course, did not create witchcraft. *Maleficium* could exist only when misfortune struck in a way that encouraged a supernatural explanation, such that a victim began to examine the recent past through the lens provided by traditional beliefs. Sometimes the presence of *maleficium* was identified merely by the speed with which misfortune struck. The rich cattle rancher assured Institoris that witchcraft was doubtless to blame for the death of his animals, since his neighbor had suffered no loss, and "when [livestock] died from disease or some other infirmity, they did not succumb suddenly, but gradually and one at a time."[81] *Maleficium* was particularly suspected when an injury could be associated with the hostile intent of a specific person reasonably supposed to be a witch. Really notorious witches could be blamed even when no animosity was apparent. A merchant of Speyer, for instance, testified that while out walking in the fields, he saw a woman a long way off. His servants identified her as a witch, and urged the man to cross himself, but the merchant arrogantly declined. Scarcely had he finished speaking, when he felt a severe pain in his left foot, so that he could scarcely move, demonstrating conclusively the guilt of the suspect.[82]

A more usual procedure, however, was for the witch to identify herself through some ambiguously worded threat which, although ignored at the time, would assume ominous significance in retrospect. Institoris and Sprenger relate that when another merchant of Speyer refused to lower his price for a certain woman, she became angry, and left, threatening that "soon you will wish you had agreed."[83] Indeed he did, for no sooner had the man turned around than his mouth stretched hideously all the way back to his ears, a deformity that remained with him for some considerable time. In another case, a priest, hastening across a bridge, rudely pushed an old woman into the mud. As he passed, she called out that he would not cross with impunity. The priest little heeded her words until he tried to rise from his bed that night, and found himself paralyzed below the waist. From that moment, "on account of her abusive words," he always suspected that the old woman had bewitched him.[84]

On the basis of such narratives, Institoris and Sprenger show that there was an intimate connection between personal animosity, threats, and witchcraft, that *maleficium* emerges out of a particular kind of hostile discourse, with its own rules and logical structures. Unfortunately, this observational acumen was not matched by the sophistication of their explanatory apparatus: why witches were so ready to incite the suspicions of their neighbors was difficult to say. Since the authors thought *maleficium* real, they could not admit the possibility that perceptions of magical harm arose only during – and because of – these exchanges. Instead, as they so often did, Institoris and Sprenger looked to the nebulous presence of the devil to explain otherwise refractory phenomena. Witches, they advised prospective judges, have a very peculiar characteristic:

> they stir up people against them, either by harmful words or deeds, as, for example, to borrow some small thing, or to inflict some kind of damage to a garden, and similar to this, so that they receive a pretext and reveal themselves in word or in deed; which exposure they have to make at the urging of demons, so that the sins of the judges may be thus aggravated as long as they remain unpunished.[85]

Witches reveal themselves so that lazy or skeptical judges will receive their due in hell, an irrational course of action, explicable only by the callous supervision of the devil. This analysis, as inherently implausible at it seems, was doubly useful, because it drew a concrete connection between definite accusations of witchcraft and rumors and malicious gossip. Because the witch's *maleficium* was firmly grounded in her social relations, wise judges should immediately seek to discover whether a consistent pattern of animosities in a suspect's personal history suggested her guilt. Judges should ask the accused, "why the common people fear her," "whether she knows that she is defamed and that she is hated," and "why she had threatened that person, saying, 'you shall not pass with impunity.'"[86]

The strength of the construction of witchcraft elaborated in the *Malleus* is that it is based upon and congruent with the narrative paradigms through which evaluations of witchcraft and the identification of witches were made on the local level. In these narratives, the various threads that comprise *maleficium* are woven together to determine the identity of witches beyond doubt. In the *Malleus*, Institoris and Sprenger raise these explanatory mechanisms to the level of learned discourse, integrating them (however uncomfortably) with a more theologically sophisticated conception of the world. In essence, the authors provide their audience with a window onto the discursive field in which their informants constructed witchcraft themselves.

As an example, let us take a fairly lengthy but otherwise typical story from Institoris' experiences in Innsbruck. An "honest married woman" had deposed that she had an arbor behind her house, adjacent to her neighbor's garden. One day she saw that a path had been beaten from the garden to the arbor, causing significant damage. As she stood, surveying the ruin, the neighbor suddenly appeared and asked whether she was suspected. The woman naturally thought her neighbor responsible, but she was frightened to say so on account of her *mala fama*. The woman therefore answered only that "The steps in the grass indicate the damage" – a vague reply, although its meaning was no doubt clear enough.[87] But however well advised, her caution was insufficient, for

Then [my neighbor] was offended, perhaps because I did not wish to entangle myself with her by litigious words for her pleasure. She left with a murmur. And although I could hear the words she uttered, I could not understand them. Indeed, after a few days, a monstrous disease struck me with pains in the stomach.[88]

The disease grew out of a quarrel marked by a singularly ambiguous verbal exchange. Neither party made her meanings clear, and both seem to have attached great importance to the opacity of their utterances. The matron tried to hide her suspicions by avoiding any direct accusation, and testifies implausibly that the very innocence of her response inspired her neighbor's subsequent indignation. The suspected witch, in her turn, walked away mumbling, and this, to the matron, was the threat: the incomprehensibility of the words invoked the danger of witchcraft.

The matron's agonies, we are told, were extreme, and her cries disturbed the whole neighborhood. Many people came to comfort her, among them a clay-worker who was having an adulterous affair with the hostile neighbor, whom the narrator now identifies for the first time unambiguously as a witch.[89] The clay-worker offered to help her find out whether her illness was, indeed, caused by witchcraft, and performed an interesting experiment. He placed a bowl of water over the woman's body and poured molten lead into the water. When the image had hardened, he examined it, and pronounced that witchcraft was present:

"Look," he said, "this infirmity has happened to you through *maleficium*, and one part of the instruments of *maleficium* has been hidden under the threshold of the door of your house. Let us go, then, and when they have been removed, you will feel better."[90]

When the threshold was examined, they discovered a wax image pierced with two needles, and little bags containing bones, seeds, and other things. When these were duly burned, the woman felt better, though not fully recovered, because there remained some other instruments of witchcraft that could not be found. When the woman asked the clay-worker how he knew to look under the threshold, he replied that his lover, the witch, had revealed it to him in an unguarded moment.[91]

No single part of this story actually proves that the neighbor was responsible for the matron's illness. Logical "proof," however, is not the objective. The narrative builds gradually upon the themes of the quarrel, "murmured" words, and the neighbor's evil reputation, so that when the sudden onset of illness raises the specter of *maleficium*, the reader is prepared for the crucial identification of "neighbor and witch." The narrative process arrives simultaneously at a determination of *malefica* and *maleficium*: the witch is joined inseparably to her witchcraft. Yet the narrative is actually divided into two quite distinct parts. The first describes the verbal exchange between the woman and her neighbor, and concludes with the illness. The actual casting of the spell happens "off camera," and brings the witch's active part in the story to a close. The remainder of the story recounts the discoveries that prove the illness to be the result of sorcery.

That the narrative genre is important to Institoris and Sprenger's understanding of witchcraft makes sense, for it is *only* in narratives that the witch and her witchcraft are firmly joined. In narratives the actual identification of the witch and of her *maleficium* (which, as a matter of actual experience are two quite different things, linked only by conjecture or occult knowledge) become two moments in an ongoing process of considerable explanatory and evidentiary power. This, of course, is why people like the clay-worker were invaluable: they confirmed suspicions and removed doubt in a conceptual arena where everything was chronically ambiguous, and ambiguity itself was threatening and dangerous.

In the *Malleus*, narratives of this type, and the structures of thought that went into them, are critical to the formal determination of a witch's guilt. As was customary, Institoris and Sprenger judged heretics sufficiently suspect to justify torture, imprisonment, and death if they were found "manifestly taken in heresy," but in the case of witches the paradigmatic expression of this degree of suspicion was provided by the posited link between a woman's ill-will or a quarrel and a subsequent injury.[92] If the injury followed immediately, as in the case of the unfortunate merchant of Speyer, the evidence was direct; if the injury followed only after the lapse of some time, as with the matron of Innsbruck, the evidence was indirect and slightly less damning. To make this determination of guilt, the inquisitors advised asking the suspect such questions as "why did you say that he would never have a day of health and so it happened?" or "why she was seen in the fields or in the stable touching the cattle?" or "why when she had one or two cows did she have more milk than her neighbors with four or six?"[93] Inconsistent responses or answers that conflicted with other testimony or physical evidence indicated the need to proceed to torture.[94] Yet, if the suspect would not confess, the stories that sufficed to put her to torture were also sufficient in themselves to convict her of witchcraft. Simply being called a witch was not enough; rather, the alleged witch had to be linked directly to some specific injury.

Recited as a dry list, the possible ways in which a woman could be caught in the "manifest heresy" of witchcraft seem ridiculously tenuous. Direct evidence of guilt might consist of the witch using threatening words, such as "you will soon know what is going to happen to you," or touching a person or beast with her hands, or even being seen in a dream prior to some affliction.[95] Nonetheless, just as these minor performances provided the necessary clues by which a witch's identity was revealed within a narrative context, so they provided the learned inquisitor with the grounds for "vehement suspicion of heresy," sufficient to justify that the witch be given over to the "torture and the squalor of prison" for up to a year, and, if confirmed by multiple witnesses, to consign her to the flames.[96]

In this, Institoris and Sprenger differed substantially from other fifteenth-century witch-theorists: although the pact may have provided the theoretical basis for the witch's heresy, and for her exceptional status among heretics, it was essentially moot in their courtroom. Instead, it was the connection between the witch and her *maleficium* that constituted their radically revised standard for "manifest heresy." A woman accused of causing an illness by touch was, for them, every bit as guilty of heresy as was a man who received communion and consolation from heretics, and showed them "reverent love."[97] For this reason, Institoris and Sprenger need not require proof that a witch had attended the Sabbat or delivered the obscene kiss, because they had made the symbolic markers of heresy dependent upon the evidence they found so readily at hand.

Superstition

However well a tautological relationship between the witch and her witchcraft might work in stories, as a logical argument it left much to be desired. For this reason, it is also a convenient illustration of the tension in the *Malleus* between the witch of narrative examples – which, as we have seen, is vitally important to the authors' argument – and the witch of theory. In effect, Institoris and Sprenger were confronted by category confusion of their own making. On the one hand, their theory was plain: the witch was defined by her pact with the devil. "Witch," in this sense, was a rigidly bounded, undifferentiated category, and so the authors consistently argue that all witches are essentially alike, despite appearances to the contrary. Yet at the same time, they endorsed a narrative-based conception of witchcraft, in which the category *malefica* was graduated, covering a wide range of individually different witches. In daily life, as in their narratives, the question "Is so-and-so a witch?" was not answered with reference to some absolutely defining parameter, but by comparison with an abstract ideal, an imagined prototype of "witch." Hence, people could either be witches, not witches, or somewhere in between.

In one sense, this category confusion was essential to Institoris and Sprenger's argument, since they used the differentiated and evaluative con-

ception of witchcraft which they found operative at the local level to fill the
otherwise empty set created by their more rigid, theoretical category.
Nonetheless, since effective persecution of witches required both a satisfactory definition and widespread acceptance that this definition was fundamen-
tally valid, Institoris and Sprenger were forced to reconcile the two.[98] This was
difficult because the rigid bounding parameters of the theologically defined
witch did not correspond in any meaningful way to the shifting, ambiguous
edges of village witchcraft. To order this intractable boundary, the authors
looked to the larger category of superstition.

Because the Church regarded all forms of magic as, at bottom, superstitious observances, notions of *maleficium* and *superstitio* had long been intertwined. Superstition, according to the authorities, consisted of "religion
observed in an excessive way, that is, religion practiced in a manner or under
circumstances that are evil or defective."[99] Superstition, in other words, was
bad religion, usually manifested in either of two closely related errors. First,
all unauthorized, erroneous, or excessive devotions to God were classified as
superstition. It was, for example, improper and superstitious to sacrifice live
animals to God after the manner of the pagans. Second, all observances,
whether in the correct form or not, were superstitious if they did not have
the proper God as their object: any prayer to Diana, indeed any recognition
of Diana's divinity, was thus superstitious. The devil created both kinds of
superstition to undermine the true faith; hence, anything accomplished
through them was done by his power and, ultimately, in his name.

This last point was very important, because here superstition and magic
converged. Demons desired various kinds of stones, plants, songs, and rites,
not because of any intrinsic quality that they might possess, but because they
were spiritual signs which signified divine honors. As Martin of Arles explained
in his treatise on superstition, witches employed various rites and apparatus
in their magic to encourage demons to respond.[100] Magicians might either
realize that they were in fact offering divine service to demons, or they might
be ignorant of the real nature of their procedures, but in either case a pact
with demons was involved. Martin further maintained that "a pact [with the
devil] is implicit in all superstitious observances, whose effect ought not to be
reasonably expected from God or from nature."[101] There was, in this sense, no
important distinction between magic *per se* and gathering medicinal herbs on
the night of St. John's feast: both were superstitious and both a diabolic pact.
Definitions of superstition differed from definitions of *maleficium* in this
respect; for while the latter was basically a descriptive category which corresponded to what victims perceived, the former was defined in purely theoretical terms and could include an almost limitless number of very different
behaviors and practices. To most people, there was a considerable difference

between a *malefica* and a woman who gave her cow holy water to drink. Not
so to the careful theologian: since holy water should not be consumed, any
effect anticipated from this procedure could not come from God. Nor could
it come from nature, since only the benediction separated holy water from
normal water. The woman was, therefore, invoking the devil in exactly the
same way as did magicians and witches.[102]

Reasoning thus, clerics often condemned superstition and magic in the
same breath. In 1402, for example, Jean Gerson abominated learned magic
and rustic superstition in identical terms, writing that

> It is necessary for me to lament passionately the pestiferous superstitions of
> magicians and the foolishness of old women who practice *sortilegium*, who
> profess to effect cures by certain accursed rites.[103]

Those guilty of magical practices, he argued, were to be burned by the secular
authorities, since all were equally guilty of apostasy through their pact with
Satan.

Although Institoris and Sprenger could certainly understand Gerson's
point, they could not accept that witches, whose crimes were immeasur-
ably more awful, were substantially equivalent to other kinds of magicians.
Magicians, they thought, belonged to several fairly distinct types: first, there
were witches, illiterate women who had given themselves body and soul to
the devil; then, there were learned magicians, who might or might not have
an explicit pact with the devil, but who did not belong to the sect of the
witches; finally, there were *superstitiosi*, who were usually guilty of only a tacit
pact with Satan. Complicating matters still further, there were also many
people who used the legitimate rites of the Church to achieve the same effects
as magicians. *Maleficae*, *superstitiosi*, and devout Catholics all used similar practices to achieve similar results, though they differed absolutely in the sources
of their power and in their relationship to that power.

In the *Malleus*, the *superstitiosi* occupy the ambiguous ground between
out-and-out witches and the lawful practitioners of useful divine observances,
where their presence permits the authors to reserve the label "witch" exclusively for those most commonly accepted as such. Take, as an example, the
magical theft of milk, butter, wine, or other agricultural products from one's
neighbors. Nider, Mamoris, and Institoris and Sprenger all refer to this magic
unambiguously as *maleficium*, and hence strongly imply that its practitioners
were witches.[104] The situation was not, however, quite this simple. This particular kind of magic might, or might not, entail an explicit pact with the devil.
Institoris and Sprenger had heard of a man who could produce witch-butter
by making strange motions while standing in a stream, but, because this *magus*

did not behave "as witches are accustomed to do," Institoris and Sprenger decided that he probably held a tacit and not an explicit pact with the devil.[105] In this case, they proposed instead that the *maleficium* of the *magus* was more akin to the magic of certain *superstitiosi*, who made off with wine in a similar manner, than to the crimes of witches.[106]

This distinction was neither arbitrary nor unreasonable. In the first place, it allowed Institoris and Sprenger to avoid having to argue that all superstitious magical practices were equivalent to witchcraft. In the second place, it allowed them to argue that not just anyone could be a witch. By distinguishing between superstitious magic and witchcraft on the basis of gender and perceptions of social deviance, Institoris and Sprenger aligned their own construction of witchcraft with that of popular usage, in which ascriptions of witchcraft commonly depended upon both the potential capacity for preternatural harm and a particular kind of social valuation. In other words, they were prepared, as other demonologists were not, to tolerate a certain amount of surreptitious traffic with the devil, provided one's résumé did not resemble that of a witch in other respects.

Institoris and Sprenger employ the concept of superstition in a similar way when they consider the problem of magical healers. Appearances could be deceiving: just as *maleficium* did not necessarily mean that one was a witch, so the use of apparently benign magic did not necessarily mean that one was not. Inconveniently, witches came in three quite different classes:

> those who cause injuries but do not have the power to cure; those who cure but who, from some singular pact entered into with the devil, do not injure; and those who both cure and cause injuries.[107]

The most powerful, and hence the most dangerous, witches were those who could do both kinds of magic, and of these the most feared were the cannibal witches, who ate newborn children, for these possessed the full panoply of diabolic powers.[108]

In their own way, however, healing witches were just as bad as more obvious *maleficae*, despite their more benign appearance, since their power was likewise derived from a explicit pact with the devil and their objectives were every bit as hostile. Healing witches sought, in effect, to exchange physical injuries for spiritual ones: by offering effective but diabolical remedies for the *maleficium* caused by their sisters, such witches entangled their victims in superstitious practices. Germany, the authors mournfully relate, was so overrun with these witches that one could be found everywhere every couple of miles.[109] They add that the unscrupulous count of Reichshofen actually made a tidy profit taxing the patrons of his local witch, and one of the authors had seen personally vast crowds of poor folk come from miles around, even in the dead of winter, to the village of Einigen to visit a celebrated witch-doctor named Hengst. "Without doubt," they comment bitterly, "so great a concourse of poor folk had never gone to any of the shrines of the Blessed Virgin either at Aachen or at Einsiedeln, such as went to that *superstitiosus*."[110]

But was Hengst a witch? Their use of the word *superstitiosus* seems to imply not. But why? Witchcraft could be undone in a number of different ways, and by diverse kinds of persons. In the worst and most obvious case, the healer simply transferred the injury from the bewitched patient to another victim, not really curing anything at all. Such a remedy was seemingly little different from open *maleficium*, and, although not absolute proof of witchcraft, the authors leave little doubt that malign healers of this sort should be treated like more conventional witches. A more difficult problem was posed by healers who employed techniques that were certainly superstitious, but that might not constitute witchcraft. Some healers, for example, undid *maleficia* through the express invocation of demons, a clearly unlawful procedure, though to Institoris and Sprenger rather less criminal than methods of the first sort. Hengst was an example of this class of magician, and he, and those like him, stood on the absolute edge of real witchcraft, to be identified by the authors as *malefici* one moment, and as *superstitiosi* or *sortilegi* the next. Finally, there were healers who used superstitious remedies but who did not invoke the devil and were not "manifest witches." These men were the least guilty, despite the probability that they worked through a tacit pact with the devil. As an example, Institoris and Sprenger describe a witch-doctor who poured molten lead into water to diagnose *maleficium*, and employed incantations to effect a cure.[111] The healer was said to attribute his success to God and to Saturn's planetary influence over lead and magic — all good and orthodox as far as it went — but, since the power by which the *maleficium* was removed was unclear, it was likely that a tacit pact with the devil was still required.

As far as Institoris and Sprenger were concerned, the use of a given supernatural agency was itself morally charged — laudable if the agent were God or his representative, sinful if the devil or his minion. To those less sensitized to the nuances of a theologically determined world, preternatural or supernatural power was morally ambiguous, relatively good or bad depending upon its effects, in other words a benign healer was separated from an evil witch by good intentions, intentions that could seem quite different to different people at different times. The ease with which a healer could slide across the boundary into witchcraft is illustrated in a narrative Institoris heard while at Innsbruck. An honest matron told him that in her youth she had been the servant of a woman who had taken ill with severe pains in the head.[112] One day, a woman arrived at the door who claimed to able to cure the affliction.

As the maid watched, the woman performed a ceremony in which water rose in a vessel, *contra naturam*. Because of this, and "considering that the pain in the lady's head was in no way mitigated by these things," the maid unwisely called the performance superstitious.[113] The irate healer then responded with an unusual variant on the damning threats of a witch: "You will know in three days whether they are superstitious or not."[114] In due course, the maid was afflicted with wracking pains of her own, which were assuaged only when her mistress's husband found the instruments of *maleficium* hidden over a tavern door.

For the most part, this is a conventional tale of witchcraft. What sets it apart is the speed and the manner with which benign healing is transformed, first into "superstition" and then into *maleficium*. For the narrator, magic was divided into three distinct conceptual fields based upon effects. Had the witch's healing performance brought immediate relief, it would have been benign; having failed, it is, perhaps, superstition; but when injury followed upon the witch's threats it is revealed as *maleficium*. Effects, not theology, mattered to the actors in this narrative, just as they did to Institoris.

In the *Malleus*, the technical distinction between a witch and a *superstitiosa* depends upon this subjective perception of the magical practitioner's intentions and the effects of his or her magic. In the author's learned model of witchcraft, the boundary between *superstitiosa* and *malefica* corresponds closely to the tenuous line that separates benign healers from evil witches in daily life. Superstition thus provides Institoris and Sprenger with a tool with which to smooth the rough edges of witchcraft's boundaries, in this case by creating a space for people who looked like witches, and were potentially witches, but whom, at a given moment, it was inconvenient or inappropriate to call witches. In a similar way, superstition helped to define an important and related category, the lawful remedial and preventative observances of the Church.

To Institoris and Sprenger, the power of God was the logical and necessary counterpart to the power of the devil. Where the witch wielded the powerfully destructive forces of evil, good Christians could turn to the equally impressive arsenal of the Church. In many respects, the witch's diabolic magic in the *Malleus* seems the mirror image of the priest's divine power. For both, supernatural power is mediated almost entirely through human agents, and is made to serve explicitly human ends. For both, this power is controlled and directed through the manipulation of material objects, sacramentals and the host in one case, the instruments of *maleficium* in the other. Finally, in both, the line between their characteristic practices and superstition was perilously thin: just as *superstitiosi* could do many of the same things as witches and still not be witches, so too could they mimic the rites of orthodox Christians, while yet invoking the devil. This apparent similarity between the observances of the Church and the witch's magic was, of course, no accident. Throughout the Middle Ages, the rituals of the Church provided models for popular magical practices, and *vice versa*. This was especially true for Institoris and Sprenger, whose understanding of the way divine power was mediated and directed for human benefit yielded the paradigm for the witch's employment of the powers of the devil in the *Malleus*. Their expansive view of the powers of witchcraft went hand in hand with their liberal endorsement of countervailing Christian observances.

From this perspective, the purpose of the *Malleus* appears almost as much a justification of popular Christian ritual as a condemnation of witchcraft, although, to the authors, these probably amounted to much the same the thing. While many of their clerical colleagues, however, began to look askance upon the thriving "economy of the sacred" that had grown up outside effective clerical control, to reform-minded clerics, superstition was, as Stuart Clark writes, "a cultural weapon," used to condemn popular belief,

> a form of proscription in terms of which many of the routine material practices of pre-industrial rural cultures, together with the categories and beliefs that shaped ordinary people's experience, were denounced as valueless.[115]

The authors of the *Malleus*, on the other hand, use notions of superstition to validate and authorize the conceptual horizons of their informants, and to defend a broad range of popular "magical" procedures by fixing a narrow limit upon those practices that were not allowed.

To begin with, Institoris and Sprenger maintained that sacramentals provided the most consistently reliable protection against witchcraft. Strictly speaking, sacramentals are blessed objects – commonly water, salt, wax, and herbs – conducive to divine grace and inimical to the devil.[116] Unlike true sacraments, they have no mechanical efficacy, being dependent upon the spiritual disposition of the user. Like the host, sacramentals provided a material point of intersection between the sacred and the profane, and access to supernatural power, and so like the host were employed to produce a variety of desired effects: to ensure the fertility of fields and animals, to extinguish fires, to repel storms, to cure illness – in short, to undo the harm wrought by destructive forces in all areas of human endeavor.[117] Disagreements arose, however, over the extent to which sacramentals could be legitimately employed as apotropaic measures, and over the requisite degree of clerical control. Because they were material objects that could be employed without immediate clerical supervision, sacramentals were obviously vulnerable to abuse; their use was especially suspect when adapted to the models provided by non-Christian magical operations. Many clerics, such as Johannes Nider and Institoris and Sprenger, did not object: so long as the charms and talismans with which people festooned their livestock conformed to the rules for proper Christian ritual, they were perfectly orthodox, even if, to untrained observers, these rules might seem arbitrary, since such operations looked completely mechanical. The temptation to extend the use of such powerful objects to performances other than those fully acceptable to the Church was irresistible. Unfortunately, the moment that happened, the operation changed diametrically in character, from Christian devotional observance to diabolic superstition.

Like most demonologists, Institoris and Sprenger liberally endorsed the use of sacramentals to counter the baleful effects of witchcraft. They recommended that all good people irrigate their thresholds with holy water, burn candles of blessed wax, scatter blessed herbs over cattle, and wear charms inscribed with holy words as protection against witches.[118] To determine whether a given usage was lawful or superstitious, Institoris and Sprenger first examined the question of efficacy. For them, as for most other late-medieval clerics, there was really no such thing as an "empty" superstition, since ritual invocations of supernatural power did indeed produce material effects – the real question was who or what was causing them? Superstitions were called "vanities" only because the ritual itself could not produce the desired effect: they communicated and mediated, but did not intrinsically possess, occult power. Under many circumstances, the efficacy of a given procedure alone could indicate whether it was lawful. For example, the authors tell of a bewitched cow that was cured when adorned with written Christian charms, as proof that such procedures are acceptable to God.[119] Because efficacy implied divine approval, it was very difficult for Institoris and Sprenger to condemn an effective observance, provided that reference was made only to God and the legitimate rituals of the Church.

Such an approach was theologically justifiable, but inherently permissive since it placed no restrictions upon the uses to which God's power might legitimately be put. Compare, for example, Institoris and Sprenger's view of superstition with that of Martin of Arles. Martin was offended by a custom of his local church, in which during times of severe drought all the people – both *clerici* and *coloni* – would assemble before the shrine of St. Peter, and then, as Martin adds, "with great devotion," would take his image down to the river with singing and with praise.[120] But then,

> some of them make a request of the image, saying, "St. Peter, help us, who have been obliged by necessity to do this, to get rain for us from God." And this is

repeated twice and three times. And when the image fails to respond to any of these requests, they cry out, "let the image of blessed Peter be submerged, if he does not obtain for us, from almighty God, the favor demanded for the need which is threatening us![121]

The statue was then submerged amid jocular debates about Peter's merits and worth, a procedure that was said to infallibly bring rain within twenty-four hours. Martin subjected this custom to lengthy analysis in the light of traditional theological authorities and concluded that "to submerge the image of blessed Peter does not pertain to the glory of God, by which the Lord is praised in his saints, but to his blame and injury."[122] Consequently, he condemned the rite as superstitious and blasphemous. In this context, the efficacy of the rite was irrelevant: one ought not to dunk St. Peter regardless of whether rains might result.

Institoris and Sprenger would probably have arrived at a similar conclusion, but through a quite different process. Where Martin chose an unacceptable superstitious usage for his test case, in the *Malleus* the most detailed discussion of the theory of superstition involved a practice that the authors ultimately endorse: the "most ancient" custom of exposing relics or the sacrament to avert oncoming storms.[123] In their opinion, any rite or observance that is not superstitious is acceptable.[124] Moreover, since witchcraft is such a terrible threat, any acceptable measure providing some degree of protection against the power of the devil should be seized upon at once, especially in this particular case, when the power of the sacrament and of relics to calm the weather was well attested both by common report and by the expert testimony of witches.

A rite was acceptable, then, if it did not violate any of the five rules for valid religious observances. First, the practice had to have as its chief aim the glorification of God (though, to the inquisitors, virtually any nonabusive use of the sacrament seemed to fulfill this condition).[125] Second, if the practice pertained to abstinence or bodily discipline, it had to be consistent with virtue and the doctrines of the Church. Third, the practice had to be in accordance with the recognized and traditional procedures of a given church or with "general custom." Fourth, the practice had to have some natural relation with the sought-after effect (though, again, in the opinion of the authors, any kind of remedial, curative, or protective effect could reasonably be expected of sacraments or the relics of saints). Finally, the practice should give no occasion for scandal or error among the uneducated, and here the authors advise the officiants merely to exercise caution and common sense. Since use of the consecrated host to avert storms was found to fulfill all five requirements, the authors therefore pronounced the custom entirely legitimate and not superstitious in the least degree.[126]

On this basis, Institoris and Sprenger did not hesitate to commend those women who gave the whole of Sunday's milk production to the poor, saying that by such means their cows gave "a greater abundance of milk and were preserved from witchcraft."[127] Above reproach, too, are those who wear prayers and charms written in Latin, even if unable to understand them; in this case it is enough, the authors say, if the patient turns his thoughts to general notions of divine goodness.[128] And they advise that the practices of peasants who weave a cross from the leaves consecrated on Palm Sunday and place it in their fields to ward off hail should be judged in a similar manner.[129] In each case, the authors approve of apotropaic and remedial observances provided a sincere appeal to divine power is made without any obvious breach of the rules.

At times this line could be perilously thin. As one possible remedy for *maleficium*, Institoris and Sprenger describe a rustic antidote to bewitched butter:

> Again, there are certain women who, when they think that they cannot finish churning their butter, as they are accustomed to do in oblong vessels made for this purpose, then, if they can quickly get some butter from the house of the suspected witch, they make three pieces or morsels from that butter, and, with an invocation to the most holy Trinity, the Father, the Son, and the Holy Spirit, throw those pieces into the churn, and so all the witchcraft is put to flight.[130]

This custom, the authors decided, was probably superstitious, since there was no natural reason why the butter had to come from the witch. At the same time, it was the mildest form of superstition, a case of opposing "vanity with vanity." That it was no worse is surprising, since the authors have just pointed out that witches often borrow dairy products as a prelude to *maleficium*. From the perspective of the "witch," these erstwhile witch curers might well have seemed guilty of witchcraft themselves. Yet Institoris and Sprenger all but give this procedure their blessing. It would be better, of course, if three random pieces of butter were used instead of those superstitiously linked to the witch, in which case the women would "remain irreproachable although not to be commended," because holy water or some other sacramental would be a more appropriate weapon against witchcraft.[131] Their phrase is curious: since the procedure was "irreproachable" one must assume that it derived its power from God, and must logically also be pleasing to God, else he would not have lent it his support. Why then would such a practice not be commendable?

I suspect that there were several reasons why Institoris and Sprenger were less than completely happy with even a revised variant of this rite. First, the element of sympathetic magic – in this case a matter of "pump-priming" the stubborn churn with butter – must have been uncomfortably obvious to ritual-sensitive clerics. Second, the narrow line that the authors drew between divine and diabolic power became more tenuous and more seemingly arbitrary the closer one got to it. This butter charm represents the far limit of legitimate "religious" observances, immediately beyond which lay the realms of demonic power. Out on this margin, the differences between the two have become essentially negligible: different butter-charm variants employed alternatively agents of God and the devil, but employed them to exactly the same ends and in exactly the same ways. By authorizing these procedures, Institoris and Sprenger have come very close to validating the view of some of their informants: that God and the devil are simply alternative sources of occult power, not the slightest bit different in kind. Finally, and probably most disturbing to the authors, viewed in the best possible light the butter charm was a kind of exorcism intended to drive destructive demonic powers from the bewitched churn. It was, however, an exorcism totally divorced from clerical control and supervision. By advising that sacramentals be used in the place of butter, Institoris and Sprenger defuse most of these issues: at the same time, the element of sympathetic magic is lost, the line between diabolic and divine power is defined, while the necessary mediative role of the Church is restored.

Given, though, the many reasons why the butter charm should be condemned, a more interesting question may be why it was not. Institoris and Sprenger were unique, insofar as I am aware, among fifteenth-century witch-theorists, in the importance and value that they ascribed to popular remedies against *maleficium*. Most of their colleagues encouraged the liberal use of sacramentals as preventative measures, but advised extreme caution when it came to undoing the effects of a witch's magic. Petrus Mamoris was both more optimistic about the efficacy of conventionally orthodox remedies, and more insistent upon the necessity for clerical mediation of divine power. For Mamoris, the most effective way to bear off the harmful effects of *maleficium* was through the normal usages of the Church: alms, prayer, the confession of sins, and communion. Since the power of the devil could be overcome only by the power of God, the bewitched were best served by appealing to God's mercy in approved and conventional ways.[132] He advised priests to counsel couples whose love had turned to hatred through witchcraft, since "they should conquer by faith . . . the enemy who endeavors to trouble them."[133] Folk remedies of all sorts he condemned as "vain superstitions which ought to be shunned just like *maleficia*."[134] The only exception to this rule was that he, like Nider, allowed that when the instruments of *maleficium* were discovered, it was licit to destroy them in hope of breaking the spell.[135]

This was an interesting exception. Since the instrument of *maleficium* was only a sign indicating the witch's complicity with the devil's design, if a spell was broken when it was destroyed it could only be through the devil's own power. Finding and removing an instrument of *maleficium* was thus technically a "vanity," in as much as the action held no intrinsic power. Most clerics took a dim view of such practices for this reason. Gerson, for example, explicitly condemned the destruction of the signs of witchcraft, as a kind of complicity with the devil little different from *maleficium*.[136] Nonetheless, various other authorities approved of this procedure. Especially notable was Duns Scotus, whom Institoris and Sprenger claim whole-heartedly approved of the destruction of the instruments of *maleficia*,

> because by destroying them he does not assent to the works of the devil, but rather believes that [the devil] is able and willing to torment him while such a sign endures, because, according to his pact, [the devil] lends his support to this torment only while that sign endures.[137]

This notion of sign, *signum*, was extremely important, for it supplied a common thread running through all types of magical operation. Sacramental observances, witchcraft, and "vain" superstitions all depended upon signs of one type or another to communicate and mediate supernatural power. Duns Scotus was, of course, speaking primarily of the destruction of magical apparatus concealed under thresholds and the like, as were Nider and Mamoris. When Institoris and Sprenger, however, explained to their readers what Duns Scotus meant by "sign," they chose a positively perverse example. They reported that when a cow's supply of milk had been depleted by witchcraft, some women would hang a pail of milk over a fire and beat it while uttering superstitious words.[138] The devil then transmitted the blows to the witch responsible. Similarly, people might drag the intestines of an animal killed by witchcraft through the streets and into their homes, and then burn them in the fire, believing that "just as the intestines grow hot and burn, so the intestines of the witch are tortured with pain and heat."[139] To Institoris and Sprenger, the bewitched cow's milk and the dying animal's intestines were both "signs" of witchcraft, and like sacramental and diabolic *signa* they could be exploited in a mechanical way. Satan, like God, was contractually obligated by his pact to behave predictably. Exactly how all this was relevant to Duns Scotus' argument remained unclear; their point, however, was that folk-remedies that did not explicitly call upon the devil, that did not involve the participation of witches, and that had the discovery or remedy of witchcraft as their aim could be tolerated even though they were clearly superstitious and implicitly dependent upon the active participation of the devil.

With this surprising conclusion, Institoris and Sprenger have again made inventive use of the category of superstition, this time to distinguish tolerable "vanities" from condemned sorcery and witchcraft. Again, the authors have used notions of superstition to define an ambiguous middle ground between legitimate magic and witchcraft. "Vanities" were not necessarily to be encouraged, and certainly were not meritorious, but they were tolerable, and were definitely not *maleficia*.

Conclusion

The image of witches and witchcraft in the *Malleus* is perhaps best understood as a representation of a contested reality. Institoris and Sprenger were merely two of many scholars, clerics, and magistrates who found traditional conceptions of a world that was almost witch-free unacceptable in the light of contemporary evidence, and their representation of witchcraft was simply one of several such models that competed for attention and influence towards the end of the fifteenth century. Their model is notable, however, in that, more successfully than most of their competitors, they reconcile the demands of experience, reason, and theologically determined truth. Their understanding of witchcraft contains features which mark it distinctively as the product of their own experience: a sensitivity to popular narrative discourse, strangely combined with an almost complete lack of understanding of the differences between oral genres; a view that supernatural powers are in a sense balanced, the power of the devil being set against the even greater power of sacramentals and the Church; a corresponding acceptance of a remarkably wide range of popular remedies against witchcraft; and especially their insistence that witchcraft is linked inextricably with the female sex. Most of the notions about witchcraft in the *Malleus* can be understood as the product of minds which – although theologically learned and aware – have a view of the world that in many respects comes extremely close to that of their informants. The incessant emphasis upon the feminine nature of witchcraft, however, requires a somewhat different explanation, and this will be the subject of our final chapter.

Notes

1 Technically, heresy consisted of an error of belief persistently and perniciously held. Thus, Robert Grosseteste defined heresy as "an opinion chosen by human perception contrary to holy Scripture, publicly held and obstinately defended." Cited in Malcolm Lambert, *Medieval Heresy* (Oxford: Basil Blackwell, 1992), 4; see also Walter L. Wakefield and Austin P. Evans, eds., *Heresies of the High Middle Ages* (New York: Columbia University Press, 1969), 1–4. Apostasy was a subspecies of heresy, in which one abandoned the faith and put some false belief in its place (Bernard of Como, *Haeretica Pravitas* (Lucerne: 1584), 14); offering any form of adoration or honor to the devil, for example, constituted apostasy.

2 See esp. Russell, *Witchcraft in the Middle Ages*, and Cohn, *Europe's Inner Demons*.

3 Augustine, *On Christian Doctrine*, c. xxiii, p. 59.

4 "Si enim per invocationes, conjurationes, sacrificia, suffumigationes, et adorationes fiunt, tunc aperte pactum initur cum demone et tunc est apostasia oris ibi." Aquinas, *Sentences*, III, dist. 7, c. 112; Lea, *Materials*, 1:200.

5 Aquinas, *Summa contra Gentiles*, 3.104–7.

6 Alexander IV, *Quod super Nonnullis*, in Hansen, *Quellen*, 1; and see Peters, 85–181.

7 Peters, 160.

8 " 'Maleficos non pateris vivere.' Maleficos qui praestigiis magicae artis et diabolicis figmentis agunt, haereticos intellige, qui a consortio fidelium qui vere vivunt, excommunicandi sunt, donec maleficium erroris in eis moriatur." *Biblia Latina cum Glossa Ordinaria* (facsimile reprint of editio princeps, Adolf Rusch, 1480/81; Turnholt: Brepols, 1992).

9 Walter Map, pt. 1, c. 30, p. 57.

10 The origins of all this are obscure, and the subject of considerable scholarly disagreement. See Ginzburg, "Deciphering the Sabbath," 121–37; Muchembled, "Satanic Myths," 139–60; and Robert Rowland, " 'Fantastical and Devilishe Persons': European Witch-beliefs in Comparative Perspective," same volume, 161–90.

11 See Lambert, 4. Early demonstrations of the collapse of defining parameters for heresy in the fourteenth century can be found in the prosecutions of "artificial" heretics: the Brethren of the Free Spirit, and the "Luciferans." See Lambert, 187–8, 212–13; Russell, *Witchcraft in the Middle Ages*, 176–80.

12 Étienne de Bourbon, 367.

13 "Ad hanc ludificacionem, que fit in sompniis, pertinet error illarum mulierum que dicunt se nocturnis horis cum Diana et Herodiade et aliis personis, quas bonas res vocant, ambulare, et super quasdam bestias equitare." *Ibid.*, 368.

14 Similar blurring of categories had occurred long before: Gregory the Great, for example, used the *lamia* as a symbolic representation of both sorcerers and heretics, a metaphor, taken perhaps more literally than Gregory intended, which remained popular among late-medieval witch-theorists. *Moralia in Job*, 34. See also Mamoris, 33.

15 Kathrin Utz Tremp and Martine Ostorero, eds., *Errores Gazariorum seu illorum, qui scobam vel baculum equitare probantur*, in Martine Ostorero, Agostino Paravicini Bagliani, and Kathrin Uzt Tremp, eds., *L'Imaginaire du Sabbat: edition critique des textes les plus anciens (1430 c.–1440 c.)*, Cahiers lausannois d'histoire médiévale 26 (Lausanne: Université de Lausanne, 1999), 278–99. See also Hansen, *Quellen*, 118–22.

16 "simul carnaliter coniunguntur solus cum sola vel solus cum solo, et aliquando pater cum filia, filius cum matre, frater cum sorore, et equo ordine nature minime observato." *Errores Gazariorum*, 290.

17 The devil gives each initiate a compact written in his or her own blood after he receives the oath of allegiance. *Ibid.*, 296–8.

18 "quod illi de secta inter ceteros fideles videntur esse meliores et communiter audiunt missam sepe in anno confitentes; et multociens capiunt sacram eucharistiam." *Ibid.*, 298.

19 Pierrette Parvay, "À propos de la genèse médiévale des chasses aux sorcières: le traité de Claude Tholasan, juge dauphinois (vers 1436)," *Mélanges de L'École française de Rome (Moyen Age – temps modernes)* 91 (1979): 333–79; see also Jeffrey Burton Russell, *Witchcraft in the Middle Ages*, 216–18; Hansen, *Quellen*, 459–67.

20 "ponunt genua ad terram, et obsculantur dyabolum qui communiter apparet eis in forma hominis et multorum diversorum animalium, et obsculantur eum in ore; dando sibi corpus et animam et alterum ex pueris suis, maxime primo genitum, quem sibi immolant et sacrificant, genibus flexis, tenendo eum sub brachiis et humeris nudum et demum extingunt et post sepulturam exhumant, et de eo, cum aliis infrascriptis, faciunt pulverem." Claude Tholosan, *Ut Magorum et Maleficiorum Errores*, in Parvay, 356.

21 "Sic quod credunt ire corporaliter de nocte, maxime diebus jovis et sabbati, in comitiva dyabolorum, ad suffocandum pueros et infirmitates incussiendum; extrahentes sagimen a pueris quos decoquunt et comedunt." *Ibid.*, 357.

22 Cohn, *Europe's Inner Demons*, 1–18.

23 Wakefield and Evans, 78–9. For a discussion of the historicity of the account, see Lambert, 9–16.

24 Wakefield and Evans, 78–9.

25 "Nam infantibus nondum baptisatis insidiamur: vel eciam baptisatis, praesertim si signo crucis non muniuntur, et orationibus, hos in cunabulis, vel ad latera iacentes parentum, ceremoniis nostris occidimus, quos postquam putantur oppressi esse, vel aliunde mortui de tumulis clam furto recipimus, in caldari decoquimus, quousque euulsis ossibus tota pene caro efficiatur sorbilis et potabilis. De solidiori huius materia vnguentum facimus nostris voluntatibus et artibus ac transmutationibus accommodatum: de liquidiori vero humore flascam aut vtrem replemus, de quo is qui potatus fuerit, additis paucis cerimoniis, statim conscius efficitur et magister nostrae sectae." Nider, *Formicarius*, 5.3; 203.

26 "Postremo de vtre bibit supradicto: quo facto, statim se in interioribus sentit imaginem nostrae artis concipere et retinere, ac principales ritus huius sectae." *Ibid.*

27 I.M. Lewis, *Religion in Context: Cult and Charisma* (Cambridge: Cambridge University Press, 1986), 67.

28 Donald Tuzin, "Cannibalism and Arapesh Cosmology," in Paula Brown and Donald Tuzin, eds., *The Ethnography of Cannibalism* (Washington, D.C.: Society for Psychological Anthropology, 1983), 62.

29 "Sunt autem he que contra humane nature inclinationem imo omnium ferarum [lupina tantummodo excepta] proprie speciei infantes vorant et comedere solent." *Malleus*, pt. 2, qu. 1, ch. 2, p. 96. Institoris and Spenger are quoting Nider's description of the witches of Lausane, although they characteristically omit Nider's immediately preceding remark, that both sexes were included among these witches: "quidam Malefici vtriusque sexus." *Formicarius*, 5.3, p. 202.

30 For the frequency with which heretics were accused of infanticide, see Russell, *Witchcraft in the Middle Ages*, 92–4; Briggs, *Witches and Neighbors*, 32.

31 This conceptual similarity, rather than any common bond with the devil, may explain the thinking of the author of one late-medieval devotional treatise who condemned "wycches & heretykes" together in one breath: "Accursed are alle þat dystroyin in þe moderys wombe ony chyld, or slene wyth drynkys, or wyth oþere craftes, after þe tym þey have lyif, or puttyn here chyldren to be fals eyres. And all wycches, & heretykes, & lollardys, & alle þat beleuyn on here heresye." Arthur Brandeis, ed., *Jacob's Well* (Early English Test Society, O.S. 115, London: Kegan Paul, Trench, Trübner and Co., 1900), 59.

32 "et ibidem abnegare coram eis Christum, eius fidem, baptisma, et uniuersalem ecclesiam. Deinde omagium praestare magisterulo, id est, paruo magistro, ita enim Daemonem et non aliter vocant . . . Sequitur postremo, de utre bibit supradicto [quo facto statim se in interioribus sentit imagines nostre artis concipere et retinere super principales ritus huius sectae]." *Malleus*, pt. 2, qu. 1, ch. 2, 98; *Formicarius*, 5.3; 203.

33 "In hac autem fascinariorum secta siue Synagoga, conueniunt non solum mulieres, sed viri, et quod deterius est, etiam Ecclesiastici et Religiosi, qui stant et loquuntur cum Daemonibus perceptibiliter." Jacquier, 41.

34 "a viginti annis citra, quendam Magnum Baronem in Galliis clam iugulasse circiter viginti pueros, ut de eorum sanguine quendam librum scriberet in obsequium Daemonum." *Ibid.*, 116. Jacquier may refer to Gilles de Rais.

35 "hoc genus superstitionis non libris aut a doctis sed omnino ab imperitis practicatur." *Malleus*, pt. 2, qu. 1, p. 91.

36 Charlton T. Lewis and Charles Short, *A Latin Dictionary* (Oxford: Clarendon Press, 1879), s.v. "maleficium" and "maleficus."

37 Both Gratian and Ivo of Chartres included the canon in their collections: "Si per sortiarias atque maleficas, occulto sed nunquam injusto Dei judicio permittente et diabolo praeparante, concubitus non sequitur." Ivo of Chartres, *Decretum*, 8.194, *Patrologia Latina* 161. See also Peters, 75.

38 Duns Scotus, *Superstitio*, c. 13, cited in Lea, *Materials* 1:169.

39 Burchard of Worms, *Corrector, Patrologia Latina*, 140, 973.

40 *Ibid.*, 971–2, 961.

41 Summaries of medieval popular and clerical perceptions of harmful magic may be found in Kieckhefer, *European Witch Trials*, 47–72, and Cohn, *Europe's Inner Demons*, 147–63.

42 Gregory of Tours, *History of the Franks*, trans. Lewis Thorpe (New York: Penguin, 1983), 248, 397, 458; references cited in Morris, 61–2.

43 Flint, 62–4.

44 Hincmar of Rheims, *De Divortio Lotharii et Tetbergae*, *Patrologia Latina* 125, 717, 718–19.

45 Lea, *Materials*, 1:178.

46 William of Paris, John of Salisbury, and Gervaise of Tilbury each discuss night-flying women and malevolent sorcerers, but each also keeps these categories quite distinct.

47 See Peters, 168; Cohn, *Europe's Inner Demons*, 225–9, although Cohn exaggerates the separation between these categories considerably.

48 Quoted in Julio Caro Baroja, *The World of the Witches*, trans. O.N.V. Glendinning (Chicago: University of Chicago Press, 1964), 277–8, from a citation in Fray Luis G.A. Getino, *Anales Salmantinos* (Salamanca, 1927), 177–9.

49 Martin of Arles, 362.

50 *Ibid.*, 413–15.

51 "Apud fere omnes per strigas sive strigones intelliguntur mulieres aut viri, qui de nocte sive domos aut per longa spatia virtute demonis discurrunt, qui etiam parvulos fascinare dicuntur . . . Huiusmodi mulieres maliarde nuncupari solent a malis, quas operantur; apud alios vero herbarie a consimilibus effectibus, fascinatrices quia pueros infasciant; gallice fastineres ou festurieres; pixidarie, in quibus unguenta ponunt; bacularie, quia a baculo feruntur virtute demonis." Jordanes de Bergamo, *Quaestio de Strigis*, in Hansen, *Quellen*, 196.

52 "Et quia nonunulli arbitrantur, strigas virtute demonis converti posse in cattas et per unctiones sive baculos transire ad diversa loca per longa spacia, virtuteque verborum sive signaculorum strigas ipsas posse producere grandines, pluvias et huiusmodi, que falso sunt, ideo tales sunt in periculo fidei et abiciendi." *Ibid.*, 200.

53 "maleficia sunt uera . . . ergo et ea que in tali ludo fiunt erunt uera: quia omnia ista fiunt arte et uersutia demonis." Visconti, a iiii.

54 *Ibid.*, b vi.

55 "eos inferre sive procurare infirmitates, languores, furias, impedimenta circa coniugia, mortes tam hominum quam pecorum, aborsus conceptiuam [sic], et impedimenta conceptionum, et frugum et plurium rerum temporalium vastationes. Cum igitur praedicta maleficia Daemonum inuocatione et patrocinio contingentia sint reales, et mali fructus maleficorum fascinatiorum [sic] cultorum et sectae et haeresis praedictae. Clarum est, quod realiter et non fantasticaei praedicti haeretici fascinarii confoederati sunt cum Daemonibus et eos colunt, obsequuntsurque." Jacquier, 43.

56 *Ibid.*, 93.

57 See Ginzburg, *Ecstasies*, 33–62; Joshua Trachtenberg, *The Devil and the Jews* (Cleveland: Meridian Books, 1961), 97–108.

58 For example, he writes that "all *malefici* commonly, and especially the heretical fascinari, are betrayers, accustomed to lying in the perpetration of black magic" ("Omnes enim malefici communiter, praesertim haeretici fascinarii sunt proditores et fictionibus assueti in maleficiorum perpetratione"). Jacquier, 93.

59 See *ibid.*, 27. Jacquier writes that Guillaume Edeline was captured with other sectaries and confessed to his heresy in 1453. In the cathedral at Evreaux he publicly admitted that he had gone to the Sabbat, worshiped the devil in the form of a goat, denied God, and done other horrible things. Jacquier, who says that he knew the man well, was especially impressed that the devil had suggested that William preach that his sect was illusory in order to deceive the people.

60 Mamoris, 6.

61 "quidam quasi hebetes opinabantur talia maleficia nihil esse: alii asserebant huiusmodi
   delusiones phantasticas tantum . . . alii autem docti magis, qui scripturas et Gentilium
   et Christicolarum legerent, dicta maleficia fieri posse firma ratione astruebant." *Ibid.*,
   6–7. See also 12–13, "Sed contra eos experientia multorum est, et multa dicta Scrip-
   turae canonicae, et auctoritates Sanctorum Doctorum," etc.

62 "[Ex istis et aliis multis pro certo tenendum est], quod deportantur aliqui nocte, vel
   die a daemone, ad loca remota atque propinqua, et ibi choreas facere possunt, daemonem adorare, homines cum mulieribus coire, et daemones eas supponere, comedere
   et bibere vere vel apparenter, mortem et infirmitates super aliquos inducere, caueas
   intrare, vinum trahere, et ad remota loca portare possunt, sopire homines, pueros a
   lateribus [sic] matrum abstrahere et assare, diuinare de futuris euentibus aliquibus, toni-
   trua et grandines excitare, ictu fulguris percutere et occidere, segetes destruere, et
   plura alia mala perpetrare auxilio daemonum." Mamoris, 42.

63 *Ibid.*, 37–8.

64 "Dicendum est quod stultorum infinitus est numerus." *Ibid.*, 38.

65 "et quod puer infirmetur, pecus moriatur, cancer vultum inficiat, et tempestas segetes
   destruat, occidat homines . . . horum omnium phantasmata daemon phantasiis talium
   obiicit, ex quibus se iudicant fecisse quod per phantasma viderunt, neque propter ista
   possunt tales personae manifeste illorum facinorum argui neque pactum cum daemone
   habuisse tacite vel occulte depraehendi." *Ibid.*, 39.

66 "[Hoc replicatur quod tales homines vel mulieres dicunt, se talia mala supradicta
   fecisse, que realiter euenerunt per pulueres, liquores, pilos, ungues, rubetas, vel per
   simulacra quae apud illos reposita inueniuntur. Ex omnibus istis supradictis pure confitentur se fecisse mala, super quibus interrogati sunt testes asserentes hoc idem realiter
   esse verum, et est vox communis quod haec mala fecerunt, et mala illa in re esse reperiuntur, et instrumenta maleficorum reseruata ab illis in secretis suis inueniuntur. Ex
   quibus omnibus colligitur] quod rei sunt maleficorum de quibus accusantur, et legal-
   ibus poenis sunt adiiciendi." *Ibid.*, 39. The passage is difficult to explain, since Mamoris
   had earlier made his belief in witchcraft perfectly clear.

67 That point may have come on the heels of William Adeline's tearful confession at
   Evreux. Mamoris recounts the story of "Guillelmus de Lure alias Hamelin" in his conclusion, and as an explicit refutation of the canon *Episcopi* (ibid., 67–8) Like Jacquier,
   he says that he was personally acquainted with William, and saw and spoke with him
   often. But if William's confession was, indeed, a turning point in Mamoris' understanding of witchcraft, it is curious that he does not follow that model more closely,
   and emphasize the notion of the diabolic cult. William Adeline's confession and the
   inquisitorial process against him of Bishop William of Evreux is in Hansen, *Quellen*,
   467–72.

68 "idcirco communi nomine maleficium nominatur et vtentes communi vocabulo malefici dicuntur: eo quod ad maleficiendum diabolos eos per illas artes inducit." Mamoris,
   51.

69 *Ibid.*, 50–1. Mamoris remarks that image magic is especially common among those
   who wish to cause bodily harm.

70 Mamoris is certainly referring to learned magicians when he writes that "ut malefici
   credunt quod in herbis et lapidis sit virtus quae possunt daemones compelli ad respon-
   dendum his a quibus inuocantur." *Ibid.*, 40.

71 *Malleus*, pt. 1, qu. 16, pp. 77–8. Their scheme is adapted from Aquinas, *Summa
   Theologiae*, 2–2, qu. 95, art. 3.

72 "Licet he omnes per expressam demonum inuocationem fiant, nulla tamen est com-
   paratio ad maleficia maleficarum cum ad nullum nocumentum hominum iumentorum
   et terre frugum tendunt directe." *Malleus*, pt. 1, qu. 16, pp. 79–80.

73 "Duplices sunt imagines, astrologice et magice que etiam ad bonum aliquod priuatum obtinendum et non ad corruptionem ordinantur." *Ibid.*, pt. 1, qu. 5, p. 37.

74 In this, the author's understanding of *maleficium* agrees with that of other recent investigations of European witchcraft. See Briggs, *Witches and Neighbors*; Devlin, 100–19; Henning K. Sehmsdorf, "Envy and Fear in Scandinavian Folk Tradition," *Ethnologica Scandinavica* (1988): 34–42; and Alver and Torunn, 28.

75 *Malleus*, pt. 2, qu. 1, ch. 14, p. 143. See George Foster, "Peasant Society and the Image of Limited Good," *American Anthropologist* 67 (1965): 293–315.

76 *Malleus*, pt. 2, qu. 14, p. 143.

77 *Ibid.*, pt. 2, qu. 2, ch. 7, p. 180.

78 For example, Institoris claimed that Innsbruck teemed with witches because there were so many men who had seduced and abandoned women. *Ibid.*, pt. 2, qu. 1, ch. 12, p. 136.

79 *Ibid.*, pt. 2, qu. 1, ch. 1, p. 95.

80 *Ibid.*, pt. 2, qu. 1, ch. 7, p. 115.

81 "quod ubi peste aut alia causali infirmitate moriuntur non subito sed paulatim et successiue deficiunt." *Ibid.*, pt. 2, qu. 1., ch. 12, p. 144.

82 "Ecce vix verba compleui, et me grauiter in pede sinistro lesum persensi ita ut sine graui dolore de loco figere pedem non potui." *Ibid.*, pt. 2, qu. 2, p. 156.

83 "in breui optasses ut annuisses." *Ibid.*, pt. 3, qu. 14, p. 210.

84 *Ibid.*, pt. 2, qu. 1, ch. 2, p. 100.

85 "Hoc enim est maleficarum proprium concitare aduersum se, vel verbis inutilibus aut factis, puta quam petit sibi praestari aliquid, aut infert ei damnum aliquod in orto [sic] et similia ad hoc vt occasionem recipiant et se manifestant in verbo vel in opere, quam manifestationem habent facere ad instantiam demonum vt sic peccata aggrauentur iudicum dum manent impunita." *Ibid.*, pt. 3, qu. 6, p. 201. Jacquier, incidently, although he gave no reasons, agreed with this assessment; he says that witches often made a point of warning their victims of the injuries that they were about to suffer, and sometimes even fixed the date when these trials would end. Jacquier, 42.

86 "Item interrogatus cur communis populus eam timeret. Et dixit. Item interrogatus an sciret se esse diffamatam et quod odio haberetur. Et dixit. Item interrogata cur illi persone obiecit, dicendo tu non transibis impune." *Malleus*, pt. 3, qu. 6, p. 201.

87 "Gressus in graminibus damna demonstrant." *Ibid.*, pt. 2, qu. 1, ch. 12, p. 135.

88 "Tunc illa indignata quia ad eius fortassis beneplacitum me litigiosis verbis cum ea implicare nolebam. Abscessit cum murmure. Et verba que protulit licet audirem tamen intelligere non potui. Post paucos vero dies ingens infirmitas mihi accidit cum doloribus ventris." *Ibid.*

89 "prefatam vicinam et maleficam." *Ibid.*

90 "Ecce inquit ex maleficio hec vobis contigit infirmitas, et subter limen hostii domus vna pars instrumentorum maleficii continetur. Accedamus ergo et illis amotis melius sentietis." *Ibid.*

91 "Ex amore quo amicus amico reuelare solet hec cognoui. Unde dum adulteram procabat et mihi vicinam agnoui." *Ibid.* Although if he knew that the instruments of *maleficium* were there in the first place, the experiment with the lead makes no sense. It is possible that this detail owes much to Institoris' prompting, since otherwise his witness was making use of diabolic countermagic.

92 *Ibid.*, pt. 3, qu. 14, p. 210.

93 "Item interrog. Item et quare dixisti quod nunquam deberet habere sanum diem et ita factum est? . . . Item. cur visa fuerit in campis vel in stabulo cum iumentum tangendo . . . Item. quod cum habeat vnam vaccam aut duas quod plus abundat lacte quod vicine habentes quator aut sex." *Ibid.*, pt. 3, qu. 6, p. 201.

94 "Inuenimus quod tu es varius in tuis professionibus utpote quod dicis tales minas

praetulisse non autem eo nocendi alio, et tamen nihilominus sunt indicia varia que sunt sufficientia te ad exponendum questionibus et tormentis." *Ibid.*, pt. 3, qu. 15, p. 211.

95 "Et talia cum sint varia videlicit aliquando per verba solum contumeliosa, dicendo, tu senties in breni [sic: brevi] que tibi euenient vel similia in effectu, vel per tactum solum, tangendo hominem aut bestiam manibus, aut per visum tantum se manifestando nocturno vel diurno tempore, certis dormientibus in cubilibus, et hoc vbi homines aut iumenta nituntur maleficiare." *Ibid.*, pt. 3, qu. 19, p. 222.

96 *Ibid.*, pt. 3, qu. 25, p. 232.

97 *Ibid.*, pt. 3, qu. 19, p. 222.

98 See R.I. Moore, *The Formation of a Persecuting Society* (Oxford: Basil Blackwell, 1987), 66–99.

99 "superstitio est religio supra modum seruata, id est, religio modis vel circumstantiis malis et defectuosis practicata." *Malleus*, pt. 2, qu. 2, ch. 6, p. 172. The authors are paraphrasing the common gloss on *Colossians* 2:23, with Aquinas and Augustine, the most common basis for fifteenth-century explications of superstition. Compare Martin of Arles, "Quid sit superstitio . . . ," 354. For a general discussion of the term's historical usage, see Mary O'Neil, "Superstition," in *The Encyclopedia of Religion*, ed. Mircea Eliade (New York: MacMillan Publishing, 1987), 14:163–6.

100 Martin of Arles, 416. Martin follows Augustine, *City of God*, c. 21, and Thomas Aquinas, *Summa Theologiae*, pt. 1, qu. 115, art. 5.

101 "Intendimus pactum esse implicitum in omni obseruatione superstitiosa, cuius effectus non debet a Deo vel natura expectari rationabiliter." Martin of Arles, 417. Martin is quoting Gerson, *De Erroribus circa Artem Magicam*; see Lea, *Materials*, 134.

102 See Gerson, *De Erroribus*,79.

103 "Incidit ut conquerer de superstitionibus pestiferis magicorum et stultitiis vetularum sortilegarum quae per quosdam ritus maledictos mederi patientibus pollicentur." *Ibid.*, 77.

104 Nider writes that both Staedelin and his teacher, Scavius, carried off up one third of a neighboring field's produce for their use, *Formicarius*, 5.4, p. 206. Mamoris tells of a maleficus who cured a nobleman's skepticism by teaching him how to magically steal wine (8). Institoris and Sprenger remarked that so common was this curse in Germany that "not the smallest farmstead is found where women do not mutually inflict the loss of milk in their cows" ("sic denique nec minima reperitur villula vbi mulieres mutuo vaccas inficere lac eas priuare"), *Malleus*, pt. 2, qu. 1, ch. 14, p. 142.

105 "vt malefici facere solent." *Malleus*, pt. 2, qu. 1, ch. 14, p. 143. The authors apparently mean that the man did not explicitly call upon the aid of the devil, but merely performed a ritual gesture.

106 *Ibid.*, 143.

107 "[in genere triplices apparent malefice vt in prima parte tractatus tactum est. Scilicet] ledentes sed curare non valentes curantes et ex aliquo singulari pacto cum demone inito non ledentes, ledentes et curantes." *Ibid.*, pt. 2, qu. 1, ch. 2, p. 95.

108 They could raise hailstorms and bring down lightning; children whom they did not devour they offered to the devil or killed in other ways; they covertly cast toddlers into water, drove horses mad, and flew through the air. They bewitched judges so that they would not prosecute them, and could magically resist the persuasive power of torture. They could cause fear in their enemies, seemed to know future events, changed the minds of men to inordinate love or hatred, and caused impotence, abortion, and other impediments to procreation. "In brief, they know how to procure all the plagues as have been mentioned before which other witches know only incompletely" ("et breviter omnia vt praemissum est pestifera que alie malefice sparsim procurare sciunt"). *Ibid.*, 96.

109 *Ibid.*, pt. 2, qu. 2, p. 155.

110 "Quod sine dubio ad quecumque loca beatissime virginis siue aquisgrani siue ad heremi-

tas tantus pauperum concursus non existit sicut ad eundem superstitiosum hominem."
Ibid., 156.

111 *Ibid.*, 156–7.

112 *Ibid.*, pt. 2, qu. 1, ch. 12, p. 134.

113 "consideransque quod ex illis dolor capitis in domina non mitigaretur aliqualiter indignata hec verba ad maleficam." *Ibid.*

114 "An sint superstitiosa vel non tercia die tu senties." *Ibid.*

115 Stuart Clark, "The Rational Witchfinder: Conscience, Demonological Naturalism, and Popular Superstitions," in Stephen Pumfrey, Paolo L. Rossi, and Maurice Slawinski, eds., *Science, Culture and Popular Belief in Renaissance Europe* (Manchester: Manchester University Press, 1991), 222–48; 234. For the "economy of the sacred" see R.W. Scribner, "Cosmic Order and Daily Life: Sacred and Secular in Pre-Industrial German Society," in R.W. Scribner, *Popular Culture and Popular Movements in Reformation Germany* (London: The Hambledon Press, 1987): 1–16; for the impetus toward clerical reform, see Charles Zika, "Hosts, Processions and Pilgrimages: Controlling the Sacred in Fifteenth-Century Germany," *Past and Present* 118 (1988): 25–64; Scribner, "Ritual and Popular Religion in Catholic Germany at the Time of the Reformation," in Scribner, *Popular Culture*, 17–47; 43.

116 Aquinas, *Summa Theologiae*, 1, qu. 84, art. 1.

117 See Scribner, "Cosmic Order and Daily Life"; Zika, "Hosts, Processions and Pilgrimages"; and R.N. Swanson, *Religion and Devotion in Europe, c.1215–c.1515* (Cambridge: Cambridge University Press, 1995), 182–4.

118 *Malleus*, pt. 2, qu. 1, pp. 86–92.

119 *Ibid.*, pt. 2, qu. 2, ch. 7, p. 180. See Nider, *Praeceptorium*, 1.11, gg.

120 Martin of Arles, 352–8.

121 "Aliqui tamen eorum quaerunt ab ipsa imagine dicentes: sancte Petre succurre nobis hac necessitate positis, vt impetres nobis a Deo pluuiam, etc., hoc 2. hoc 3. Et cum ad singula nihil respondeat, clamant dicentes: submergatur beatissimi Petri imago si nobis apud Deum omnipotentem gratiam expostulatam pro imminenti necessitate non impetrauerit." *Ibid.*

122 "Constat autem quod submergere imaginem beati Petri non pertinet ad Dei gloriam, qua laudatur dominus in sanctis eius, sed ad vituperium et iniuriam." *Ibid.*, 358.

123 *Malleus*, pt. 2, qu. 2, ch. 7, pp. 181–2.

124 "Ad premium, quod quia hoc dicitur licitum in cultu christiane religionis quod non est superstitiosum." *Ibid.*, pt. 2, qu. 2, ch. 6, p. 171.

125 Or, as Institoris and Sprenger put it, "the transport of reliquaries or sacraments for calming the weather does not seem to militate against this rule" ("deportatio sacramenti vel reliquarum ad auram sedandam non videtur contra hanc regulam militare"). *Ibid.*, pt. 2, qu. 2, ch. 7, p. 181.

126 These rules were taken from Nider, and, ultimately, from Aquinas, who, however, had phrased them more flexibly. See Nider, *Praeceptorium*, 1.11, dd.; Aquinas, *Summa Theologiae*, 2–2, qu. 93, art. 2. The progressive elaboration of Aquinas's strictures, making them more detailed and more rigid, tended to imply that any usage that did not transgress the rules was valid. The net effect of this change was that it became increasingly possible to justify doubtful usages through a narrow interpretation of the rules.

127 "asserunt vaccas etiam sub ubertate ampliori lactis a maleficiis preseruari." *Malleus*, pt. 2, qu. 2, ch. 7, p. 180.

128 Provided, of course, that the charms contained no unknown names or other suspect characters, and that their efficacy was left in the hands of God. *Ibid.*, pt. 2, qu. 2, ch. 6, p. 173.

129 *Ibid.*, pt. 2, qu. 2, ch. 7, p. 179.

130 "Praeterea sunt certe mulieres que dum sentiunt quod in coagulando butirum nil perficiunt, sicut in vasis oblongis ad hoc aptis laborare solent, tunc si subito ex suspecte

malefice domo modicum butiri habere possunt, tria frusta seu bolos ex illo butiro faciunt, et sub sanctissime trinitatis inuocatione patris et filii et spiritus sancti illa frusta in vasculum proiiciunt et sic omne maleficium fugatur." *Ibid.*, pt. 2, qu. 2, ch. 7, p. 180.

131 "irreprehensibilis maneret licet commendanda non esset." *Ibid.*

132 Mamoris, 36–7, 58–9. He concludes his discussion of remedies quite simply: "And therefore, for such *maleficia*, let us have recourse with sincere faith to Christ, to the blessed Virgin, to the saints, and to the prayers and exorcisms of the Church" ("Ad Christum igitur et ad beatam virginem, et ad sanctos, et ad preces et exorcismos Ecclesiae in talibus maleficiis cum sinceritate fidei recursum habeamus").

133 "Et debet confessor dicere quod oportet vt vincant per fidem, adhaerendo Iesu Chriso Domino nostro, inimicum qui eos nititur perturbare." *Ibid.*, 36–7.

134 "praedicta remedia quae dicta sunt superstitiosa vana et vitanda esse tanquam malefi-cia." *Ibid.*, 59.

135 *Ibid.*, 31; Nider, *Praeceptorium*, 1.11, x.

136 Gerson, *De Erroribus*, 84–5.

137 "quia destruens non assentit operibus diaboli, sed credit eum posse et velle fatigare, dum durat tale signum quia ex pacto non assistit ad hoc nisi dum illud durat." *Malleus*, pt. 2, qu. 2, p. 153.

138 *Ibid.*

139 "sicut intestine calesciunt et ardent, ita intestine malefice calore et doloribus cru-ciantur." *Ibid.*, 158. Similar types of sympathetic magic are well known from modern Europe: in nineteenth-century France, a common way to detect a witch was to boil the innards of a dead animal. See Devlin, 111.

7

Witchcraft as an expression of female sexuality

That "a greater multitude of witches is found among the weaker sex of women than among men" was so obviously a fact to the authors of the *Malleus* that, despite scholastic custom, it was completely unnecessary to deduce arguments to the contrary.[1] Witches, in their view, were entirely more likely to be women than men. The experience of the next two hundred years appeared to vindicate this judgment. Throughout most of central and western Europe, where witchcraft persecution was most intense, between 70 and 80 percent of convicted witches were women.[2] Institoris and Sprenger's learned successors in the sixteenth and seventeenth centuries – demonologists and their skeptical opponents alike – concurred with their evaluation: to the well informed, witches were almost always women.

It is possible, however, that Institoris and Sprenger's own construction of witchcraft prejudiced the issue: were women singled out for persecution by later witch-hunters precisely because Institoris and Sprenger had already arbitrarily defined witches as women? Was, in Christina Larner's apt phrase, witch-hunting actually woman-hunting?[3] Or are Institoris and Sprenger basically right – that without any learned coaching, people more often accused women of witchcraft than men? In other words, is the gender bias of texts like the *Malleus* descriptive or prescriptive in nature?

Many modern scholars incline toward the latter view, and look to medieval clerical misogyny, masculine anxieties about the changing social, economic, or familial roles of women, women's control over proscribed medicinal or magical activities, or changing notions of gender to explain why witches were women.[4] Institoris and Sprenger, however, are adamant that their characterization of witches as predominately female is no more than an accurate description of reality: their own first-hand experience and the reliable testimony of trustworthy witnesses show this to be true.[5] Though this claim of objectivity has often been dismissed by scholars, who point out that prior to the *Malleus* men were at least as often identified as witches in learned treatises

as were women, it may have substantial validity.[6] Notions of gender intersected
the various constituent categories of witchcraft in different ways, and because
different authors had quite different notions about what witchcraft was, their
opinion of the probable gender of witches varied accordingly.

Some of the categories out of which late-medieval witchcraft evolved
were more closely associated with women than others. There was, for
example, universal agreement among clerics that women most generally held
the beliefs condemned by the canon *Episcopi*. It was further agreed that not
only did women believe that they rode at night in the company of fairies (or
demons), but that the beings whom they followed were exclusively female as
well. Not only were Diana, Herodias, Holda, and company all female, but so
were their malign counterparts, the *lamiae*, *strigae*, *unholdas*, and other blood-
sucking, night-flying hags that provided an archetype in legend and folklore
for the witch in her most monstrous form. This archetype could also be actu-
alized in the form of an accusation against real women. The sixth-century *Pactus
Legis Salicae* orders that a *stria* who is proven to have eaten a man is liable to a
fine of 8000 denarii.[7] In later law codes, it was rather the belief in such creatures that was more often condemned, with women who were accused of being
monstrous witches frequently entitled to compensation. The continuing presence of such laws testifies to the durability of the belief that certain women
could be *strigae* in fact, as do similar entries in early-medieval penitentials and
the later *exempla* of preachers, and this popular belief existed side by side with
the educated, clerical position approved by the canon *Episcopi*. Women were
thus liable to attack from two sides. As their beliefs became progressively more
demonized, and as judicial and ecclesiastical authorities began to place more
credence in charges that they committed real crimes, women associated
with these beliefs became open to accusations of heresy, and, eventually, of
witchcraft.

For theorists who based their model of witchcraft on such traditional
beliefs, witches, logically, tended to be women. Thus, the witches of Girolamo
Visconti and Ambrosius de Vignate were generally women. Likewise, Alphonso
de Spina's witches are unmistakably female: he reported that demons deceived
"cursed old women" ("vetulas maledictas") into thinking that they went by
night to the Sabbat, and that vast numbers of such "perverse women" had
overrun Dauphiné and Gascony, although many had already been convicted of
heresy and burned.[8]

These women were not, however, accused of *maleficium*, but heresy:
insofar as they complied with the devil's promptings, they were guilty of
demonolatry, even if their crimes were committed while they slept. Worse
still, such women did not renounce their imagined nocturnal crimes when they

awoke, but reveled in their sin. So ran the usual argument. But although the heretical nature of their beliefs might appear clear, this itself raised another problem: the demography of heresy was well known, and heretical sects, unlike the company who flew with the *bonae res*, or even the legions of the superstitious, were not noticeably biased toward female members. The more reliant a definition of witchcraft was upon the model provided by diabolic heresy, the less could witchcraft be confined to women. Girolamo Visconti faced this problem when he turned to the question of whether his *strigae* and *lamiae* were guilty of heresy. Before he could assure his readers that witches were, indeed, heretics – regardless of the objective reality of their crimes – and that, contrary to the canon *Episcopi*, men as well as women went to the *ludus*, he had also to admit – somewhat sheepishly – that women were certainly more numerous at these gatherings, and that "because there are more such women than men, there is more to say of them."[9]

Demonologists and witch-theorists who structured their notions of witchcraft more precisely around the familiar paradigms provided by heretical sects were more emphatic. Nicholas Jaquier's diabolic sect of *fascinarii*, for example, contained both men and women, with men usually taking their expected roles as leaders. This allowed him to use the gender specificity of the canon *Episcopi* to his advantage, and argue that the canon could not be applied legitimately to the modern sect of witches, because while it spoke of a delusion found solely in women, both sexes were found among the *fascinarii*.[10] Similarly, the gender of witches was of no particular moment to the author of the *Errores Gazariorum*, who merely remarked that the heretics attempted to recruit members from both sexes into their sect, and that at their orgies both men and women were adequately represented.[11] In *La Vauderye de Lyonois en brief* (c. 1460), the sex of the sectaries is not mentioned at all; instead, the author notes with care "that people of all ranks and conditions belong to this damnable sect."[12]

Logically, where such heresy-based constructions of witchcraft were most widely accepted, women should not have been singled out for persecution. Susanna Burghartz has compared the witch-trials in Lucerne and nearby Lausanne during the fifteenth and sixteenth centuries, looking specifically for gender bias.[13] In Lucerne, where witches were tried by the secular authorities, over 90 percent of those accused of witchcraft between 1398 and 1551 were women. Judges in this region had a quite rudimentary knowledge of contemporary demonology, and focused principally upon the concerns of the witnesses themselves, especially *maleficium*. In Lausanne, on the other hand, witchcraft prosecution was controlled by the episcopal inquisition, for whom heresy and demonolatry were major concerns, and only 38 percent of those prosecuted were women. Thus, a learned construction of witchcraft appears actually to have ameliorated the gender bias inherent in popular assessments of *maleficium*.

Unfortunately, the problem is seldom so clearly defined, since for both judges and scholarly authors an understanding of witchcraft was often derived from the assimilation of competing categories. While heresy may have been more or less gender neutral, superstition certainly was not: for centuries, superstition and magic had been conceived as particularly feminine vices, and for theorists who constructed witchcraft principally around notions of *maleficium*, this tradition informed witches' gender.

Clerical authors had for centuries been unanimous in their opinion that women were more prone to superstitious beliefs and observances of all types than were men. In the penitentials of the early Middle Ages, women were consistently singled out as the most likely practitioners of condemned magic and superstition. Burchard of Worms regularly identifies forbidden superstitious and pagan practices with allusions to "the vanities which women do" or to "what some women do at the instigation of the devil."[14] Throughout the high Middle Ages, clerical *exempla* echoed this general perception. Stephen of Bourbon condemns women who make charms with the sacrament or with sacred things.[15] The thirteenth-century *Liber Exemplorum* tells of evil and superstitious women who make a man of straw while one of their number is in labor, and dance and sing around this idol.[16] Endless stories of this type were available, making the village wise woman, along with shrewish wives and grasping usurers, a stock character in Sunday homilies.

Like witches, these wise women combined a reputation for occult powers with a propensity to interfere in the sexual and marital affairs of their neighbors. Jacques de Vitry tells of a young man who was hopelessly in love with a girl who would have nothing to do with him. In desperation, the youth turned for help to a certain old woman, who concocted a clever plan. First, she told the would-be lover to pretend to be gravely ill. Then, she fed mustard seed to her little dog to make the animal shed tears, and brought it to the maiden in question, telling her that the animal had once been a woman who had allowed a suitor to die for the love of her, adding ominously that the girl had then been turned into a dog by magical spells, "which God permitted on account of her sin."[17] To avoid such a fate, the girl accepted the young man as her lover. Foolish old women such as this, Jacques tells us, had no real occult power, but they used their reputations as sorceresses and their knowledge of popular superstitions to work extensive evil. They were, in his words, "the enemies of Christ, ministers of the devil, and the foes of chastity."[18]

Although greatly exaggerated and distorted, such tales offer a legitimate representation of the world as medieval preachers saw it. The use of various stereotypical characters in *exempla* was intended to denounce real and not imaginary sins, and if they were not perceived to have had a legitimate relationship with contemporary society, they would not have been effective. This is not, of course, to say that medieval women were more superstitious than men in any absolute sense, only that they were commonly perceived to be so.

The authorities of the late-medieval Church agreed that, by their very nature, women were more superstitious than men. John of Frankfurt, writing in 1412, remarked that

> women are less vigorous in reason and understanding than men, and this is why they are more readily held in the snare of superstitions and are less easily dissuaded from them.[19]

Jean Gerson argued that similar mental weaknesses made "old women, girls and boys, and the slow-witted more prone to observing and believing such superstitions."[20] Nider in his *Praeceptorium* elaborated upon this theme, and gave what would become the three canonical reasons for women's inclination to superstitious practices. First, women were simply more credulous than men, and since false and erroneous faith was a principal aim of the devil, he mercilessly exploited this weakness. Second, women were especially vulnerable to diabolic assaults because their impressionable natures made them more apt than men to the influences and revelations of spiritual beings. Finally, because they had "slippery tongues," women were unable to conceal from their sisters what they had learned by their magic arts, and, since they were not strong, they were easily inclined to seek revenge though *maleficium*.[21]

Nider's concluding remark is especially relevant, because it links superstitious belief directly with the practice of black magic. Of course, as has already been pointed out, the practice of *maleficium* was a species of superstition, and insofar as women were more prone to superstition, it made sense to assume that they were also especially prone to witchcraft. Gerson was making just this point when he wrote that because of their propensity for superstitious practices, old women had earned their French epithet "old sorceresses."[22] Nider, however, suggests that women who practice witchcraft are guilty of a specifically moral error rather than an intellectual one. Associating women with superstition, Nider combines ideas drawn from a somewhat different tradition in which women, specifically, were suspected of being *maleficae*.

Throughout the Middle Ages, women were often accused of malign sorcery. Clerical *exempla* make it clear that village wise women were sometimes thought guilty of more than just sharp practice. Although Jacques de Vitry (c. 1180–c. 1240) usually scoffs at the occult powers of old women, he also tells of certain *maleficae mulieres* who seemed to turn a woman into a mare, until the deception of the devil was revealed and undone through the prayers of a saint.[23] Jacques does not tell the story in full, but in his source, the *Vitae Patrum*, the woman was bewitched because she had spurned an evil man's advances, who then had recourse to magic to gain his revenge. This is, then, almost the same story as Jacques's tale of the old woman and her weeping dog, but here the power of old wives is not trivial. Tellingly, Jacques made a significant adjustment to his text: in the original, the magician was a man; for Jacques, however, this kind of magic was typical of women.

Other sources, too, attributed harmful sorcery especially to women. As Nider observed, because women were thought less able than men to gratify their thirst for revenge through overt violence, they were widely believed to employ occult means. In his penitential, Burchard warned that some women, "filled with the discipline of Satan," would remove turf from the footprints of unsuspecting victims "and hope thereby to take away their health or life."[24] In a canon devoted to the sins of women, the Anglo-Saxon penitential of Egbert also remarked upon the female propensity for magical harm, charging that

> If a woman works witchcraft and enchantment and [uses] magical philters, she shall fast for twelve months . . . If she kills anyone by her philters she shall fast for seven years.[25]

In the late twelfth century, Peter of Blois accused women of making wax and clay figurines either for the purposes of love magic or for straightforward revenge.[26] Aragonese laws of the same century condemned to death women guilty of harming men or beasts through ligatures, herbs, or *facticiosa*.[27] Late thirteenth-century Swedish law similarly stated that a woman who killed a man through *maleficium* should be burned.[28] In short, although the sources are not unanimous, and although men were certainly thought able to work magic if so inclined, it seems, as Nider in effect argued, that the common association of women with superstitious practices in general, and their inability to exact revenge through other means, combined to make them especially liable to charges of practicing *maleficium*.[29]

Studies of sixteenth and seventeenth-century witch-beliefs support this conclusion. In his examination of witchcraft accusations in seventeenth-century Yorkshire, J.A. Sharpe concludes that the witch embodied a peculiarly feminine kind of negative power, "the power to make trouble"; *maleficium* at the local level was a manifestation of tension and conflict centering on this perceived power of women.[30] Clive Holmes agrees, and argues that in popular belief, "the mysterious powers that constituted witchcraft would normally be possessed by women."[31] Christina Larner is similarly inclined to see the prosecution of female witches as simply the reflection of a widespread consensus that women especially work magical harm.[32] Although medieval records do not permit the same sort of extensive investigation of local-level witchcraft belief through trial records and depositions that is possible for later periods, anecdotal evidence may suggest that similar patterns held true. Thus in Ghent during the 1370s, accusations of *maleficium* emerged out of women's quarrels, jealousies, and rumors, precisely as they are described in the *Malleus*.[33] Since, moreover, there is no reason to assume that patterns of witch-belief changed dramatically on the local level after 1500, it is quite possible that accusations of harmful magic tended to cluster around women during the Middle Ages just as they did in later years. This is, at any rate, the position of the many late-medieval demonologists and witch-theorists who accepted without hesitation the proposition that women, in general, were more often *superstitiosae et maleficae* than men.

Maleficium was not, however, a clearly defined, homogeneous category, but an amalgamation of harmful conditions that could in some way be linked with particular superstitious practices (from the perspective of the learned observer), particularly meaningful events, or particularly motivated individuals (from the perspective of the victim). Some effects, motivations, and practices were more closely associated with the domain of women than were others. To take the most obvious example, love magic of various sorts was invariably recognized as the specific provenance of female magicians. Magic of this type acted principally to increase or diminish sexual passion and marital affection, or to cause sexual dysfunction, sterility or abortion.[34] There were many practices associated with these kinds of *maleficium*, but ligatures, weaving, and binding magic were most common.[35] For this reason, clerical authorities thought that magical operations of this sort were among the most common, and, because they seemed so obviously superstitious and diabolical, they provided clerics with a basic paradigm for "popular" magic. The constant insistence on the part of theologians that such magic was, indeed, diabolical cast women's magic in an increasingly sinister light from the thirteenth century onwards.

Moreover, because problems of impotence, loss of marital affection, and infertility remained widespread, reports and accusations of this type of magic intruded regularly into the pastoral experiences of the clergy. By the fifteenth century, among both witch-theorists like Institoris and Sprenger and clerics less intimately involved in the witch debates, love magic came to be seen not so much as a species of superstition, but as evidence of an overt and explicit pact with the devil. Gabriel Biel (d. 1496) was one of many clerics whose interest in *maleficium* was restricted principally to its practical effects upon marriage, but who nonetheless agreed with the witch-theorists that women did not work their spells through any power of their own, but only "through the help of demons whose pacts and sacraments they employ."[36]

Just as love magic was an area of undoubted female expertise, other kinds of sorcery were more often associated with men. Learned magic of various sorts provides the most obvious example of an almost entirely masculine occult domain. The Middle Ages recognized a whole range of magical operations for which literacy and extensive book learning were prerequisites. At one end of the spectrum was the *scientia magica* of Ficino and Giovanni Pico della Mirandola, an enormously complex and intellectually difficult attempt to understand God and his creation through ritual and meditation.[37] At the other, there were the crude magical practices and recipes found in books of necromancy and compilations of miscellaneous sorcery. Between these two extremes was an extensive middle ground comprising alchemy, astrology and assorted divinatory practices, the manufacture of magical talismans and amulets, and the use of herbs, stones, and other materials in magical and quasi-magical ways.[38] At various times, all of these practices were condemned by the Church, although with greatly varying degrees of severity, and never as consistently or intensely as were the characteristic magical practices of women. In many cases, learned magicians were able to mount sophisticated defenses of their procedures and acquit themselves of charges of superstition and idolatry. In others, licit practices were coupled with the suspect in a confusing melange that defied easy condemnation. Most of all, though, "book" magic was less often identified with *maleficium* than were other magical practices, and so there was never the same victim-driven impetus for persecution. Similarly, whereas love magic was a matter of practical daily concern for many clerics, learned magic was a problem principally of theoretical interest. Thus, the most typically masculine forms of magical practice remained largely insulated from the persecutions of the late Middle Ages, and were never successfully integrated into learned constructions of witchcraft.

Nonetheless, between these two clearly gendered poles of medieval magical practice, there were many kinds of magical operations, some of which were indifferently ascribed to men and women alike, and some of which were, at times, perceived to be more sex-specific. Despite his general claim that women were inherently inclined toward magic and superstition, Johann Nider was also careful to distinguish between the magic of male and female sorcerers. He writes that while it was a *malefica* or a *maga* who caused destructive rain to fall with her broom, it was the *maleficus* who made magical images from wax or lead.[39] Similarly, while *malefici* could make imperfect animals after the manner of Pharaoh's magicians, with the help of demons, only women hurt children with their poisonous glances.[40] To Nider, it would seem that harmful magic was much less the single, undifferentiated category that it became in the *Malleus*, but a more complicated system of categories specific to gender and culture.

In Martin of Arles's examination of local superstition, he made similar distinctions between typically male and female magic. Following traditions laid down in antiquity, Martin used the masculine form of the words for witch, magician, and sorcerer, when speaking generically: *maleficus, magus, incantator, praestigiosus*, and so on. When he turned to specific kinds of magic, however, he chose the gender of his words very carefully. Male magicians, Martin tells us, practiced learned magic, image magic, astrology, and divination of all sorts.[41] The evil eye and *maleficium* that impeded procreation, on the other hand, belonged to *maleficae* and *vetulae sortilegae*.[42] Logically, when Martin looks at the traditions of the night-flying women commonly known as *broxae*, he refers only to "mulieres sortilegae et maleficae."[43] Finally, he specifically mentions that the ranks of magicians who used various kinds of stones, herbs, woods, animals, songs, and rites to invoke demons to do their will included both *malefici* and *maleficae* in their number.[44]

Institoris and Sprenger's innovation was not their insistence that women were naturally prone to practice *maleficium* – in this they were simply following long-standing clerical traditions. Rather, it was their claim that harmful magic belonged *exclusively* to women that was new. If this assertion was granted, then the presence of *maleficium* indicated decisively the presence of a female witch. In the *Malleus*, the field of masculine magic is dramatically limited and male magicians are pointedly marginalized; magic is no longer seen as a range of practices, some of which might be more characteristic of men, some of women, and some equally prevalent among both sexes. Instead, it was the effects of magic that mattered most, and harmful magic, the magic most characteristic of witches, belonged to women. Men might be learned magicians, anomalous archer wizards, or witch-doctors and *superstitiosi*, but very seldom did they work the broad range of *maleficium* typical of witches.

The simplest explanation for this change is to accept, as Institoris and Sprenger claim, that it derives from their own experience as witch-hunters. Since their professional activities were restricted geographically to southern Germany and Austria, and since their investigations tended to focus upon charges of *maleficium* most often associated with women, it is not unreasonable to suppose that most of the accused witches whom they encountered were women. Nor was their conclusion some kind of inquisitorial idiosyncrasy. Their contemporary, Ulrich Molitor, though in other respects a man with quite different ideas about witchcraft, also assumed that witches were female as a matter of course: they were women driven to devote themselves to the devil "either because of desperation, or poverty, or the hatred of neighbors, or other temptations sent by the devil."[45] Although men could certainly work magic with the aid of the devil, Molitor tended to restrict masculine magical enterprises to comparatively benign activities such as fortune-telling: as a general rule, witches who worked *maleficium* were *maleficae mulieres*, while *magi* or *malefici* predicted the future.[46]

That witches were women was a conclusion that Institoris and Sprenger's contemporaries would not have found especially alarming – extreme, perhaps, but not so radical as to leave the pale of accepted clerical tradition.[47] On the other hand, what the authors of the *Malleus* did with this observation, how they explained it, and how they made it integral to their understanding of witchcraft, was quite unusual indeed. To explain the phenomenon they assembled a formidable catalogue of authorities, ancient and modern, to testify to feminine weakness, sinfulness, and perfidy.[48] After a polite enough nod to the glories of the Virgin, admitting that, just as an evil woman exceeds all others in iniquity, so a good woman is a model of righteousness, the authors begin to show how a propensity for witchcraft is the logical and necessary result of women's nature. To Nider's traditional explanation for women's inclination to superstitious beliefs, Institoris and Sprenger graft a veritable *summa* of late-medieval misogynist commonplaces. "Since women," they write, "are deficient in all strengths, as much of mind as of body, no wonder that they cause a great deal of witchcraft to be done to those who oppose them."[49] Intellectually, women are childlike, so feeble-minded that they are of a completely different order from men.[50] Their minds are warped, twisted like the rib from which Eve was first formed; and just as the first woman could not keep faith with God, so all women are faithless. This, the authors add, is shown by the very etymology of the word for "woman," "for it is said that *femina* is from *fe* and *minus* because a woman always has and keeps less faith."[51] Women also have weak memories, and from this defect "it is a natural vice in them to refuse to be governed, but to follow their impulses without any due reserve."[52] Their will, too, is warped, because they are inordinately passionate, more prone to violent love and hate, and so often turn to witchcraft to gratify these desires.[53] Women are natural born liars, proud and vain, and their hearts are ruled by malice.[54] And all of these defects made women the devil's ready dupes or willing slaves.

Institoris and Sprenger's misogynist arguments ought not to be taken for granted. Although such views were, no doubt, common in the late Middle Ages, nowhere else are they so forcefully linked to notions of witchcraft. No other fifteenth-century demonologist, not even a man such as Molitor, went much beyond Nider's brief enumeration of women's relevant weaknesses. Institoris and Sprenger, however, conceived of witchcraft as essentially rooted in and defined by women's sins, and as all but inconceivable without it.

Nonetheless, although their misogynist views are violent and striking, they occupy a relatively small part of Institoris and Sprenger's text, being for the most part confined to the single *questio* devoted to women and their natures. This chapter is also more straightforwardly a collection of classical and scriptural passages than is any other in the *Malleus*; on the subject of women, the authors' personal experience, so evident elsewhere, is notably absent. Neither is their pervasively misogynist argument entirely self-consistent, since, if all or most women were indeed so thoroughly evil, then all or most women should be prospective witches, and this is clearly not the case – only certain identifiable women are likely to be witches.

Although the *Malleus* represents women with a variety of shared, inherent weaknesses, and although these weaknesses created a propensity for a variety of sins, one weakness and one sin – carnality and lust, respectively – were especially characteristic of witches. Women, Institoris and Sprenger observed, are more carnal than men, "as their many carnal depravities make clear."[55] By this defect, woman are more enslaved to their desires and the lusts of the flesh, and are correspondingly less rational, spiritual, and intelligent than men. So closely are women and the sin of lust identified in the minds of the authors that they use the very word "woman" as a kind of metaphorical shorthand for lust. Institoris and Sprenger advise that whenever one reads censures of women, these "can be interpreted to mean bodily concupiscence, such that 'woman' is always understood to refer to the lusts of the flesh."[56]

From women's unsatisfied sexual desires sprang their unequaled malice: the most malicious of women were the most lustful; and the most lustful of women were witches, whose sexual appetite was insatiable, and who, "for the sake of quenching their lusts, excite themselves with devils."[57] A witch's perverse sexuality was echoed in her magic: the sexual dysfunction caused by her spells, impeding procreation and legitimate sexual relations, revealed "that witchcraft arises more often from adulteresses, fornicatresses, etc."[58] Other vices characterizing witches, notably infidelity and ambition, paled beside the witch's sexual demands. For this reason, the authors add, "those among ambitious women who burn more to satisfy their depraved lusts – as do adulteresses, fornicatresses, and the concubines of the great – are more infected." This was of enormous concern to Institoris and Sprenger, who worried that, through their magic, witches were gradually insinuating themselves into the highest ranks of European society. A witch in such a position had the power to poison her lover's mind, infecting him with a mad love that no shame or reason could gainsay,

> which threatens both the extermination of the faith and intolerable daily danger, because witches know how to change their minds so that they will permit no harm to be done to them, either by their lovers themselves or by others. And so their numbers daily increase.[59]

In this way, in a few sentences, the authors transform the lust of women into witchcraft, and then into an apocalyptic vision of a world overrun with witches and sexual deviance.

The worthy inquisitors certainly did not invent the perverse sexuality of witches out of whole cloth; both heretics and night-traveling women were linked in masculine imagination with traditions of deviant sexuality. Indiscriminate and orgiastic couplings were a familiar topos in clerical descriptions of heretical cults, and Nicholas Jacquier was merely following this tradition when he claimed that

> nearly all worshipers in the heresy and sect of witches or sorcerers' cults, many of whom, of both sexes, have revealed this willingly and by the sign of their blushes, assert that at their meeting which they hold for the worship of demons, they themselves, along with the demons which appear, are at times carnally pleasured in turn without measure so forcefully that it is brought about that many of them remain afterwards afflicted and debilitated for some days.[60]

But this was not at all the same kind of sexual sin as preyed upon the minds of Institoris and Sprenger; this was rather the deviant sexuality of the heretical cult. Both men and women alike, as Jacquier was careful to observe, participated in this filthiness, and their perverse lusts had no wider connotations: sexual sin is simply a generic characteristic of the heretic to Jacquier, and not a logically necessary part of a larger whole.

In the *Malleus*, however, witchcraft, femininity, and sexual sin form a tight constellation of interrelated ideas: unbridled feminine sexuality led to witchcraft, which expressed itself most typically in sexual, reproductive, or marital dysfunction; the defining act of the witch was sexual intercourse with the devil; men who committed adultery, whose lusts were unrestrained like a woman's, became liable to the spells of witches; and this feminine vice led directly to a second inversion of the natural order, because such men then allowed themselves to be dominated by women. To Institoris and Sprenger, witchcraft, adultery, and feminine domination lead logically to a coherent, closely interconnected conception of a wide-ranging occult conspiracy against society.

In an interesting passage, the authors ask rhetorically: what is the use of finding remedies for witchcraft when men are so sunk in depravity, and when

> the landed magnates, prelates, and other rich men are most often involved with this wretchedness; indeed this is the time of women . . . , since now the world is full of adultery, especially among the nobles – why should those who hate the remedies write about them?[61]

Institoris and Sprenger believe themselves to be living in an age of adultery, an age of witchcraft – an age of women. The "wretchedness" referred to, which emasculates the great men of the world and makes them subject to their mistresses, may be either witchcraft or adultery, but it matters little, since in Institoris and Sprenger's minds sexual and diabolical sins are so closely identified. Thus, the relationship between sexual deviance and witchcraft was reciprocal: disordered sexual relationships engendered witches, and witchcraft, in turn, disordered sexual relationships.[62]

To Institoris and Sprenger, notions of "witches" and "witchcraft" served to reify, in the form of a wholly corrupt female body, the threats and the anxieties posed by human sexuality. Categorizing witches as embodiments of sinful female sexuality provided the authors with a useful means to control the unbridled sexuality of women that led to misfortune and disaster.[63] As Guido Ruggiero puts it, witches were "sexual outsiders," whose activities, from the perspective of the dominant culture, threatened the natural order of society with the wrath of God.[64] Faced with the possibility of another Sodom, Institoris and Sprenger defined witchcraft so as to localize the responsibility for sexual sin in the bodies of particular women, bodies which could be discovered, punished, and burned. Further, by the very act of categorization order *was* imposed: through the creation of an ordered semantic and intellectual system, Institoris and Sprenger provided the necessary terms for a satisfactory symbolic discussion of human sexuality, order, and power. In this new conceptual field, disordered sexuality is identified with the devil, inverted gender roles and sexual dysfunction with witchcraft, and defective social and political hierarchies with women and women's sins. None of this, however, is possible without the use of witches and witchcraft as an ordering term; witchcraft, as it were, provides the conceptual grid which binds this cognitive map together.

In theoretical terms, such a model makes considerable sense. If one accepts the fiction that women were controlled within an imposed sexual hierarchy, and that feminine power and influence within society were subsumed within a discourse of gender and sexuality, then any disordering manifestation of women's power, influence, or behavior must be understood in terms of sexual perversity. In other words, because men in late-medieval and early-modern Europe tended to view women as sexual beings, existing within a rigidly defined sexual hierarchy, any perception of feminine deviance could logically be interpreted as a manifestation of sexual deviance.[65] As soon as *maleficium* began to be seen as a particularly feminine crime, it became correspondingly necessary to view witchcraft within the rubric provided by sexual perversity. Such a construction seems even more probable if the village discourse of magic conceals a hidden discourse of women's power and of negotiated female social roles. The gendered aspects of Institoris and Sprenger's construction of witchcraft, I suggest, thus reflects their own experience of *maleficium* as principally a woman's crime, understood in terms of what they conceived "woman" to mean.

As a point of comparison, Stanley Brandes has described a very similar complex of ideas in his study of gender construction in modern Andalusia.[66] In Andalusian society, gender boundaries are comparatively rigid, and women's behavior and social roles are quite restricted. Nonetheless, men feel themselves constantly under threat by the dangerous and potent forces under women's command. Much of this fear is specifically sexual, since Andalusian men fear the debilitating effects of an adult woman's sexual appetite, which "threatens in various ways to rob them of their masculinity and convert them symbolically into females."[67] Women are insatiable, lustful seductresses, whose temptations men are all but powerless to resist. Women also command formidable and malign magical and supernatural powers, linked directly to their sexuality. Menstrual magic is especially potent, as is the magic of widowed, non-virgical, and/or sexually unsatisfied women.[68] Men in this society constantly stress their own moral and social superiority over women – they equate themselves with God and women with the devil – yet they also fear the disordering sexual and magical powers of women. Both masculinity and social order are defined against a rigidly controlled, powerfully sexualized notion of femininity; anxiety about the stability of these structures expresses itself here, as in the *Malleus*, in terms of fears of occult harm and deviant sexuality.

On a more abstract level, this analysis parallels Bruce Kapferer's interpretation of Sinhalese concepts of the feminine and demonic.[69] Kapferer suggests that Sinhalese women provide their culture with central mediating and articulating symbols precisely because their subordination to men is so central to their society. In his view,

> Sinhalese women are vital symbols at once responsive to, and concentrating in their being, the forces and processes ordering and disordering the cultural and social universe of action and experience.[70]

The point is that if the social position of women in society is symbolically linked to a wider conceptual field (and in the late Middle Ages the cult of the Virgin alone would demonstrate that this was true), then perceived deviations from the approved norm carry correspondingly greater meaning and are of proportionally more concern, depending upon the breadth and centrality of women symbolically. Furthermore, the reverse is also true: just as perceived feminine deviance carries the threat of more general disorder, so misfortune and failure may be perceived to be the result of women's misbehavior. Thus Sinhalese women understand that, as women, their bodies pose a unique threat to ordered social hierarchies, and so "are culturally motivated to incorporate within themselves the misfortune and suffering that strikes at the household."[71] Lyndal Roper has similarly shown that political power and authority were conceived metaphorically in terms of the sexual dominance of husband over wife in post-Reformation Augsburg.[72] For the urban patriarchate, women's sexual sins were acutely felt to be a threat to established structures of order, and "women's lusts were to be feared as unbridled and demonic."[73]

Taken as a kind of symbolic discourse, the construction of witchcraft and the constellation of related ideas that revolve around it in the *Malleus* are thus neither unique nor unreasonable. It is in this context, perhaps, that we should understand Institoris and Sprenger's otherwise risible fascination with the penis-stealing exploits of witches. It is doubtless true, as Mary O'Neil has suggested, that much of the evidence for this practice was found in a tradition of bawdy, rustic joking which the inquisitors lamentably misunderstood.[74] But, while it may seem absurd to suggest that anyone could seriously believe that a witch could steal a man's penis and keep it alive and well in a bird's nest on a diet of oats, and that, when the owner finally came to retrieve his missing property, the witch would admonish him to put back the largest of those he found because it belonged to a secular priest, it is not absurd to suggest that, by so doing, the witch is only doing in a singularly literal way what she and her sisters were accustomed to do more figuratively: make a man into a woman.[75]

A similar conceptual move may explain why one of the most common forms of *maleficium* was to cause impotence. The fact that men were peculiarly susceptible to such magic suggests that masculine sexuality was itself fragile and easily disturbed: physically, witches could prevent erections and inhibit the flow of semen; psychologically, witches could cool the desire necessary for satisfactory sexual performance.[76] When enchantments permitted a man to perform sexually only with a witch, he acquired a passive, "feminine" social role, a role that mirrored the witch's own sexual servitude to the devil.

Inversions of the sexual and social order were characteristic of witches in other ways as well. In another tale of symbolic emasculation and sexual inversion, Institoris and Sprenger relate that a well-born citizen of Speyer was cursed with an obstinate and evil-tempered wife, who, no matter how much he might try to please her, repaid him with recalcitrance and insults. One day when the man tried to escape his wife's incessant abuse, she dared him to strike her, saying that "unless he thrashed her, he had neither honesty nor honor left in him."[77] Goaded at last to violence by these "heavy words," the man slapped his wife lightly on the rear and at once toppled senseless to the floor. Thereafter he was confined to bed for many weeks. For this unfortunate, appropriately masculine behavior was the immediate cause of his bewitchment: while he patiently endured his wife's taunts, while he accepted a passive, "womanish" social role, his wife was content merely to abuse him. When, on the other hand, he finally dared to act like a man, he was struck down and left even more feminized: weak, bedridden, domesticated, and dependent.

Amid so much talk of passive, emasculated men, it is surprising that Institoris and Sprenger have so little to say on the subject of sodomy.[78] Even their demons, like their witches, are primly heterosexual, and would never consider participating in a sexual act *contra naturam*. Of course, one perfectly plausible explanation for this omission is that Institoris and Sprenger are writing specifically about witches, whereas sodomy is a crime most often associated with men. In consequence, although it too, is closely associated with lust, inverted gender roles, and sexual perversion, it does not directly intrude upon the purely feminine world of witchcraft. On the other hand, we may also note the words with which Institoris and Sprenger conclude their diatribe against the female sex:

> And blessed be the Most High, who up to the present has preserved from so vile a disgrace [as witchcraft] the male sex, in which He chose to be born and suffer for us, and therefore accorded it this privilege.[79]

These words unmistakably echo a phrase of William of Paris, who praised the Almighty in similar terms, but for quite different reasons: William thanked God that men, at least, had never been sodomized by fallen angels, although demons were theoretically quite capable of such an act.[80]

In the corresponding passage of the *Malleus*, on the other hand, witchcraft replaces sodomy as the "unthinkable" abomination for men. Here the authors do semantically precisely what Institoris did conceptually in his discussion of the young demoniac who could not be freed of his devil on account of "the Lombards" (that is, because of the sin of sodomy): "the worst vice of lust" is ignored in order to focus entirely upon the witch.[81] Such odd substitutions demonstrate the similarities between the authors' conception of witchcraft and contemporary notions of sodomy: both are sexually disordering, both threaten masculine sexuality and gender identity, and for these reasons both are symbolically linked to a wider cognitive field. In each case, they are crimes uniquely offensive to God and to man; they are treason – *lèse majesté* – offenses "against divine order and against the commonwealth."[82] Like the witch, the sodomite so offended God that his whole community was liable for his sin: plagues and natural disasters were only a foretaste of the apocalypse that could ensue from the wrath of an angry God, and for this reason aggressive persecution of the guilty was absolutely required.[83] Institoris and Sprenger's description of witchcraft reminds one irresistibly of Jonathan Goldberg's description of sodomy in late-medieval and early-modern thought: "It names something unnamable, something that goes beyond the evidentiary and the logical; it is a category of violation and violates categories."[84] Witchcraft could well be described in similar terms with this exception: in Institoris and Sprenger's mind witchcraft was not an "utterly confused" category, but a logical and eminently "thinkable" one. As a pervasive and central cultural symbol, witchcraft allowed the inquisitors to replace confused, difficult, and potentially dangerous concepts and relationships with ones that were more artificial, but for this reason also safer, more logical, and more readily controlled.

Throughout the *Malleus*, Institoris and Sprenger try to establish a reciprocally defining relationship between their construction of witchcraft and the persons of real individuals who might plausibly be suspected of such a crime. For this endeavor they created a very detailed image of the archetypal witch. She was a woman, certainly, but she was not just any woman – so inclusive an ascription would have made nonsense of the category the authors worked so hard to make sensible. Rather the witch of the *Malleus* was determined first by the parameters of the category which Institoris and Sprenger had constructed: more than anything else, a witch to them was a person with a reputation for possessing and using harmful occult powers. Yet Institoris and Sprenger were not satisfied to model their witch so straightforwardly upon popular perceptions of unwelcome sorcerers. The unmodified village magician provided them with no easy points of contact with the larger conceptual field of witchcraft as they understood it. True, any use of magic could be diabolized through the theory of the demonic pact, but there was a considerable difference in their minds between magic, even of the most diabolic stripe, and witchcraft. Much of this difficulty evaporated, however, as soon as the authors chose to emphasize the essentially feminine nature of witchcraft. With witches defined exclusively as women, a fortuitous homology was formed between them, night-flying *strigae*, and the women of the *bonae res*, traditions which formed the core of numerous alternative visions of witchcraft.

Yet the witch in the *Malleus* was also not simply a female sorcerer; she was also the personification of deviant or "bad" female sexuality. For all their misogyny, Institoris and Sprenger never accuse chaste virgins of witchcraft. Indeed, one of the most remarkably virtuous characters to be found in their text is a woman, a "poor little virgin and most devout," who was able to cure bewitched persons by merely reciting the Lord's Prayer with complete faith.[85] Witches instead were adulteresses, murderous midwives, and evil mothers, women defined by the authors as personifications of feminine sexuality. The witch's relationship with the devil was not defined in terms of conventional notions of heretical cults, but through sexual relations: the witch did not worship the devil, she slept with him. The link thus established between female sexuality and physical harm of all sorts gave Institoris and Sprenger's conception of witchcraft an explanatory power that rival conceptions lacked. Witch-craft provided a coherent system through which a whole constellation of socially disordering forces could be understood; it created a conceptual field in which anxieties about social order and material well-being could be arranged, understood, and, at least potentially resolved.

Notes

1 "Cur in sexu tamen fragili mulierum maior multitudo maleficarum reperitur quam inter viros, et quidem in contrarium in argumenta deducere non expedit." *Malleus*, pt. 1, qu. 6, p. 40.

2 See Robin Briggs, "Men against Women: The Gendering of Witchcraft," ch. 7 of *Witches and Neighbors*; E. William Monter, "The Pedestal and the Stake: Courtly Love and the Witchcraze," in R. Bridenthal and C. Koonz, eds., *Becoming Visible* (Boston: Houghton Mifflin, 1977), 130–4; Brian Levack, *The Witch-Hunt in Early Modern Europe* (London: Longman, 1987), 124.

3 Christina Larner, *Enemies of God: The Witch-Hunt in Scotland* (Baltimore: Johns Hopkins University Press, 1981), 100.

4 A concise summary of these explanations for a prescriptively gendered construction of witchcraft appears in Brauner, 13–27.

5 That witches were most usually women, the authors remark, "cum ipsa experientia preter verborum et fidedignorum testimonia talia facit credibilia." *Malleus*, pt. 1, qu. 6, p. 40. The point is important enough to bear repetition; a few pages later the authors again observe that "in these modern days this perfidy [witchcraft] is more commonly discovered among women than among men, as actual experience teaches" ("Sed quia adhuc modernis temporibus hec perfidia amplius in mulieribus quam in viris inuenitur vt ipsa experientia docet"). *Ibid.*, 42.

6 See Brauner, 13; and, in a somewhat different context, Marianne Hester, "Patriarchal Reconstruction and Witch Hunting," in Jonathan Barry, Marianne Hester, and Gareth Roberts, eds., *Witchcraft in Early Modern Europe* (Cambridge: Cambridge University Press, 1996): 288–306. Contra Cohn, *Europe's Inner Demons*, 239–51.

7 Katharine Fischer Drew, trans., *The Laws of the Salian Franks* (Philadelphia: University of Pennsylvania Press, 1991), 64.3

8 "quia nimium habundant tales peruerse mulieres in delphinatu et in gaschonia." Spina, consid. 10.

9 "Sciendum est quod nedum mulieres uadunt ad ludum; sed etiam uiri, sed quia plures sunt mulieres uiris ideo de eis magis fit sermo." Visconti, c. v.

10 Jacquier, 41. Jacquier was refining an argument made earlier by Jean Vineti, an inquisi-tor at Carcassone, in his *Tractatus contra Daemonum Invocatores* (c. 1450), Hansen, *Quellen*, 125.

11 *Errores Gazariorum*, 279–81.

12 "Item, ex omni statu et condicione hominum dicunt de hac dampnabili secta esse." *La Vauderye de Lyonois en brief*, Hansen, *Quellen*, 188–95; 191.

13 Susanna Burghartz, "The Equation of Women and Witches: A Case Study of Witchcraft Trials in Lucerne and Lausanne in the Fifteenth and Sixteenth Centuries," in Brian Levack, ed., *Articles on Witchcraft, Magic, and Demonology*, 10 vols. (New York: Garland Publishing, 1992), 10 (*Witchcraft, Women and Society*): 67–83.

14 Burchard of Worms, *Corrector, Patrologia Latina* 140, 961–73.

15 Étienne de Bourbon, no. 371.

16 A.G. Little, ed., *Liber Exemplorum ad Usam Praedicantium*, in *The British Society of Francis-can Studies* 1 (1908), 153.

17 "Hec fuit quedam mulier que permisit mori juvenem amore ipsius. Cumque graviter

infirmaretur, quibusdam sortilegiis ut se vindicaret de illa, mutavit illam in catellam, quod Deus permisit pro peccato suo." Jacques de Vitry, no. 250.

18 "Huiusmodi autem vetule leve sunt inimice Christi et ministre diaboli atque hostes castitatis." *Ibid.*, 251.

19 "Ipse quidem mulieres minus vigent in racione et intelligencia quam viri, et hinc est quod magis istis superstitionibus illaqueate tenentur et difficilius amoventur." John of Frankfurt, *Questio, utrum potestas cohercendi demones fieri possit per caracteres . . .* , in Hansen, *Quellen*, 76.

20 "ex phantasiae et imaginativae virtutis debilitatione, cuius signum est quod vetulae et pueri et puellae et idiotae proniores sunt ad tales superstitiones credendas vel observandas;" Jean Gerson, *Contra Superstitiosam Dierum Observantiam*, in *Oevres complètes* no. 503; 7:120.

21 Nider, *Praeceptorium*, 1.11, bb. This passage would retain considerable currency, and was quoted virtually verbatim in the *Malleus*, pt. 1, ch. 6; See also Bernard Basin's, *Tractatus de Artibus Magicis ac Magorum Maleficiis* (1482; reprint, 1600: NP, Frankfurt), 16; and in Martin of Arles, 446.

22 "Unde ortum habuit illud de vetulit epitheton: vetulae sortilegae, gallice vieilles sorcières." Gerson, *Contra Superstitiosam Dierum Observantiam*, 120.

23 Jacques de Vitry, no. 262.

24 Burchard of Worms, *De Erroribus*, 974. For an account of a much later but remarkably similar practice, see Mary R. O'Neil, "Missing Footprints: *Maleficium* in Modena," *Acta Ethnographica Hungarica* 37 (1991/92): 123–42.

25 *The Confessional of Egbert*, 29, in McNeill and Gamer, 246. "Witchcraft" is given by the editors along with "druid-craft" for the Old English "dry-cræft."

26 Lea, *Materials*, 1:144.

27 Lea cites the provisions granted by Alfonso II of Aragon in 1176. *Ibid.*, 139–40.

28 Cohn, *Europe's Inner Demons*, 150.

29 Yet Nider himself does not gender witches consistently, and his most fully described *maleficus*, the arch-witch Staedelin, is a man. It is likely, however, that here we glimpse a contradiction between Nider's own conception of witchcraft, and the beliefs and experiences of his informant, Peter Gruyères of Bern. See Blauert, 57–9.

30 J.A. Sharpe, "Witchcraft and Women in Seventeenth Century England: Some Northern Evidence," *Continuity and Change* 6 (1991): 179–99; 194. See also Sharpe, *Witchcraft in Seventeenth Century Yorkshire: Accusations and Countermeasures*, Bothwick Paper 81 (1992), 18; Briggs, *Witches and Neighbors*, 265–71.

31 Clive Holmes, "Women: Witnesses and Witches," *Past and Present* 140 (1993), 45–78; 51.

32 Christina Larner, *Enemies of God*, 88–90.

33 See David Nicholas, *The Domestic Life of a Medieval City:Women, Children and the Family in Fourteenth-Century Ghent* (Lincoln: University of Nebraska Press, 1985), 21.

34 Thus Ivo of Chartres wrote that on occasion God permitted the devil to prevent sexual intercourse through the actions of "female sorceresses and witches" ("Si per sortiarias atque maleficas, occulto sed nunquam injusto Dei judicio permittente et diabolo praeparante, concubitus non sequitur"). *Panormia*, c. 117, *Patrologia Latina* 161.

35 To give just one of many possible examples, Burchard condemns love magic done by weaving and ligatures as sins specifically characteristic of women, *Corrector, Patrologia Latina* 140, 961, 972.

36 "Non autem mulierculae illa faciunt sua naturali virtute aut rerum aliarum quarum utuntur ministerio; sed ministerio daemonum quorum utuntur pactis et sacramentis." Gabriel Biel, *Supplementum in XXVIII Distinctiones Ultimas Quarti Senteniarum*, dist. 34, q. 1, in Lea, *Materials*, 1:170.

37 See Scholz Williams; D.P. Walker, *Spiritual and Demonic Magic* (1958, reprint, Notre Dame: University of Notre Dame Press, 1975). The humanist scholar Giovanni Pico was

the author of *Adversus Astrologiam*, among other things, and should not be confused with Gianfrancesco Pico, the author of the dialogue on witchcraft, *Strix*.

38 For a concise summary of these practices, see Kieckhefer, *Magic in the Middle Ages.*

39 Nider, *Praeceptorium*, 1.11, v.

40 *Ibid.*, 1.11, l, ee.

41 Martin of Arles, 367–75, 405–7.

42 *Ibid.*, 385–6, 415.

43 *Ibid.*, 362.

44 "quod daemones alliciuntur per varia genera lapidum, herbarum, lignorum, animalium, carminum, rituum . . . His ergo rebus vtitur maleficus vel malefica instinctu daemonis per pactum inuocationis tacite vel expresse." *Ibid.*, 416.

45 "vel ob desperationem, vel paupertatem, vel odia vicinorum, vel alias tentationes per Diabolum immissas, [quibus non resistunt] . . . sese Diabolo deuouendo." Molitor, c. 10, p. 714.

46 "Diabolus per se, siue Magos seu Maleficos vera et futura praedicere alteri non potest." *Ibid.*, 713–14.

47 An exception is Institoris and Sprenger's insistence that midwives were especially prone to witchcraft, and that midwife witches were the most powerful and most abominable of the breed. These women, they claim, "exceed all other witches in their villainy," and, worse still, were so numerous "that there is not the smallest hamlet where a witch of this kind may not be found" ("Incidentaliter reducuntur et obstetrices malefice omnes alias maleficas in flagiciis excedentes . . . quarum etiam tantus numerus vt ex earum confessionibus compertum est quod non estimatur villula vbi huiusmodi non reperiantur existit [sic]"). *Ibid.*, pt. 3, qu. 34, p. 252. Despite the assurance of this ringing denunciation, the testimony of contemporary witch-theorists and the evidence of trials indicates that, in this case, the authors were wrong: midwives were neither widely identified with witches nor singled out for prosecution. See David Harley, "Historians as Demonologists: The Myth of the Midwife-Witch," *Social History of Medicine* 3.1 (1990): 1–26; and Ritta Jo Horsley and Richard A. Horsley, "On the Trial of the 'Witches:' Wise Women, Midwives and the European Witch Hunts," in Marianne Burkhard and Edith Waldstein, eds., *Women in German Yearbook* 3 (Lanham, Maryland: University Press of Amherst, 1986): 1–28. Institoris and Sprenger's idiosyncratic and obsessive interest in midwife-witches may stem from the disproportionate weight they assign to the testimony of the single "repentant witch" of Breisach, whose confession – mentioned each time the subject of midwife-witches arises – provided the authors with what they considered unimpeachable expert testimony. *Ibid.*, pt. 1, qu. 12, and pt. 2, qu. 1, chs. 2 and 13.

48 *Malleus*, pt. 1, qu. 6.

49 "in omnibus viribus tam anime quam corporis cum sint defectuose non mirum si plura maleficia in eos quos emulantur fieri procurant." *Ibid.*, 42.

50 *Ibid.*, 42.

51 "Dicitur enim femina fe et minus quia semper minorem habet et seruat fidem." *Ibid.*, 42. Where the authors came across this famous and thoroughly ridiculous stab at etymological learning is unknown.

52 "Quantum insuper defectum in memorativa potentia cum hoc fit in eis ex natura vitiium nolle regi sed suos sequi impetus sine quacunque pietate." *Ibid.*, 43.

53 *Ibid.*, 42–3.

54 *Ibid.*, 44.

55 "Ratio naturalis est, quia plus carnalis viro existit vt patet in multis carnalibus spurcitiis." *Ibid.*, 42.

56 "Unde vituperationes leguntur in concupiscentiam carnis interpretari possunt vt semper mulier per carnis concupiscentia intelligatur." *Ibid.*, 41.

57 "Unde et cum demonibus causa explende libidinis se agitant." *Ibid.*, 45.

58 "Secundo eadem veritas scilicet quod adultere fornicarie etc., amplius existunt malefice

ostenditur per impedimentum maleficale super actum generatiue potentie." *Ibid.*, pt. 1, qu. 8, p. 52.

59 "Et quibus etiam et exterminium fidei seu periculum intolerabile quotidie imminet quod eorum animos immutare taliter sciunt quod eis nullum siue per se siue ab aliis fieri permittant sicquod quotidie crescunt." *Ibid.*, 45–6.

60 "Cum itaque fere omnes haereses et sectae maleficorum siue fascinariorum cultores, quorum plures ex eis, vtriusque sexus, hoc sponte et cum signis erubescentiae fateantur, asserant, quod in congregatione sua, quam faciunt ad cultum Daemonum, ipsi cum Daemonibus apparentibus, quandoque ad inuicem inordinate carnaliter voluptantur, adeo vehementer, vt praetactum est, quod plures ex eis inde postea per aliquot dies manent afflicti et debilitati." Jacquier claimed that this proved that the deeds of the witches were real, since everyone knew that "operations of Venus or the carnal passions cannot be completed or consummated by those sleeping" ("quia experientia manifeste docet, quod operationes Venereae et passiones carnalis voluptatis perfici siue consumari non possunt a dormientibus."). Jacquier, 37.

61 "Item ubi . . . Optimates praelati et alii diuites sepissime his miseriis inuoluuntur. Et quidem hoc tempus muliebre . . . cum iam mundus plenus sit adulterii praecipue in optimatibus, et quod opus scribere de remediis qui remedia abhorrent." *Malleus*, pt. 2, qu. 2, ch. 3, p. 164.

62 Innsbruck, the town overrun with abandoned women and witches is a case in point.

63 Institoris and Sprenger's attitude toward women and toward the disordering or emasculating powers of feminine forces is in this respect curiously similar to their near contemporary, Niccolo Machiavelli. See Hanna Fenichel Pitkin, *Fortune is a Woman* (Berkeley: University of California Press, 1984), 285–306 and *passim*.

64 Guido Ruggiero, *The Boundaries of Eros* (New York: Oxford University Press, 1985), 140.

65 See Sherry B. Ortner and Harriet Whitehead's introduction to Ortner and Whitehead, eds., *Sexual Meanings: The Cultural Construction of Gender and Sexuality* (Cambridge: Cambridge University Press, 1981): 1–27.

66 Stanley Brandes, "Like Wounded Stags: Male Sexual Ideology in an Andalusian Town," in Ortner and Whitehead, 216–39; see also James M. Taggart, *Enchanted Maidens. Gender Relations in Spanish Folktales of Courtship and Marriage* (Princeton: Princeton University Press, 1990).

67 Brandes, 224.

68 Taggart, 5.

69 Bruce Kapferer, *A Celebration of Demons* (Providence, Rhode Island: Berg Publishers and the Smithsonian Institution, 1991).

70 *Ibid.*, 141.

71 *Ibid.*, 150.

72 Lyndal Roper, *The Holy Household* (Oxford: Oxford University Press, 1989), 56–88.

73 *Ibid.*, 131.

74 Mary R. O'Neil, "Tall Tales and Sober Truth: Storytellers before the Inquisition," *Æstel* 3 (1995): 1–18.

75 See the *Malleus*, pt. 2, qu. 1, ch. 7; O'Neil, "Tall Tales," 8.

76 *Malleus*, pt. 1, qu. 8, p. 53.

77 "quod nisi eam verberaret nulla probitas aut honestas sibi inesset." *Ibid.*, pt. 1, qu. 18, p. 85.

78 They confine their remarks to the brief discussion of the devil's abhorrence for sodometrical sexuality and the reasons for his preference. See Chapter 3 above. For a recent discussion of the sin of sodomy in a medieval theological context, see Mark Jordan, *The Invention of Sodomy in Christian Theology* (Chicago: University of Chicago Press, 1997).

79 "Et benedictus altissimus qui virilem speciem a tanto flagitio vsque in praesens sic praeseruat in quo utique cum pro nobis nasci et pati voluit, ideo et ipsum priuilegiauit." *Malleus*, pt. 1, qu. 6, p. 45.

80 "But blessed be the Most High, who has so preserved the male sex among people from

their disgraceful acts up to this day, so that no man has been heard to have been polluted hitherto by that abominable lust" ("Benedictus autem altissimus, qui virilem speciem in hominibus a flagitiis eorum usque hodie sic servavit, ut nullus virorum ista nefaria libidine pollutus adhuc auditus sit"). William of Paris, 1071.

81 *Malleus*, pt. 2, qu. 1, ch. 10, pp. 127–8.

82 See Marc Boone, "State Power and Illicit Sexuality: The Persecution of Sodomy in Late Medieval Bruges," *Journal of Medieval History* 22 (1996): 135–53; 138.

83 Felix of Hemmerlin maintained that not only did the acts of sodomites "pollute the elements," but that so too did speaking and hearing of such crimes; such pollution was abhorrent as an offense against God, and because sodomy "generates pestilence and tempests." Felix of Hemmerlin, *Tractatus de Exorcismis* (c. 1455), printed in *Malleus Maleficarum* (Frankfurt: 1600), 2:418. See also Ruggiero, 109–13. Sodomy was also linked to notions of heresy: by the fifteenth century, throughout northern Europe, sodomites were called *bougres*, a word derived from "Bulgars" and associated with Manicheans in general.

84 Jonathan Goldberg, *Sodometries* (Stanford: Stanford University Press, 1992), 196.

85 "quadam virgine paupercula et ideo plurimum devota." *Malleus*, pt. 2, qu. 2, ch. 6, p. 171.

Bibliography

Primary works

Albertus Magnus. *Summa Theologiae*. In *Opera Omnia*, ed. Dionysius Siedler *et al.* Aschendorf: Monasterium Westfalorum, 1978.

———. *De Animalibus*. Trans. James J. Scanlan. Binghamton: Medieval and Renaissance Texts and Studies, 1987.

———. *Physica*. In *Opera Omnia*, ed. Paulus Hossfeld. Aschendorf: Monasterium Westfalorum, 1993.

Ambrosius de Vignati. *Tractatus de Haereticis*. In Hansen, *Quellen*, 215–27.

Ammann, Hartmann. "Der Innsbrucker Hexenprocesse von 1485." *Zeitschrift des Ferdinandeums für Tirol und Vorarlberg* 34 (1890): 1–87.

Aquinas, Thomas. *Expositio in Job*. In *Opera Omnia*, iussu Leonis XIII P. M. edita, t. 26. Rome: Ad Sanctae Sabinae, 1965.

———. *Questiones Disputatae*. Ed. Raymondi Spiazzi, et al. Taurini (Turin): Marietti, 1961.

———. *Sentences*. Ed. P. Mandonnet, Paris: P. Lechielleux, 1929.

———. *Summa contra Gentiles*. Ed. P. Marc, C. Pera, and P. Caramello. Taurini (Turin): Marietti, 1961.

———. *Summa Theologiae*. Ed. Institutio Studiorum Medievalium Ottaviensis. Ottowa: Studii Generalis O. Pr., 1941.

———. *The Summa Theologica*. Trans. Fathers of the English Dominican Province. London: Burns, Oates and Washbourne, 1914.

Athanasius. *The Life of St. Antony*. Trans. Robert T. Meyer. Westminster, Maryland: The Newman Press, 1950.

Augustine of Hippo. *On Christian Doctrine*. Trans. D.W. Robertson, Jr. Indianapolis: Bobbs-Merrill/Library of Liberal Arts, 1958.

———. *City of God*. Trans. Henry Bettenson. London: Penguin, 1972.

———. *De Civitate Dei*. Corpus Christianorum Series Latina 47–8. Turnhout: Brepols, 1955.

———. *The Divination of Demons*. Trans. R.W. Brown. In *Saint Augustine. Treatises on Marriage and Other Subjects*, ed. Roy J. Deferrari. New York: Fathers of the Church, 1951.

———. *Sermones de Vetere Testamento*. Ed. Cyrillus Lambot. Corpus Christianorum Series Latina 41. Turnhout: Brepols, 1961.

———. *Sermons*. Ed. John E. Rotelle. Trans. Edmund Hill. Brooklyn: New York City Press, 1992.

Bardin, Guillaume. *Chronicon Bardini*. In J. Vaissete, *Histoire générale de Languedoc*, ed. Auguste Molinier. vol. 10. Toulouse, privately published: 1885.

Basin, Bernard. *Tractatus de Artibus Magicis ac Magorum Maleficiis*. Frankfurt, 1600.

Bernard of Como. *Haeretica Pravitas*. Lucerne: 1584.

———. *Tractatus de Strigibus*. In *Haeretica Pravitas*, 140–54.

Bernardin of Siena. *Sermons*. Ed. Nazareno Orlandi. Trans. Helen Josephine Robins. Siena: Tipografie sociale, 1920.

Biblia Latina cum Glossa Ordinaria. Facsimile reprint editio princeps, Adolf Rusch, 1480/81. Turnholt: Brepols, 1992.

Brandeis, Arthur, ed. *Jacob's Well*. Early English Test Society, O.S. 115. London: Kegan Paul, Trench, Trübner and Co., 1900.

Burchard of Worms. *Corrector*. In Hansen, *Quellen*, and *Patrologia Latina* 140.

———. *Decreta*. *Patrologia Latina* 140, 537–1058.

Caesarius of Heisterbach. *Dialogus Miraculorum*. 2 vols. Ed. Joseph Strange. 1851. Reprint, Ridgewood New Jersey: Gregg Press, 1966.

Damiani, Peter. *De Castitate*. *Patrologia Latina* 145, 709–16.

[Pseudo-] Dionysius the Areopagite. *The Complete Works*. Trans. Colm Luibheid. New York: Paulist Press, 1987.

Dodo, Vincente. *Apologia*. In Hansen, *Quellen*, 274–8.

Errores Gazariorum. In Hansen, *Quellen*, 118–22; and in Ostorero, Bagliani, and Tremp, 267–300.

Étienne de Bourbon. *Anecdotes historiques*. Ed. A. Lecoy de la Marche. Paris: Libraire Renouard, 1877.

Gerson, Jean. *Contra Superstitiosam Dierum Observantiam* and *De Erroribus circa Artem Magicam*. In *Oeuvres complètes*. 8 vols. Ed. Palemon Glorieux. Paris: Desclée, 1960–66.

Gervaise of Tilbury. *Otia Imperialia*. Ed. Felix Liebrecht. Hanover: Carl Rümpler, 1856.

Giraldus Cambrensis. *Itinerarium Kambriae*. In *Opera*, vol. 6, ed. James F. Dimock. London: Longmans, Green, Reader, and Dyer, 1866.

Gregory the Great. *Morals on the Book of Job*. Ed. James Bliss. Oxford: John Henry Parker, 1844.

———. *Dialogues*. Trans. O.J. Zimmerman. New York: Fathers of the Church, 1959.

Gregory of Tours. *History of the Franks*. Trans. Lewis Thorpe. New York: Penguin, 1983.

Grillandus, Paulus. *Tractatus de Sortilegiis*. Frankfurt am Main, 1592.

Guibert of Nogent. *De Vita Sua*. In *Opera Omnia*, *Patrologia Latina* 156, 837–962.

Guillaume de Lorris and Jean de Meun. *The Romance of the Rose*. Trans. Charles Dahlberg. Hanover: University Press of New England, 1971.

Hansen, Joseph, ed. *Quellen und Untersuchungen zur Geschichte des Hexenwahns und der Hexenverfolgung im Mittelalter*. 1901. Reprint, Hildesheim: Georg Olms Verlagsbuchhandlung, 1963.

Hemmerlin, Felix (Felix Malleolus). *Tractatus de Credulitate Daemonibus Adhibenda*. In Institoris and Sprenger, *Malleus Maleficarum*, 1600.

———. *Tractatus de Exorcismis*. In Institoris and Sprenger, *Malleus Maleficarum*, 1600.

———. *Dialogus de Nobilitate et Rusticitate*. In Hansen, *Quellen*, 109–12.

Herolt, Johannes. *Miracles of the Blessed Virgin*. Trans. C.C. Swinton Bland. London: George Routledge and Sons, 1928.

Hincmar of Rheims. *De Divortio Lotharii et Tetbergae*. *Patrologia Latina* 125, 620–733.

Hrabanus Maurus. *De Magicis Artibus*. *Patrologia Latina* 110, 1095–110.

Institoris, Henricus. *Tractatus Varii*. N.P., 1496.

Institoris (Krämer), Henricus, and Jacobus Sprenger. *Malleus Maleficarum*. 1487. Facsimile reprint, Göppingen: Kümmerle Verlag, 1991.

———. *Malleus Maleficarum Maleficas et Earum Heresim ut Phramea Potentissima Conterens*. Lyon: Jean Marion, 1519.

———. *Malleus Maleficarum*. Frankfurt am Main: Nicolaus Bassaeus, 1580.

———. *Malleus Maleficarum*. 2 vols. Frankfurt am Main: Nicholas Bassaeus, 1600.

———. *The Malleus Maleficarum*. Trans. Montague Summers. 1928. Reprint, New York: Dover, 1971.

———. *Le Marteau des sorcières*. Ed. and trans. Amand Danet. Paris: Civilisations et mentalités, 1973.

Isidore of Seville. *Etymologiae*. Ed. W.M. Lindsay. Oxford: Clarendon, 1911.

Ivo of Chartres. *Decreti*. *Patrologia Latina* 161, 47–1022.

———. *Panormia*. *Patrologia Latina* 161, 1041–344.

Jacques de Vitry. *The Exempla of Jacques de Vitry*. Ed. Thomas Frederick Crane. London: David Nutt, 1890.

Jacquier, Nicholas. *Flagellum Haereticorum Fascinariorum*. Ed. Ioannes Myntzenbergius. Frankfurt am Main: Nicholas Bassaeus, 1581.

James, M.R. "Twelve Medieval Ghost Stories." *English Historical Revue* 37 (1922): 413–22.

John of Frankfurt. *Questio, utrum potestas cohercendi demones . . .* In Hansen, *Quellen*, 71–82.

Jordanes de Bergamo. *Questio de Strigis*. In Hansen, *Quellen*, 195–200.

The Laws of the Salian Franks. Trans. Katharine Fischer Drew. Philadelphia: University of Pennsylvania Press, 1991.

Lea, Henry Charles. *Materials Toward a History of Witchcraft*. 3 vols. Ed. Arthur C. Howland. 1939. Reprint, New York: Thomas Yoseloff, 1957.

Little, A.G., ed. *Liber Exemplorum ad Usum Praedicantium*. In *The British Society of Franciscan Studies* 1 (1908).

Mamoris, Petrus. *Flagellum Maleficorum*. Lugdunum [Lyon]: 1621.

Map, Walter. *De Nugis Curialium*. Ed. M.R. James. Oxford: Clarendon Press, 1914.

Martin of Arles. *Tractatus de Superstitionibus*. In Jacquier, *Flagellum Haereticorum Fascinariorum*.

McNeill, John T., and Helena M. Gamer, eds. and trans. *Medieval Handbooks of Penance*. New York: Columbia University Press, 1938.

Molitor, Ulrich. *Tractatus de Pythonicis Mulieribus*. In Institoris and Sprenger, *Malleus Maleficarum*, 1580.

Nicholas of Cusa. *Opera*. Paris, 1514. Facsimile reprint, Frankfurt am Main: Minerva, 1962.

Nider, Johannes. *Praeceptorium Legis s. Expositio Decalogi*. Strassburg: Georg Husner, 1476.

──. *Formicarius*. 1480. Facsimile reprint, Graz: Akademische Druck- und Verlagsanstalt, 1971.

Ostorero, Martine, Agostino Paravicini Bagliani, and Kathrin Utz Tremp, eds. *L'Imaginaire du Sabbat: édition critique des textes les plus anciens (1430 c.–1440 c.)*. Cahiers lausannois d'histoire médiévale 26. Lausanne: Université de Lausanne, 1999.

Parvay: see Tholosan.

Pico della Mirandola, Gianfrancesco. *Strix*. Argentoratum [Strassburg]: Carole Weinrichius, 1612.

Ponzinibio, Gianfrancesco. *Tractatus de Lamiis*. In Paulus Grillandus, *Tractatus de Sortilegiis*.

Prieras, Sylvester (Sylvestro Mazzolini). *De Strigimagarum, Daemonumque Mirandis, Libri Tres*. Rome: 1521.

Rather of Verona. *The Complete Works of Rather of Verona*. Ed. and trans. Peter L.D. Reid. Binghamton: Medieval and Renaissance Texts and Studies, 1991.

Regino of Prüm. *De Ecclesiasticis Disciplinis*. Patrologia Latina 132, 185–400.

Robert of Brunne. *Handlyng Synne*. Ed. F.J. Furnivall. London: Early English Text Society, 1901.

Roger of Howden. *Chronica Rogeri de Hoveden*. Ed. William Stubbs. Rolls Series 52. London: Longman and Greens, 1869.

Rollins, H.E., ed. *The Pepys Ballads*. Cambridge, Massachusetts: Harvard University Press, 1931.

Salimbene de Adam. *The Chronicle of Salimbene de Adam*. Ed. and trans. Joseph L. Baird. Binghamton: Medieval and Renaissance Texts and Studies, 1986.

Samuel de Cassini. *Question de le Strie*. (1505). In Hansen, *Quellen*, 262–73.

Spina, Alphonso de. *Fortalitium Fidei*. Lugdunum [Lyon]: Gulielmus Balsarin, 1487.

Suso, Henry. *The Exemplar*. Ed. Nicholas Heller. Trans. Ann Edward. Dubuque: The Priory Press, 1962.

Tholosan, Claude. *Ut Magorum et Maleficiorum Errores*. In Pierette Parvay, "À propos de la genèse médiévale des chasses aux sorcières: le traité de Claude Tholasan, juge dauphinois (vers 1436)." *Mélanges de L'École française de Rome (Moyen Age – Temps modernes)* 91 (1979): 354–79.

Thomas of Cantimpré. *Bonum Universale de Apibus*. NP: 1627.

Vincent, Jean (Johann Vincentii). *Liber adversus Magicas Artes*. In Hansen, *Quellen*, 227–31.

Vineti, Jean (Johannes Vinetus). *Contra Daemonum Invocatores*. Cologne: Ludwig von Renchen, c. 1487.

Visconti, Girolamo. *Lamiarum sive Striarum Opuscula*. Milan: Leonardus Pachel, 1490.

Wakefield, Walter L., and Austin P. Evans, eds. *Heresies of the High Middle Ages*. New York: Columbia University Press, 1969.

Weyer, Johann. *De Praestigiis Daemonum*. Trans. John Shea as *Witches, Devils, and Doctors in the Renaissance*. Binghamton: Medieval and Renaissance Texts and Studies, 1991.

William of Malmesbury. *De Gestis Regum Anglorum*. Ed. William Stubbs. London: Longmans, Green, Reader and Dyer, 1887–1889.

William of Paris (Guilielmus Parisiensis). *De Universo*. In *Opera Omnia*. Paris: 1674. Reprint, Frankfurt am Main: Minerva, 1963.

Wright, Thomas, ed. *A Selection of Latin Stories*. London: The Percy Society, 1842.

Secondary works

Accati, Luisa. "The Spirit of Fornication: Virtue of the Soul and Virtue of the Body in Friuli, 1600–1800." In *Sex and Gender in Historical Perspective*, ed. Edward Muir and Guido Ruggiero, trans. Margaret A. Gallucci, with Mary M. Gallucci and Carole C. Gallucci, 110–40. Baltimore: Johns Hopkins University Press, 1990.

Allport, Gorden W., and Leo Postman. *The Psychology of Rumor*. New York: Henry Holt, 1947.

Alver, Bente Gullveig, and Torunn Selberg. "Folk Medicine as Part of a Larger Concept Complex." *ARV* 43 (1987): 21–44.

Ammann, Hartmann. "Eine Vorarbeit des Heinrich Institoris für den *Malleus Maleficarum*." *Mitteilungen des Institutes für Österreichischen Geschichtsforschung* 8 (1911): 461–504.

Anglo, Sydney. "Evident Authority and Authoritative Evidence: The *Malleus Maleficarum*." in *The Damned Art: Essays in the Literature of Witchcraft*, ed. Sydney Anglo, 1–31. London: Routledge and Kegan Paul, 1977.

Ankarloo, Bengt, and Gustav Henningsen, eds. *Early Modern European Witchcraft*. Oxford: Clarendon Press, 1990.

Ardener, Edwin. "Social Anthropology, Language and Reality." In *Semantic Anthropology*, ASA Monograph 22, 1–14. London: Academic Press, 1982.

———. *The Voice of Prophecy and Other Essays*. Ed. Malcolm Chapman. Oxford: Basil Blackwell, 1989.

Baroja, Julio Caro. *The World of the Witches*. Trans. O.N.V. Glendinning. Chicago: University of Chicago Press, 1964.

———. "Witchcraft and Catholic Theology." In Ankarloo and Henningsen, 19–43.

Barry, Jonathan. "Introduction: Keith Thomas and the Problem of Witchcraft." In Barry, Hester, and Roberts, 1–45.

Barry, Jonathan, Marianne Hester, and Gareth Roberts, eds. *Witchcraft in Early Modern Europe*. Cambridge: Cambridge University Press, 1996.

Barstow, Anne Llewellyn. "On Studying Witchcraft as Women's History: A Historiography of the European Witch Persecutions." *Journal of Feminist Studies in Religion* 4 (Autumn, 1988): 7–19.

Behringer, Wolfgang. "Witchcraft in Austria, Germany and Switzerland." In Barry, Hester, and Roberts, 64–95.

———. *Hexenverfolgung in Bayern*. Munich: R. Oldenbourg, 1988.

———. *Chonrad Stoekhlin und die Nachtschar*. Munich: Piper, 1994.

Belmont, Nicole. "Levana; or, How to Raise Up Children." In *Family and Society*, ed. Robert Forster and Orest Ranum, trans. Elborg Forster and Patricia Ranum, 1–15. Baltimore: Johns Hopkins University Press, 1976.

Bennet, R.F. *The Early Dominicans*. Cambridge: Cambridge University Press, 1937.

Bernstein, Alan. "Theology between Heresy and Folklore: William of Auvergne on Punishment after Death." *Traditio* 38 (1982): 4–44.

Bertolotti, Maurizi. "The Ox's Bones and the Ox's Hide: A Popular Myth, Part Hagiography and Part Witchcraft." In *Microhistory and the Lost Peoples of Europe*, ed. Edward Muir and Guido Ruggiero, trans. Eren Branch, 41–70. Baltimore: Johns Hopkins University Press, 1991.

Blakeborough, Richard. *Yorkshire Wit, Character and Folklore*. 1898. Reprint, Wakefield: EP Publishing Limited, 1973.

Blauert, Andreas. *Frühe Hexenverfolgungen*. Hamburg: Junius, 1989.

Blécourt, Willem de. "Witch Doctors, Soothsayers, and Priests: On Cunning Folk in European Historiography and Tradition." *Social History* 19.3 (1994): 285–303.

Boone, Marc. "State Power and Illicit Sexuality: The Persecution of Sodomy in Late Medieval Bruges." *Journal of Medieval History* 22 (1996): 135–53.

Borst, Arno. "The Origins of the Witch-Craze in the Alps." In *Medieval Worlds*, trans. Eric Hansen, 101–22. Chicago: University of Chicago Press, 1992.

Bossy, John. *Christianity and the West 1400–1700*. Oxford: Oxford University Press, 1985.

Bovenschen, Sylvia. "The Contemporary Witch, the Historical Witch and the Witch Myth: The Witch, Subject of the Appropriation of Nature and the Object of the Domination of Nature." Trans. Jeannine Blackwell, Johanna Moore, and Beth Weckmueller. In *Articles on Witchcraft, Magic and Demonology*, ed. Levack, 10:131–67.

Boyce, Georgina. "Belief and Disbelief: An Examination of Reactions to the Presentation of Rumor Legends." In *Perspectives on Contemporary Legend*, ed. Paul Smith, 64–78. Sheffield: CECTAL Conference Papers Series no. 4, 1984.

Boyer, Paul, and Stephen Nissenbaum. *Salem Possessed: The Social Origins of Witchcraft*. Cambridge Massachusetts: Harvard University Press, 1974.

Brandes, Stanley. "Like Wounded Stags: Male Sexual Ideology in an Andalusian Town." In *Sexual Meanings: The Cultural Construction of Gender and Sexuality*, ed. Sherry B. Ortner and Hariet Whitehead, 216–39. New York: Cambridge University Press, 1981.

Brauner, Sigrid. *Fearless Wives and Frightened Shrews: The Construction of the Witch in Early Modern Germany*. Ed. Robert H. Brown. Amherst: University of Massachusetts Press, 1995.

Briggs, Katherine M. *A Dictionary of British Folktales*. 2 vols. Bloomington: University of Indiana Press, 1971.

———. *The Vanishing People*. London: B.T. Batsford, 1978.

Briggs, Robin. *Communities of Belief: Cultural and Social Tension in Early Modern France*. Oxford: Clarendon Press, 1989.

———. "Women as Victims? Witches, Judges and the Community." *French History* 5.4 (1991): 438–50.

———. *Witches and Neighbors: The Social and Cultural Context of European Witchcraft*. New York: Viking, 1996.

———. "'Many Reasons Why': Witchcraft and the Problems of Multiple Explanation." In Barry, Hester, and Roberts, 49–63.

Brown, Peter. "Sorcery, Demons, and the Rise of Christianity from Late Antiquity into the Middle Ages." In Douglas, 17–45.

Burghartz, Susanna. "The Equation of Women and Witches: A Case Study of Witchcraft Trials in Lucerne and Lausanne in the Fifteenth and Sixteenth Centuries." In Levack, ed., *Articles on Witchcraft, Magic, and Demonology*, 10:67–83.

Burr, George Lincoln. *The Witch Persecutions*. Philadelphia: University of Pennsylvania Press, 1903.

Clark, Stuart. "Inversion, Misrule and the Meaning of Witchcraft." *Past and Present* 87 (1980): 98–127.

———. "French Historians and Early Modern Popular Culture." *Past and Present* 100 (1983): 62–99.

———. "The 'Gendering' of Witchcraft in French Demonology: Misogyny or Polarity?" *French History* 5.4 (1991): 426–37.

———. "The Rational Witchfinder: Conscience, Demonological Naturalism, and Popular Superstitions." In Stephen Pumfrey, Paolo L. Rossi, and Maurice Slawinski, eds., *Science, Culture and Popular Belief in Renaissance Europe*. Manchester: Manchester University Press, 1991, 222–48.

———. *Thinking with Demons: The Idea of Witchcraft in Early Modern Europe*. Oxford: Oxford University Press, 1997.

Clark, William. "Witches, Floods and Wonder Drugs: Historical Perspectives on Risk Management." In R.C. Schwing and W.A. Albers, Jr, eds., *Societal Risk Assessment: How Safe is Safe Enough?* New York: Plenum Press, 1980, 287–313.

Clarke, Garret. "Women and Witches: Patterns of Analysis." *Signs* 3 (1977): 461–70.

Cohn, Norman. "The Myth of Satan and his Human Servants." In Douglas, 3–16.

———. *Europe's Inner Demons*. New York: Basic Books, 1975.

Coudert, Allison P. "The Myth of the Improved Status of Protestant Women." In Levack, ed., *Articles on Witchcraft, Magic and Demonology*, 10:85–113.

Crick, Malcolm. *Explorations in Language and Meaning: Towards a Semantic Anthropology*. New York: John Wiley and Sons, 1976.

Davidson, Jane P. "Wolves, Witches, and Werewolves: Lycanthropy and Witchcraft from 1423 to 1700." *Journal of the Fantastic in the Arts* 2 (1990): 47–67.

Dégh, Linda. "Satanic Child Abuse in a Blue House." In *Narratives in Society: A Performance-Centered Study of Narration*, Folklore Fellows Communication 255, 358–68. Helsinki: Academia Scientiarum Fennica, 1995.

Dégh, Linda, and Andrew Vázsonyi. "Legend and Belief." *Genre* 4 (1971): 281–304.

Delumeau, Jean. *La Peur en occident*. Paris: Fayard, 1978.

———. *Sin and Fear: The Emergence of a Western Guilt Culture, 13th–18th Centuries*. Trans. Eric Nicholson. New York: St. Martin's Press, 1990.

Demos, John Putnam. *Entertaining Satan:Witchcraft and the Culture of Early New England.* New York: Oxford University Press, 1982.

Devlin, Judith. *The Superstitious Mind. French Peasants and the Supernatural in the Nineteenth Century.* Newhaven: Yale University Press, 1987.

Ní Dhuibhne, Éilís. "'The Old Woman as Hare': Structure and Meaning in an Irish Legend." *Folklore* 104 (1993): 77–85.

Dienst, Heide. "Lebensbewältigung durch Magie: alltägliche Zauberei in Innsbruck gegen Ende des 15. Jahrhunderts." In Alfred Kohler and Heinrich Lutz, eds., *Alltag im 16. Jahrhunderts.* Vienna: Verlag für Geschichte und Politik, 1987, 80–116.

Dinzelbacher, Peter. "Der Realität des Teufels im Mittelalter." In Segl., ed., *Der Hexenhammer,* 151–75.

Douglas, Mary, ed. *Witchcraft Confessions and Accusations.* London: Tavistock Publications, 1970.

Duerr, Hans Peter. *Dreamtime.* Trans. Felicitas Goodman. Oxford: Basil Blackwell, 1985.

Duffy, Eamon. *The Stripping of the Altars:Traditional Religion in England c. 1400–c. 1580.* New Haven: Yale University Press, 1992.

Ehrenreich, Barbara, and Diane English. *Witches, Midwives and Nurses.* London: Readers and Writers, 1976.

Eire, Carlos M.N. *War against the Idols:The Reformation of Worship from Erasmus to Calvin.* Cambridge: Cambridge University Press, 1986.

Eliade, Mircea. *Shamanism: Archaic Techniques of Ecstasy.* Trans. Willard R. Trask. Princeton: Princeton University Press, 1964.

Elliott, Dyan. *Fallen Bodies: Pollution, Sexuality, and Demonology in the Middle Ages.* Philadelphia: University of Pennsylvania Press, 1999.

Endres, Rudolf. "Heinrich Institoris, sein Hexenhammer und der Nürnberger Rat." In Segl, ed., *Der Hexenhammer,* 195–216.

Epstein, Scarlett. "A Sociological Analysis of Witch Beliefs in a Mysore Village." In John Middleton, ed., *Magic, Witchcraft and Curing,* 137–54. Garden City: The Natural History Press, 1967.

Evans-Pritchard, E.E. *Witchcraft, Oracles and Magic among the Azande.* Oxford: Basil Blackwell, 1937.

Favret-Saada, Jeanne. *Deadly Words:Witchcraft in the Bocage.* Trans. Catherine Cullen. Cambridge: Cambridge University Press, 1980.

Fernandez, James. "The Mission of Metaphor in Expressive Culture." *Current Anthropology* 15 (1974): 119–45.

———. "Historians Tell Tales: Of Cartesian Cats and Gallic Cockfights." *Journal of Modern History* 60 (1988): 113–27.

Fichtenau, Heinrich. *Living in the Tenth Century.* Trans. Patrick J. Geary. Chicago: University of Chicago Press, 1991.

Flint, Valerie J. *The Rise of Magic in Early Medieval Europe.* Princeton: Princeton University Press, 1991.

Forbes, Thomas Rogers. *The Midwife and the Witch.* New Haven: Yale University Press, 1966.

Foster, George. "Peasant Society and the Image of Limited Good." *American Anthropologist* 67 (1965): 293–315.

Funkenstein, Amos. *Theology and the Scientific Imagination: From the Middle Ages to the Seventeenth Century.* Princeton: Princeton University Press, 1986.

Galpern, A.N. "The Legacy of Late Medieval Religion in Sixteenth Century Champagne." In Charles Trinkhaus and Heiko A. Oberman, eds., *The Pursuit of Holiness in Late Medieval and Renaissance Religion.* Leiden: E.J. Brill, 1974, 141–76.

Geertz, Clifford. *The Interpretation of Cultures.* New York: Basic Books, 1973.

Gentilcore, David. *From Bishop to Witch.* Manchester: Manchester University Press, 1992.

Gijswijt-Hofstra, Marijke. "The European Witchcraft Debate and the Dutch Variant." *Social History* 15.2 (1990): 181–94.

Ginzburg, Carlo. *The Night Battles.* Trans. John and Anne Tedeschi. Baltimore: The Johns Hopkins University Press, 1992.

———. "Deciphering the Sabbath." Trans. Paul Falla. In Ankarloo and Henningsen, 121–37.

———. *Ecstasies: Deciphering the Witches' Sabbath.* Trans. Raymond Rosenthal. New York: Pantheon Books, 1991.

Goddu, André. "The Failure of Exorcism in the Middle Ages." In Albert Zimmerman, ed., *Soziale Ordnungen im Selbstverständnis des Mittelalters.* Berlin: Walter de Gruyter, 1980, 540–77.

Goldberg, Jonathan. *Sodometries.* Stanford University Press, 1992.

Graf, Antonio. *The Story of the Devil.* Trans. Edward Noble Stone. New York: Macmillan, 1931.

Greilsammer, Myriam. "The Midwife, the Priest, and the Physician: The Subjugation of Midwives in the Low Countries at the End of the Middle Ages." *Journal of Medieval and Renaissance Studies* 21 (1991): 285–329.

Grimm, Jacob. *The German Legends of the Brothers Grimm.* Ed and trans. Donald Ward. 2 vols. Philadelphia: Institute for the Study of Human Issues, 1981.

Grohman, W.A. Baille. *Gaddings with a Primitive People, Being a Series of Sketches of Tyrolese Life and Customs.* New York: Henry Holt, 1878.

Hansen, Joseph. "Der *Malleus Maleficarum*, seine Druckausgaben und die gefälschte Kölner Approbation vom J. 1487." *Westdeutsche Zeitschrift für Geschichte und Kunst* 17 (1898), 119–68.

———. *Zauberwahn, Inquisition und Hexenprozess im Mittelalter.* 1900. Reprint, Munich: Scientia Verlag Aalen, 1964.

Harley, David. "Historians as Demonologists: The Myth of the Midwife-Witch." *Social History of Medicine* 3.1 (1990): 1–26.

Harner, Michael. "The Role of Hallucinogenic Plants in European Witchcraft." In Michael Harner, ed., *Hallucinogens and Shamanism,.* New York: Oxford University Press, 1972, 127–50.

Harris, Marvin. "The Great Witch Craze." In Marvin, *Cows, Pigs, Wars and Witches: The Riddles of Culture.* New York: Vintage Books, 1978.

Hastrup, Kirsten. *Island of Anthropology.* Odense, Odense University Press, 1990.

Helder, E. van der. "Drama and Its Intellectual Climate: The Roles of Mary and Christ in Some German Miracle and Eschatological Plays." *Parergon* 4 (1986): 117–33.

Henderson, William. *Folklore of the Northern Counties of England and the Borders.* 1866. Reprint, Wakefield: EP Publishing, 1973.

Henningsen, Gustav. " 'The Ladies from the Outside': An Archaic Pattern of the Witches' Sabbath." In Ankarloo and Henningsen, 191–215.

Hester, Marianne. *Lewd Women and Wicked Witches.* London: Routledge, 1992.

———. "Patriarchal Reconstruction and Witch Hunting." In Barry, Hester, and Roberts, 288–306.

Hinnebusch, William A. *The History of the Dominican Order.* 2 vols. New York: Alba House, 1973.

Hinton, Norman. "The Werewolf as *Eiron*: Freedom and Comedy in William of Palerne." In Nona C. Flores, ed., *Animals in the Middle Ages.* New York: Garland Publishing, 1996, 133–46.

Holmes, Clive. "Women: Witnesses and Witches." *Past and Present* 140 (1993): 45–78.

Honko, Lauri. "Memorates and the Study of Folk Belief." In Reimund Kvideland and Henning K. Sehmsdorf, eds., *Nordic Folklore.* Bloomington: Indiana University Press, 1989, 100–9.

Hopkin, Charles Edward. *The Share of Thomas Aquinas in the Growth of the Witchcraft Delusion.* Philadelphia: University of Pennsylvania Press, 1940.

Horsley, Richard A. "Who were the Witches? The Social Role of the Accused in the European Witch Trials." *Journal of Interdisciplinary History* 9 (1979): 689–715.

Horsley, Ritta Jo, and Richard A. Horsley. "On the Trail of the "Witches:" Wise Women, Midwives and the European Witch Hunts." In Marianne Burkhard and Edith Waldstein, eds., *Women in German Yearbook* 3. Lanham, Maryland: University Press of Amherst, 1986, 1–28.

Hoyt, Charles Alva. *Witchcraft.* Carbondale: Southern Illinois University Press, 1989.

Janssen, Johannes. *History of the German People after the Close of the Middle Ages.* Trans. A.M. Christie. New York: AMS Press, 1966.

Jordan, Mark. *The Invention of Sodomy in Christian Theology.* Chicago: University of Chicago Press, 1997.

Kapferer, Bruce. *A Celebration of Demons.* Providence, Rhode Island: Berg Publishers and the Smithsonian Institution, 1991.

Karlson, Carol F. *The Devil in the Shape of a Woman.* New York: W.W. Norton, 1987.

Keck, David. *Angels and Angelology in the Middle Ages.* Oxford: Oxford University Press, 1998.

Kelly, Henry Ansgar. *The Devil at Baptism.* Ithaca: Cornell University Press, 1985.

Kieckhefer, Richard. *European Witch Trials.* Berkeley: University of California Press, 1976.

———. *Repression of Heresy in Medieval Germany.* Philadelphia: University of Pennsylvania Press, 1979.

———. *Unquiet Souls: Fourteenth Century Saints and Their Religious Milieu.* Chicago: University of Chicago Press, 1984.

———. *Magic in the Middle Ages.* Cambridge: Cambridge University Press, 1989.

Klaits, Joseph. *Servants of Satan*. Bloomington: Indiana University Press, 1985.

Klaniczay, Gábor. *The Uses of Supernatural Power*. Ed. Karen Margolis. Trans. Susan Singerman. Cambridge: Polity Press, 1990.

Kluckhohn, Clyde. *Navaho Witchcraft*. Boston: Beacon Press, 1944.

Kors, Alan, and Edward Peters, eds. *Witchcraft in Europe: 1100–1700*. Philadelphia: University of Pennsylvania Press, 1972.

Kunze, Michael. *Highroad to the Stake*. Trans. William E. Yuill. Chicago: University of Chicago Press, 1987.

Kvideland, Reimund, and Henning K. Sehmsdorf, eds. *Scandinavian Folk Belief and Legend*. Minneapolis: University of Minnesota Press, 1988.

Lakoff, George. *Women, Fire and Other Dangerous Things*. Chicago: University of Chicago Press, 1987.

Lambert, Malcolm. *Medieval Heresy*. Oxford: Basil Blackwell, 1992.

Larner, Christina. *Enemies of God: The Witch-Hunt in Scotland*. Baltimore: Johns Hopkins University Press, 1981.

———. *Witchcraft and Religion*. Oxford: Basil Blackwell, 1984.

Lea, Henry Charles. *A History of the Inquisition in the Middle Ages*. 3 vols. 1888. Reprint, New York: The Harbor Press, 1955.

Lecouteux, Claude. "Hagazussa – Striga – Hexe." *Hessische Blätter für Volks- und Kulturforschung* N.F. 18 (1985): 57–70.

———. *Geschichte der Gespenster und Wiedergänger im Mittelalter*. Köln: Böhlau Verlag, 1987.

———. *Fées, sorcières et loups-garous au Moyen Âge: histoire du double*. Paris: Imago, 1992.

Le Court, Marc. "Comment la sagesse vient aux femmes: Ethnologies d'Europe et d'ailleurs." *Civilisations* 36 (1986): 61–6.

Leff, Gordon. *The Dissolution of the Medieval Outlook*. New York: Harper and Row, 1976.

Le Goff, Jacques. "The Learned and Popular Dimensions of Journeys in the Otherworld in the Middle Ages." In S.L. Kaplan, ed., *Understanding Popular Culture*. Berlin: Mouton, 1981, 39–51.

Levack, Brian. *The Witch-Hunt in Early Modern Europe*. London: Longman, 1987.

———, ed. *Articles on Witchcraft, Magic, and Demonology*. 10 vols. (vol. 10: *Witchcraft, Women and Society*). New York: Garland Publishing, Inc., 1992.

Lewis, Charlton T., and Charles Short. *A Latin Dictionary*. Oxford: Clarendon Press, 1879.

Lewis, I.M. *Religion in Context: Cult and Charisma*. Cambridge: Cambridge University Press, 1986.

List, Edgar A. "Is Frau Holda the Virgin Mary?" *German Quarterly* 32 (1953): 80–4.

———. "Holda and the Venusberg." *Journal of American Folklore* 73 (1960): 307–11.

MacCulloch, J.A. *Medieval Faith and Fable*. Boston: Marshall Jones Company, 1932.

MacDonald, Scot. "Theory of Knowledge." In *The Cambridge Companion to Aquinas*, ed. Norman Kretzmann, Eleanor Stump, 160–95. Cambridge: Cambridge University Press, 1993.

Macfarlane, Alan. *Witchcraft in Tudor and Stuart England*. London: Routledge and Kegan
     Paul, 1970.
———. "Witchcraft in Tudor and Stuart Essex." In Douglas, 81–99.
Mair, Lucy. *Witchcraft*. New York: World University Library, 1969.
Martin, Ruth. *Witchcraft and the Inquisition in Venice 1550–1650*. Oxford: Basil
     Blackwell, 1989.
Marwick, M.G. "The Sociology of Sorcery in a Central African Tribe." In John
     Middleton, ed., *Magic, Witchcraft and Curing*. Garden City: The Natural History
     Press, 1967, 101–26.
Meehan, Francis X. *Efficient Causality in Aristotle and Thomas Aquinas*. The Catholic
     University of America Philosophical Studies 56. Washington, D.C.: The Catholic
     University of America Press, 1940.
Michelet, Jules. *La Sorciere*. 2 vols. 1863. Reprint, Paris: Libraire Marcel Didier, 1956.
Midelfort, H.C. Erik. "Recent Witch Hunting Research, or Where do we go from
     here?" *Bibliographical Society of American Papers* (1968): 373–420.
———. *Witch-Hunting in Southwestern Germany 1562–1684*. Stanford: Stanford Univer-
     sity Press, 1972.
———. "Witchcraft, Magic and the Occult." In Steven Ozment, ed., *Reformation Europe:
     A Guide to Research*. St. Louis: Center for Reformation Research, 1982,
     183–209.
Monter, E. William. "The Historiography of European Witchcraft: Progress and
     Prospects." *Journal of Interdisciplinary History* 11 (1972): 435–51.
———. *Witchcraft in France and Switzerland*. Ithaca: Cornell University Press, 1976.
———. "The Pedestal and the Stake: Courtly Love and the Witchcraze." In R.
     Bridenthal and C. Koonz., eds., *Becoming Visible*. Boston: Houghton Mifflin,
     1977, 119–36.
———. *Ritual, Myth and Magic in Early Modern Europe*. Athens, Ohio: Ohio University
     Press, 1983.
Moore, R.I. *The Formation of a Persecuting Society*. Oxford: Basil Blackwell, 1987.
Morris, Katharine. *Sorceress or Witch? The Image of Gender in Medieval Iceland and
     Northern Europe*. Lanham: University Press of America, 1991.
Muchembled, Robert. *La Sorcière au village*. Paris: Éditions Julliard/Gallimard,
     1979.
———. "The Witches of Cambrésis." Trans. Susan Darnton. In *Religion and the People,
     800–1700*, ed. James Obelkevich, 221–76. Chapel Hill: University of North
     Carolina Press, 1979.
———. *Popular Culture and Elite Culture in France 1400–1750*. Trans. Lydia Cochran.
     Baton Rouge: Louisiana State University Press, 1985.
———. "Satanic Myths and Cultural Reality." In Ankarloo and Henningsen, 139–60.
Muller, Frederick. *The Roots of Witchcraft*. Plymouth: Clarke, Doble, and Brenden,
     1973.
Müller, K.O. "Heinrich Institoris, der Verfasser des Hexenhammers un seine Tätigkeit
     als Hexeninquisitor in Ravensburg im Herbst 1484." *Württemburgerische Viertel-
     jahreshefte für Landesgeschichte* N.F. 19 (1910): 397–417.

Murray, Margaret. *The Witch Cult in Western Europe*. 1921. Reprint, Oxford: Oxford University Press, 1962.

——. *The God of the Witches*. 1931. Reprint, London: Oxford University Press, 1970.

Needham, Rodney. *Primordial Characters*. Charlottesville: University Press of Virginia, 1978.

——. *Against the Tranquility of Axioms*. Berkeley: California University Press, 1983.

Nicholas, David. *The Domestic Life of a Medieval City: Women, Children and the Family in Fourteenth-Century Ghent*. Lincoln: University of Nebraska Press, 1985.

Nildin-Wall, Bodil, and Jan Wall. "The Witch as Hare or the Witch's Hare: Popular Legends and Beliefs in Nordic Tradition." *Folklore* 104 (1993): 66–76.

Oakley, Francis. *Omnipotence, Covenant, and Order*. Ithaca: Cornell University Press, 1984.

Oberman, Heiko. *The Dawn of the Reformation*. Edinburgh: T. & T. Clark, 1986.

——. "Fourteenth Century Religious Thought: A Premature Profile." In Oberman, *Dawn of the Reformation*, 1–17.

——. "The Shape of Late Medieval Thought: The Birthpangs of the Modern Era." In Oberman, *Dawn of the Reformation*, 18–38.

——. "*Via Antiqua* and *Via Moderna*: Late Medieval Prolegomena to Reformation Thought." *Journal of the History of Ideas* 48 (1987): 23–40.

O'Neil, Mary R. "Superstition." In *The Encyclopedia of Religion*, ed. Mircea Eliade, 14:163–6. New York: MacMillan Publishing, 1987.

——. "Missing Footprints: *Maleficium* in Modena." *Acta Ethnographica Hungarica* 37 (1991/92): 123–42.

——. "Tall Tales and Sober Truth: Storytellers before the Inquisition." *Æstel* 3 (1995): 1–18.

Ortner, Sherry B., and Harriet Whitehead. Introduction to Ortner and Whitehead, eds., *Sexual Meanings: The Cultural Construction of Gender and Sexuality*. Cambridge: Cambridge University Press, 1981, 1–27.

Otton, Charlotte F., ed. *A Lycanthropy Reader*. Syracuse: Syracuse University Press, 1986.

Palmer, Roy. *The Folklore of Warwickshire*. Totowa, New Jersey: Rowman and Littlefield, 1976.

Peters, Edward. *The Magician, the Witch, and the Law*. Philadelphia: University of Pennsylvania Press, 1978.

Pitkin, Hanna Fenichel. *Fortune is a Woman*. Berkeley: University of California Press, 1984.

Pócs, Éva. *Fairies and Witches at the Boundary of South-Eastern and Central Europe*. Folklore Fellows Communication 243. Helsinki: Academia Scientiarum Fennica, 1989.

Porter, Enid. *Cambridgeshire Customs and Folklore*. London: Routledge and Kegan Paul, 1969.

Quétif, Jacobus, and Jacobus Echard. *Scriptores Ordinis Praedicatorum*. 2 vols., 2 pts. 1719–23. Reprint, New York: Burt Franklin, 1960.

Rapp, Ludwig. *Die Hexenprozesse an ihre Gegne aus Tirol.* Innsbruck: Verlag des Wagner'schen Universitäte Buchhandlung, 1874.

Rheinheimer, Martin. "Die Angst vor dem Wolf. Werwolfglaube, Wolfsagen und Ausrottung der Wölfe in Shleswig-Holstein." *Fabula* 36 (1995): 25–78.

Rheubottom, David. "The Seeds of Evil Within." In David Perkin, ed., *The Anthropology of Evil.* Oxford: Basil Blackwell, 1985, 77–91.

Robbins, Rossell Hope. *The Encyclopedia of Witchcraft and Demonology.* New York: Crown Publications, 1963.

———. "The Imposture of Witchcraft." *Folklore* 74 (1963): 545–64.

Roper, Lyndal. *The Holy Household.* Oxford: Oxford University Press, 1989.

———. *Oedipus and the Devil.* London: Routledge, 1994.

Rosch, Eleanor. "Principles of Categorization." In Eleanor Rosch and B.B. Lloyd, eds., *Cognition and Categorization.* Hillsdale: Lawrence Erlbaum Associates, 1978, 27–48.

Rose, Elliot. *A Razor for a Goat* (Toronto: Toronto University Press, 1962).

Rothkrug, Lionel. *Religious Practices and Collective Perceptions: Hidden Homologies in the Renaissance and Reformation.* In *Historical Reflections,* 7.1 (1980).

Rowland, Robert. "'Fantastical and Devilishe Persons': European Witch-beliefs in Comparative Perspective." In Ankarloo and Henningsen, 161–90.

Ruggiero, Guido. *The Boundaries of Eros.* New York: Oxford University Press, 1985.

Runeberg, Arne. *Witches, Demons and Fertility Magic.* Societas Scientiarum Fennica Commentationes Humanarum Litterarum 14. Helsinki: Centraltryckeri och Bokbinderi, 1947.

Russell, Jeffrey Burton. *Witchcraft in the Middle Ages.* Ithaca: Cornell University Press, 1972.

———. *A History of Witchcraft.* London: Thames and Hudson, 1980.

———. *Satan: The Early Christian Tradition.* Ithaca: Cornell University Press, 1981.

———. *Lucifer: The Devil in the Middle Ages.* Ithaca: Cornell University Press, 1984.

Russell, Jeffrey Burton, and Mark W. Wyndham. "Witchcraft and the Demonization of Heresy." *Mediaevalia* 2 (1976): 1–21.

Sabean, David. *Power in the Blood: Popular Culture and Village Discourse in Early Modern Germany.* Cambridge: Cambridge University Press, 1984.

Sahlins, Marshall. "Raw Women, Cooked Men, and Other 'Great Things' of the Fiji Islands." In Paula Brown and Donald Tuzin, eds., *The Ethnography of Cannibalism.* Washington D.C.: Society for Psychological Anthropology, 1983, 72–93.

Samos, Nicholas P. "Witchcraft in Histories of Psychiatry: A Critical Analysis and an Alternative Conception." *Psychological Bulletin* 85 (1978): 417–39.

Schmitt, Jean-Claude. *The Holy Greyhound.* Trans. Martin Thom. Cambridge: Cambridge University Press, 1983.

———. *Les Revenants.* Paris: Gallimard, 1994.

Schnyder, André. "Der *Malleus Maleficarum*: Fragen und Beobachtungen zu seiner Druckgeschichte sowie zur Rezeption bei Bodin, Binsfeld und Delrio." *Archiv für Kulturgeschichte* 74 (1992): 325–64.

———. *Malleus Maleficarum: Kommentar zur Wiedergabe des Erstdrucks von 1487.* Göppingen: Kümmerle, 1993.

——. "Der Inquisitor als Geschichtenerzähler." *Fabula* 36 (1995): 1–24.

Scholz Williams, Gerhild. *Defining Dominion: The Discourses of Magic and Witchcraft in Early Modern France and Germany.* Ann Arbor: The University of Michigan Press, 1995.

Scribner, R.W. *Popular Culture and Popular Movements in Reformation Germany.* London: The Hambledon Press, 1987.

——. "Cosmic Order and Daily Life: Sacred and Secular in Pre-Industrial German Society." In Scribner, *Popular Culture,* 1–16.

——. "Ritual and Popular Religion in Catholic Germany at the Time of the Reformation." In Scribner, *Popular Culture,* 17–47.

——. "Sorcery, Superstition and Society: The Witch of Urach, 1529." In Scribner, *Popular Culture,* 257–75.

——. "The Reformation, Popular Magic, and the 'Disenchantment of the World.'" *Journal of Interdisciplinary History* 23.3 (1993): 475–94.

Segl, Peter. "Heinrich Institoris: Persönlichkeit und literarisches Werk." In Segl, ed., *Der Hexenhammer,* 103–26.

——, ed. *Der Hexenhammer.* Cologne: Böhlau Verlag, 1988.

Sehmsdorf, Henning K. "Envy and Fear in Scandinavian Folk Tradition." *Ethnologica Scandinavica* (1988): 34–42.

Sharpe, J.A. "Witchcraft and Women in Seventeenth Century England: Some Northern Evidence." *Continuity and Change* 6 (1991): 179–99.

——. *Witchcraft in Seventeenth Century Yorkshire: Accusations and Countermeasures.* Bothwick Paper 81 (1992).

Smith, Kathryn C. "The Role of Animals in Witchcraft and Popular Magic." In J.R. Porter and W.M.S. Russell, eds., *Animals in Folklore.* Ipswich: D.S. Brewer, 1978, 96–109.

Spence, Donald P. "The Mythic Properties of Popular Explanations." In Joseph de Rivera and Theodore Sarbin, eds., *Believed-In Imaginings: The Narrative Construction of Reality.* Washington, D.C.: American Psychological Association, 1998, 217–28.

Sperber, Dan. *Rethinking Symbolism.* Cambridge: Cambridge University Press, 1975.

Stewart, Charles. *Demons and the Devil: Moral Imagination in Modern Greek Culture.* Princeton: Princeton University Press, 1991.

Swanson, R.N. *Religion and Devotion in Europe, c. 1215–c. 1515.* Cambridge: Cambridge University Press, 1995.

Taggart, James M. *Enchanted Maidens: Gender Relations in Spanish Folktales of Courtship and Marriage.* Princeton: Princeton University Press, 1990.

Tavenner, Eugene. "Canidia and Other Witches." Reprinted in *Witchcraft in the Ancient World and Middle Ages,* ed. Brian Levack, 2:14–39. New York: Garland Publishers, 1992.

Taylor, Larrisa. *Soldiers of Christ: Preaching in Late Medieval and Reformation France.* Oxford: Oxford University Press, 1992.

Thomas, Keith. "The Relevance of Social Anthropology to the Historical Study of Witchcraft." In Douglas, 47–80.

——. *Religion and the Decline of Magic.* New York: Charles Scribner's Sons, 1971.

Thomas, Keith, and Hildred Geertz. "An Anthropology of Religion and Magic." *Journal of Interdisciplinary History* 6 (1975): 71–109.

Thompson, Stith. *Motif Index of Folk-Literature*. Bloomington: Indiana University Press, 1955.

Thorndike, Lynn. *A History of Magic and Experimental Science*. 8 vols. New York: Columbia University Press, 1923–58.

Trachtenberg, Joshua. *The Devil and the Jews*. Cleveland: Meridian Books, 1961.

Trevor-Roper, H.R. "The European Witch-Craze." In Trevor-Roper, *The European Witch-Craze of the Sixteenth and Seventeenth Centuries and Other Essays*. New York: Harper Torchbooks, 1969.

Turberville, A.S. *Medieval Heresy and the Inquisition*. 1920. Reprint, London: Archon Books, 1964.

Tuzin, Donald. "Cannibalism and Arapesh Cosmology." In Paula Brown and Donald Tuzin, eds., *The Ethnography of Cannibalism*. Washington, D.C.: Society for Psychological Anthropology, 1983, 61–71.

Walker, D.P. *Spiritual and Demonic Magic*. 1958. Reprint, Notre Dame: University of Notre Dame Press, 1975.

Wiesner, Merry E. "Early Modern Midwifery: A Case Study." In Barbara Hanawalt, ed., *Women and Work in Preindustrial Europe*. Bloomington: Indiana University Press, 1986, 94–113.

Wilson, Eric. "Institoris at Innsbruck: Heinrich Institoris, the *Summis Desiderantes* and the Brixen Witch-Trial of 1485." In Bob Scribner and Trevor Johnson, eds., *Popular Religion in Germany and Central Europe 1400–1800*. New York: St. Martin's Press, 1996, 87–100.

Wirth, J. "Against the Acculturation Thesis." In Wirth, *Religion and Society in Early Modern Europe, 1500–1800*, 56–78. Boston: Allen and Unwin, 1984.

Zika, Charles. "Hosts, Processions and Pilgrimages: Controlling the Sacred in Fifteenth-Century Germany." *Past and Present* 118 (1988): 25–64.

Zilboorg, Gregory. *The Medical Man and the Witch during the Renaissance*. Baltimore: The Johns Hopkins Press, 1935.

Index

Note: "n." after a page reference indicates the number of a note on that page. Literary works can be found under authors' names.

Printed in the United States
72018LV00003B/175-210

9 780719 064418